# DATE DUE

DISCARD

RED FAMILIES V. BLUE FAMILIES

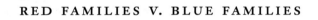

NAOMI CAHN AND JUNE CARBONE

# RED FAMILIES
# V.
# BLUE FAMILIES

*Legal Polarization and the*
*Creation of Culture*

OXFORD
UNIVERSITY PRESS
2010

## OXFORD
UNIVERSITY PRESS

Oxford University Press, Inc., publishes works that further
Oxford University's objective of excellence
in research, scholarship, and education.

Oxford   New York
Auckland   Cape Town   Dar es Salaam   Hong Kong   Karachi
Kuala Lumpur   Madrid   Melbourne   Mexico City   Nairobi
New Delhi   Shanghai   Taipei   Toronto

With offices in
Argentina   Austria   Brazil   Chile   Czech Republic   France   Greece
Guatemala   Hungary   Italy   Japan   Poland   Portugal   Singapore
South Korea   Switzerland   Thailand   Turkey   Ukraine   Vietnam

Copyright © 2010 by Oxford University Press, Inc.

Published by Oxford University Press, Inc.
198 Madison Avenue, New York, New York 10016

www.oup.com

Oxford is a registered trademark of Oxford University Press.

Library of Congress Cataloging-in-Publication Data
Cahn, Naomi R.
Red families v. blue families : legal polarization and the creation
of culture / Naomi Cahn and June Carbone.
    p.   cm.
Includes bibliographical references and index.
ISBN 978-0-19-537217-5
    1. Domestic relations—Social aspects—United States.
2. Social change—United States.   I. Carbone, June.   II. Title.
KF505.C34 2010
306.850973—dc22      2009048788

5 7 9 8 6 4

Printed in the United States of America
on acid-free paper

# Contents

# Acknowledgments

We will never be able to look at a map of the United States again without seeing purple—and red and blue.

This is the place/space/location for us to thank friends and colleagues who have supported us over the years that we have been involved in this project. First, we thank each other for our conversations, which have occurred over more than a decade and spanned several continents. As we've worked through our agreements—and disagreements—we've learned much about red and blue families, and about our own families. Second, we appreciate the extensive discussions, editing, and support—and vetting—that we've received from numerous colleagues, friends, and family members. Thank you to Bill Black, Deirdre Bowen, Paul Callister, Jane Curry, Tony Gambino, Vivian Hamilton, Brad Joondeph, Nancy Levit, Linda McClain, Rachel Rebouche, Carol Sanger, Mike Selmi, Mary Lyndon Shanley, Jana Singer, Mary Ellen and Charles Taylor, and Jeff Thomas. We've also benefited from presenting early pieces of this book at numerous conferences, including a cathartic meeting of the Baltimore/Washington Feminist Law Prof Group and "Red States v. Blue States: The Judicial Role in an Era of Partisanship at the University of Missouri at Kansas City. We've been fortunate to work with Dave McBride as our editor at Oxford University Press and with his assistant, Alexandra Dauler.

We'd also like to thank the research assistants who worked in Santa Clara, Kansas City, and Washington: Megan Monk, Lindsey Nelson, Christine Waltz, and Annie Wang; and Kasia Solon, our George Washington University library liaison, who answered all of our questions and helped us to answer ones we hadn't yet asked. Naomi would like to express her gratitude to Fred Lawrence, who so ably supports faculty development.

To our own families—Abigail, Louisa, and Tony, Bill, Galen, Genina, and Kenny—you color our rainbows!

RED FAMILIES V. BLUE FAMILIES

# Introduction

F
AMILIES ARE ON the front lines of the culture wars. Controversies over abortion, same-sex marriage, teen pregnancy, single-parenthood, and divorce have all challenged our images of the American family. Some Americans seek a return to the "mom, dad, and apple pie" family of the 1950s, while others embrace all of our families, including single mothers, gay and lesbian parents, and cohabiting couples. These conflicting perspectives on life's basic choices affect us all—at the national level, in state courts and legislatures, in drafting local ordinances, and in our own families.

In this book, we go behind the overblown rhetoric and political posturing of the family values conflict. What we have found is that the new information economy is transforming the family—and doing so in ways that create a crisis for marriage-based communities across the country.

The "blue families" of our title are on one side of the cultural controversy. These families have reaped the handsome rewards available to the well-educated middle class who are able to invest in both their daughters' and sons' earning potential. Their children defer family formation until both partners reach emotional maturity and financial independence. Blue family champions celebrate the commitment to equality that makes companionate relationships possible and the sexual freedom that allows women to fully participate in society. Those who have embraced the blue family model have low divorce rates, relatively few teen births, and good incomes. Yet, the ability to realize the advantages of the new blue family system appears to be very much a class-based affair. Women who graduate from college are the *only* women in American society whose marriage rates have increased, and they and their partners form the group whose divorce rates have most appreciably declined.

The terms of the successful blue family order—embrace the pill, encourage education, and accept sexuality as a matter of private choice—are a direct affront to the "red families" of our title and to social conservatives who see their families in peril. Driven by religious teachings about sin and guilt and based in communities whose social life centers around married couples with children, the red family paradigm continues to celebrate the unity of sex, marriage, and procreation. Red family champions correctly point out that the growing numbers of single-parent families threaten the well-being of the next generation, and they accurately observe that greater male fidelity and female "virtue" strengthen relationships. Yet, red regions of the country have higher teen pregnancy rates, more shotgun marriages, and lower average ages at marriage and first birth. What the red family paradigm has not acknowledged is that the changing economy has undermined the path from abstinence through courtship to marriage. As a result, abstinence into the mid-20s is unrealistic, shotgun marriages correspond with escalating divorce rates, and early marriages, whether prompted by love or necessity, often founder on the economic realities of the modern economy, which disproportionately rewards investment in higher education. Efforts to insist on a return to traditional pieties thus inevitably clash with the structure of the modern economy and produce recurring cries of moral crisis.

The intractability of the differences between the two perspectives has dominated legal and political debate. Part of the reason for the intensity of the conflict is geographic. The blue family model has taken hold most completely in urban areas, along the coasts, and in the increasingly Democratic areas of the country—from the Research Triangle in North Carolina to the Microsoft-dominated areas of Seattle—that have profited most from technological innovation. In contrast, red families generally, and the Republican strongholds in which they predominate, are more likely to be religious, rural, less educated, and less mobile, and the political leadership in these regions is more likely to value tradition and continuity. Geographic separation along demographic lines means that the two groups have increasingly less in common, and as the two political parties have become more ideological, these different values orientations have become increasingly partisan—making family form in the twenty-first century one of the most accurate predictors of political loyalties.

This partisan conflict at the national level, which pits two powerful constituencies against each other, obscures the ways in which family issues have magnified a growing economic inequality. The emergence of the blue family paradigm came with women's ability to control the timing of pregnancy and childbirth. For those with the resources and discipline to take advantage of these techniques, family formation occurs at the point when adults can be expected to do the right thing—and have the emotional and financial resources to manage their children—with a minimum of external assistance. The prescription to delay family formation until after graduate-school age, however, carries little suasion for those who will not complete college. Red families would accordingly like to reinforce parental control over wayward teens and make it harder to escape the consequences of improvident conduct. Yet, the most likely effect of restricting the availability of the morning-after pill to 18-year-olds is to increase the number of non-marital pregnancies, and the emphasis on abstinence education has dramatically raised the odds that a poor African-American teen will have her first sexual experience without any information about contraception. The irony is that blue families, who overwhelmingly oppose these policies, simply accompany their daughters to the pharmacy while more-conservative families—with many minority parents approving of the measures—disproportionately bear the consequences.

To get beyond the existing divisions, therefore, we believe that the time has come for a more realistic and comprehensive conversation that begins with the recognition that the crisis in family values is real. The new information economy has exacerbated income inequality, and the three-quarters of Americans on the losing end of this transformation have seen not only their employment, but also their familial stability, decline. Marriage has effectively disappeared from the poorest communities, and more stable communities are now seeing divorce rates plateau at high levels and nonmarital births continue to rise. While well-educated single parents may ably provide for their children, these changes in family structure reduce the resources available for the most vulnerable members of the next generation.

Genuine engagement also requires a recognition that leadership couched in the terms of one paradigm may needlessly antagonize the other. The blue family paradigm is built on a model of responsible parenthood that assumes that good things come to those who wait. Yet, the most visible representatives of blue family values bristle at restrictions on sexuality, insistence on marriage, or the stigmatization of single parents. Their secret, however, is that they encourage *their* children to simultaneously combine public tolerance with private discipline, and their children then overwhelming choose to raise their own children within two-parent families. The leaders in more troubled communities, including many African-American and Latino clergy, are often more socially conservative precisely because external authority is more critical where private discipline is harder to instill—and they understandably resent those who would denigrate their efforts.

Conversely, the fact that greater moral authority is needed and valued does not mean that government imposition of traditional values is necessarily appropriate or effective. Studies of evangelicals show, for example, that the most devout (roughly a quarter of the group) do abstain from sexual activity to a greater degree than other teens and that shared religious faith contributes to stronger marriages and lower divorce rates. These same studies also show that evangelicals as a group, in part because of income and class differences, begin sexual activity earlier than members of religions with more-flexible attitudes toward sexuality. In this context, emphasizing strict religious values, even if it strengthens the practices of regular churchgoers, may leave the less devout of the same faith ill-prepared for participation in a secular world.

This dynamic of class and regional antagonisms, of a clash between religious and secular world views, of different symbolic and practical needs, offers enormous opportunities for shortsighted and cynical policies when it combines with partisan electoral politics. The values divide (indeed, what Justice Antonin Scalia referred to as a "culture war") has become intractable because politicians have intentionally chosen to focus on the most intrinsically divisive issues. Psychologist Drew Westen, for example, writes that Republicans have been "unequivocal" in conflating abortion and murder, setting out "an uncompromising stance as the only *moral* stance one could take, get[ting] the 30 percent of Americans with the least tolerance for ambiguity on moral questions to the polls," and allowing the Democrats to splinter in their approach to the issue.[1] Abortion thus increases in political importance *because* it is incapable of resolution and serves to reinforce political identity. The last Republican congressional representative from New England, Christopher Shays, defeated for reelection in 2008, complained that it is one thing to oppose abortion; it is another to have to vote on abortion-related provisions 80 times a year, whether or not they have any prospects of passage.

Political scientists have found that polarization on moral questions was largely nonexistent in the early 1960s—disagreements about issues such as abortion or homosexuality did not depend on region, church attendance, or party. In the twenty-first century, in contrast, the better-educated and more politically active are strikingly polarized on these questions. While political scientists debate whether the country as a whole is more divided, they agree that the college-educated have stronger views than those completing high school, and party stalwarts have become even more divided and ideological than the college grads. Among the public generally, divisions on moral issues such as abortion and same-sex marriage have increased dramatically since the 1980s.[2] While Americans still prefer compromise on most issues, if pollsters ask if someone is "strongly pro-choice," "strongly pro-life," or only "somewhat committed" to one of the positions, 70% of the public identify with one of the two poles.[3] Even those who question the existence of the culture wars acknowledge that "[m]oral issues have become increasingly important over the past 30 years. Such issues have grown from insignificance to a clear second dimension in American elections."[4] The 2008 election suggests that, even though the presidency shifted parties, political parties remain aligned with differences in family composition—and, as the famous election maps in red and blue illustrate, those differences are regional in nature.

If there is a hopeful sign, however, it is that the number of *conservatives* calling for a greater separation of religion and politics and the

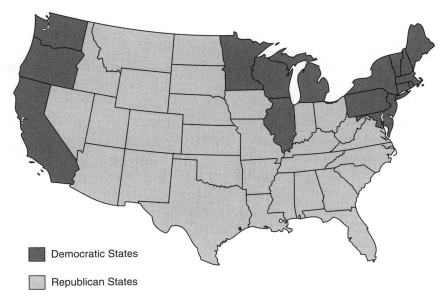

■ Democratic States

☐ Republican States

FIGURE I.I: 2004 Electoral Map

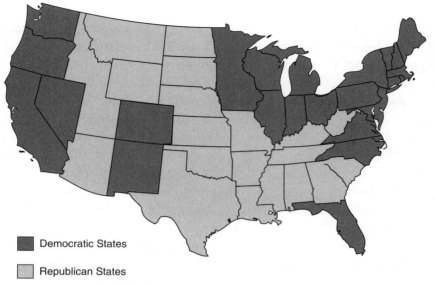

Democratic States

Republican States

FIGURE I.2: 2008 Electoral Map

number of *liberals* favoring affirmation of marital fidelity and commitment have both increased. The book takes a comprehensive look at the relationship among moral anxiety about family form, ideologically driven family laws, and the prospect for more constructive approaches to family change.

We conclude that genuine family law reform requires a more honest conversation about the changed and changing terms of family stability. Doing so starts with the recognition that red families and blue families are living different lives with different symbolic and practical needs. The blue paradigm is at the other end of the sexual revolution. Its families *have* been remade and the remaking is a huge success. For red families, it is family ideals that are in crisis. As Barbara Dafoe Whitehead, the codirector of the National Marriage Project, points out, the growing separation of the beginning of sexuality and marriage, a separation that is not appreciably shorter for evangelicals than for the rest of the population, is a source of anguish for the older generation. So, too, are the rising divorce and nonmarital birth rates that disproportionately affect those ready to form families at younger ages. The decline of marriage in communities built around married families undermines the fabric of community life in much more fundamental ways than an increase in the number of urban singles.

Accordingly, even if some degree of convergence were possible politically, the practical agendas *should* not be the same. The challenge is to get past the divisive partisan rhetoric to the policies capable of rebuilding support for family life in all of its variety. We believe that the secret to doing so lies in changing the subject. The most divisive issues—abstinence education, homosexuality and abortion—have dominated the family debate for the last decade. Yet, we live in a federal system designed to permit and defuse regional differences. Family law decision making has traditionally belonged to the states. The framers recognized that states and municipalities can draw more effectively than the national government on shared values to reshape community norms, and have done so in ways that promote progressive, as well as conservative, values. It is time to rediscover the ideal of more localized family law, and to embrace the shift in emphasis a federal system might facilitate. We believe that a revitalized family agenda would, quite literally, change the subject in three significant ways:

First, *change the subject* of family values promotion *from sex* (and sex ed) *to commitment* (and marriage ed). The real threat to the red family world—and to the well-being of all but the top group of American families—is declining marriage and high divorce rates for those who do not complete college. Preaching abstinence—and increasing the penalties for improvident sexuality—will do nothing to improve the stability of the early marriages and families that follow from such efforts. Red family advocates and, indeed, many blue family champions believe that long-term, stable relationships ideally promote family well-being. Most adults would choose to raise their children in families with two supportive parents who have a long-term commitment to each other and to the children. Social science research, while inconclusive on many fundamental questions with respect to children's well-being, suggests that children appear to do better if their parents avoid destructive conflict—and stay together.[5] The issue, however, is not the ideal, but how to achieve it. New efforts at marriage promotion suggest that delayed marriage, financial planning, more-effective communication, mutual respect and commitment, shared interests, and recognizing the warning signs of domestic violence (both in oneself and in potential mates) all enhance relationship stability. Marriage promotion programs that teach these strategies show some small early signs of success—in contrast with abstinence-only efforts, which have proven to be ineffective or counterproductive. These programs, however, can only be effective if tailored to regional sensibilities: let the states design and implement the programs of their choice.

Second, *change the subject from abortion to contraception*. Abortion is an intrinsically divisive issue, and it has become a focal point for values conflict *because* it offers no middle ground. In contrast, attitudes toward contraception are on a continuum—over 95% of sexually active women will use contraception at some point in their lives. More critically, the intensity of the abortion conflict obscures the real tragedy: the United States has the highest rates of unplanned teen pregnancies in the industrialized world. Thirty percent of American girls will become pregnant before they turn 20, and 80% of the pregnancies are unplanned. Moreover, nonmarital births have skyrocketed because of high rates of unplanned pregnancies for unmarried women in their early 20s, the age-group least likely to have health insurance. The only way to genuinely address family values is to reconsider the terms of family formation. The dramatic story of the '90s was a national decline in teen births, a decline most dramatic for the poorest and most-vulnerable Americans and one concentrated much more heavily in the states most committed to the availability of birth control and abortion. That decline in births occurred at the same time that teen pregnancy and abortion rates fell, and it depended on both greater abstinence and more-effective contraceptive use. Yet, the beneficial effects of these efforts never carried over to women beyond the high school years, and in the early twenty-first century, teen births have crept back up, with the largest rise for African-Americans. Commentators attribute the increase to some combination of the worsening economy (a bright future is the best contraceptive), increasing amounts of abstinence-only education (the poorer the woman, the more likely she is to receive no information about contraception before her initial sexual encounter), and less access to contraception. At the same time, the morning-after pill and nonsurgical abortion (RU-486) have blurred the line between contraception and abortion for the middle class, increasing the ease of access for those with medical care and worsening the plight of women with the least resources as abortion later during pregnancy becomes harder to secure.

If there is a middle ground in the cultural fight, it should be on the importance of moving family formation out of the teen years. Early marriage derails education and increases the likelihood of divorce. As the National Campaign to Prevent Teen and Unplanned Pregnancy points out, young teen mothers are less likely to complete high school, and their children do not perform as well in school as do children of older parents.[6] While abstinence reinforcement can play a useful role, few successful couples will forgo contraceptive use altogether—whether within marriage or without. Comprehensive approaches to deterring improvident childbirth, with special attention to the needs of poorer, minority, and evangelical teens, should command greater support. After all, those who succeed in avoiding unplanned births

become more likely to marry, stay married, and bear children who replicate more-stable family patterns.

Third, *change the subject from family to work*. The changing family
is part of a long-term restructuring of the interaction between work
and family. Yet, family dynamics have responded to workplace needs
more readily than the workplace has changed to accommodate family
responsibilities. This failure to restructure the workplace to accommodate the changes in family needs affects everyone. Since the late 1980s,
the largest increase in perceptions that work interferes with family
involves *men's* jobs. The design of full-time positions on the assumption that the worker has a full-time homemaker/spouse serves neither
the interests of modern men who have assumed a larger share of childrearing responsibility, nor those of more-traditional women who may
have no choice but to work to support their families.

The blue family model, which defers family formation in response
to the greater demands of the modern workplace, has resulted in lower
fertility rates. More family-friendly workplaces would encourage middle-class births by helping men and women feel comfortable that they
can combine work and family. At the same time, the disappearance of
stable blue-collar jobs for young people has undermined family formation altogether for the less-prosperous parts of society. Greater attention to the transition to adulthood, perhaps with mandatory service,
more-flexible educational opportunities, a higher minimum wage and/
or expansion of the earned income tax credit, and more opportunities
for apprenticeships, may also pay off in terms of relationship stability
and investment in children.

The nation's reactions to Sarah Palin's daughter Bristol clearly illus-
trated the clash between our blue and red paradigms. Not long after
John McCain's announcement in August 2008 that he had chosen
Alaska governor Sarah Palin as his running mate, Palin acknowledged
that her 17-year-old daughter was pregnant and engaged to the teen-
aged father. The prototypical blue family was, predictably, appalled—a
17-year-old, married or not, is not ready for parenthood. Palin's social
conservative base, which might otherwise have been expected to disapprove of the nonmarital sex that produced the pregnancy, applauded
Bristol's decision to keep the child and the betrothal that followed. The
wedding never happened. We could have predicted that Levi Johnston
would not feel "mature" enough at age 19 to assume all of the familial
responsibilities associated with having a wife and child, so when he
announced that the engagement was off, we were not surprised. We

also smiled at the irony when Bristol became a spokesperson against teen pregnancy. She may be a far more effective representative of family reconciliation than her elders precisely because she is the one who is living with the consequences.

In the intense aftermath of the 2004 election, researchers John Green and Mark Silk concluded that "[g]eography matters in American politics today above all" and ultimately, "those first-day stories about moral values—and the red-and-blue maps that went with them—conveyed something real."[7] Throughout this book, we will use geography as an organizing theme in an effort to capture the relationships between different family patterns and different political and ideological packages. The first part of the book, "Family Maps," literally maps changing family lives onto different regions of the country and discusses the relationships among our brains, our politics, and our maturity. We show that the demographic story is overwhelmingly about the age at family formation. The "reddest" areas of the country, both in terms of their politics and the lives of their families, marry and have children at younger ages and are most likely to see the embrace of traditional values as critical to community well-being. The "bluest" areas of the country, and particularly the urban Northeast, have the highest averages ages of family formation and demonstrate the greatest support for the mechanisms that effectively deter teen births. The second and third chapters in this section explain the history that has produced these regional divisions and the biology that makes age such an important cultural marker. The final chapter in the section addresses the intersection of religion, culture, and politics. The greatest political polarization since the 1980s among the public at large has occurred with respect to the issue of moral values. We show how the disappearance of the center in American religion has exacerbated regional differences and set the stage for the political exploitation of cultural conflict.

In undertaking this study, we recognize that the state maps may cloak diversity within their boundaries. Urban Kansas City, for example, is strikingly different from the rural Missouri of the Ozarks politically, ethnically, and demographically. Yet, the state-by-state divisions are important partly because the family law decisions we map take place at the state level and partly because the regional divisions reflect different values orientations in different parts of the country. Nonetheless, our descriptions of what makes a place red or blue may obscure certain important distinctions. First, the differences between red and blue themselves are not entirely parallel. The blue paradigm, as an ideological construct that combines political and family orientations, most tellingly describes college graduates who live in blue regions. University education itself is an important element of socialization into shared perspectives, and the successful middle-class families who have embraced a commitment to deferred family formation are in many ways more uniform, wherever they may live, than other parts of the population. In contrast, quintessential red families include poor Appalachian whites with relatively high teen pregnancy rates, Utah Mormons with higher educational attainment and lower teen birthrates but younger average ages at marriage, mountain families in Wyoming and Montana with strong libertarian traditions, and suburban and rural midwestern families from Kansas, Nebraska, and the Dakotas.

Second, one of the effects of the red-blue discourse is to mask racial effects. Blue urban areas, for example, include large African-American and Latino populations with relatively early ages of family formation, and regional differences among African-Americans in states such as Wisconsin, Louisiana, New Hampshire, and Iowa are more likely to reflect the socioeconomic status of the African-Americans within those states than differences in black attitudes or values. Minority communities are neither united nor monochromatic on family issues. Approximately 50% of blacks and Latinos, compared to 33% of whites, for example, believe that unwed mothers are a big problem in their communities. A 2007 poll found further that more than 60% of blacks believed that the values of poor and middle-class blacks had become increasingly different; only 53% of the respondents believed it still made sense to talk of blacks as a single race (37% did not), and more than half believed that the values of whites and blacks had become more similar over the past decade. Nonetheless, neither the family practices of minority communities nor the internal divisions within them translate automatically into the same construction of red and blue paradigms, nor do they necessarily carry the same political salience. The world views we are constructing in this volume, while they overlap with the views of many individual minorities, do not adequately address either the way the debate is framed within minority communities nor the way minority communities might prioritize their own family needs.

The second part, "The Legal Map," shows the correlation between cultural divisions and legal rules. While the demographic picture is shaped by age at family formation, the legal picture concerns the regulation of sexuality. As this part shows, there are significant differences in laws between red states as a whole and blue states as a whole. For example, although most states—both red and blue—do not recognize same-sex civil unions and marriages, *all* of those that provide broad rights to same-sex unions are blue. The fact that the laws differ and that they differ in accordance with the strength of the Democratic or Republican vote is not, however, the point. Instead, the book shows how the acceptance of a new family regime translates into types of legal decision making.

Red cultural beliefs reaffirm the control of sexuality while blue cultural beliefs give more weight—symbolic and practical—to the promotion of equality. These beliefs, however, play out differently in legislatures than in courts, in decisions that affect many versus those limited to the few, and with respect to issues that engage the powerful as opposed to the disenfranchised.

The book illustrates these patterns by focusing on five distinct areas of contention: contraception and the pathways to blue family life in chapter 5, abortion, law and the cognitive map in chapter 6, abstinence-only education in chapter 7, the marrying law, including marriage promotion and same-sex marriage, in chapter 8, and the role of nonmarital cohabitation in custody decisions in chapter 9. At the symbolic level, all involve control of sexuality. At a practical level, they also address the circumstances that make greater equality possible between men and women and between rich and poor. They depend on different decision makers—executive officers, legislators, federal and state courts, initiative voters—with different incentives to inflame or diffuse cultural tensions. Together, they illustrate how different sections of the country address family change.

The final part, "The Map to the Future," addresses looming policy issues and the prospects for renewed consensus. The construction of red and blue family types, of course, does not depict absolutes, nor are they mutually exclusive. Nonetheless, each paradigm reflects a different response to a social and economic restructuring that affects the country as a whole. Whether we like it or not (and whether the intensely red parts of the country resist more than the intensely blue), globalization, technology, and changing gender roles have revolutionized society. Within families, this may mean greater resistance to the values parents would like to instill in their children—resistance that may produce different understandings in the next generation. Within the larger community, those holding red and blue family values must face the same changing economic conditions that have eliminated jobs paying adequate wages for less-educated young people and that have made both partners' incomes critical to middle-class status.

Chapter 10, "Marriage Advice in Shades of Pink," shows that Americans have higher marriage, divorce, and unintended pregnancy rates than much of the industrialized world and has less of a social safety net to cushion the impact of family instability. Revitalization of the norms of commitment is accordingly critical to children's well-being and much of the tension over family values concerns the content of those norms. The advice in this chapter is in "shades of pink" or "light red" in three senses. First, marriage *is* the primary issue for red America: marriage channels sexuality, connects it to childrearing, and continues to be the foundation for community life in much of the United States. Focusing on strategies to deter divorce makes sense, though such efforts will neither completely satisfy those who wish to bring back traditional families nor ultimately succeed without taking on the larger issues of family economic support. Hence, the efforts will be "pink" rather than true red. Second, for blue America, the primary issue is whether to recognize a continuum of adult relationships or to revitalize the special status of marriage by moving it away from its patriarchal past. Marriage continues to be an important institution in the creation of commitment, and recognition of same-sex marriage is critical to more-egalitarian understandings of the institution. These reform efforts are "pink" both in their embrace of gay and lesbian participation and in their evolving definitions of the role of marriage as a defining element of family life. Finally, since marriage will continue to play a more influential role in the United States than elsewhere in the industrialized world, revitalization of the institution will benefit from greater attention to local nuance and shades of meaning sensitive to regional context.

Chapter 11, "Making Ready for Baby: Painting the Nursery Sky Blue," addresses policies for the dual issues that underlie fertility control: first, the systematic provision of birth control to allow the entire population to choose the timing of births more effectively, and second, greater attention to the fertility efforts of those who may have passed the optimum period for conception. The United States is one of few industrialized countries with births above the replacement rate only because poor women's high unintended pregnancy rates mask the plummeting fertility levels of better-off Americans. Existing policies thus fail to address family planning in the multiple contexts in which family formation occurs, including older women struggling with fertility issues, sexually active women in their early 20s without reliable partners or health care coverage, and teens who vary in their ability and willingness to postpone the beginning of sexual activity. The failure to recognize the diversity of interests and needs systematically disadvantages the most-vulnerable women. While the discussion of marriage in chapter 10 addresses core red paradigm concerns, the discussion of contraception in chapter 11 embraces central elements of the blue paradigm. Yet, it concludes that encouraging the births of more *wanted* children should be an objective both models share.

The final chapter in this section, "Retooling the Foundation in Deep Purple," concludes that the essential next step for red and blue families alike is a reconsideration of the relationship between work and family. Dual-income families increasingly list both men's and women's working hours as a top concern. Poorer families face impoverishment if they deviate from the new middle-class ideal of deferred childbearing. The challenge for everyone is the creation of new strategies that make childrearing less destructive of continued education and employment. For blue families, where human capital acquisition precedes family formation, the challenge is to structure the workplace to make room for family. For red families, where family formation may come first, the challenge is to restructure the relationship to the workplace to make room for continued human capital acquisition.

Finally, there is one critical area where genuine convergence between the two models might ultimately transform the debate. This final area involves thinking about the circumstances that might persuade our prototypical red family to delay family formation to the mid-20s and our prototypical blue family to start a bit earlier.

We are pessimistic, however, that genuine family transformation can occur without addressing the growing inequality that has exacerbated the pressures on family life. Our well-educated, middle-class families, who might prefer earlier childbearing, increasingly do not form stable, mature partnerships until later in life. Our poorer red families, who might benefit from delayed childbearing, may be more likely to miss out on family life altogether if they wait, partly because, in marriage-oriented communities, marital prospects decline more with age and partly because of the increased—and expensive to remedy—infertility issues that come with later childbearing. Existing patterns of family formation, however, have their own dynamic, undermining the life chances of the children born to young parents and lowering the number of children born to older ones. Rebuilding family life and thinking about how it fits within the country's overall development require the consideration of family issues together with education and employment, region and class, and, ultimately, the legal and institutional support for all of our families.

PART I

# FAMILY MAPS

## CHAPTER I

# Moral Demography

INCE WE STARTED this research, we see discussions of red v. blue everywhere—election maps in red and blue, public opinion maps with color-coded states and counties, red cooking tips v. blue ones. What we did not see is a comprehensive explanation of whether "red" *families* differ from "blue" ones. To find out, we decided to see if we could find a geographic pattern in the statistics that corresponded to our understandings of red v. blue family strategies.

We started with what we know about family change over the last half century. During that period the United States has undergone enormous changes. We have been at the center of a technological revolution, and we have become wealthier because of it. We have dramatically changed our patterns of marriage (we do it at older average ages), divorce (we do it substantially more often), childbearing (we want and have substantially fewer children), and the likelihood that we will raise our children in two-parent families. These changes, however, have not played out evenly by class, race, or region. Instead, a growing literature suggests that family structure itself exacerbates the growing income inequality in the United States and serves as a cultural marker that increase the divisions between regions, races, and classes.

To explore this hypothesis, we looked at the regional distribution of family patterns and whether they explain the emergence of "red" and "blue" strategies. The biggest differences between red and blue families center on age: age at marriage and age at first birth. Teen marriage and childbirth were once commonplace. In both 1900 *and* 1960 (though not necessarily in between), the average woman married by the age of 20. Since 1960, these statistics have changed dramatically. The average age at first marriage for women around the country has risen to 25; teen births, which were once overwhelmingly within marriage, now overwhelmingly take place without; and teen pregnancy, which occurs at dramatically lower rates than in earlier eras, has been coded as a social problem—in most of the country. The regional distribution of teen births thus provides some important clues to the tensions that underlie family values debates, with the most telling connections occurring between white teen births and moral values concerns.

To determine whether people in different parts of the country are living different lives, we looked at how age matters to several major life events. We identified the top 5 and the bottom 5 states in each of our demographic measures, because these 10 states show the poles of the distribution of differences. Other scholars have run more-sophisticated calculations; as we document in the notes, they find that family characteristics in the 50 states strongly predict political outcomes.[1] Unlike the political scientists, however, we are not attempting to show the correlation between family issues and political loyalties. Nor are we attempting to show a statistical connection between social policies (e.g., opposition to abortion) and their potential consequences (e.g., higher teen birthrates). We also are not attempting to control for factors such as race, income, and religious beliefs, factors that strongly affect reproductive practices, though we note the existence of such factors as potential explanations for the patterns we find. Instead, by looking at these overall state averages, we are trying to describe cultural patterns. Do people in different parts of the country experience family formation through different lenses as a result of what they see around them? To capture these differences, we start with what happens to teens.

## THE TEEN DIVIDE

What happens during the teen years establishes the paths to adulthood. If teens postpone their assumption of adult roles, such as parenting or leaving school, until their mid-20s, they invest more in education, acquire independence, and learn how to navigate in the world before they marry. Conversely, those who marry before they turn 21 and have children soon after are likely to bear more children, interrupt their educations, and negotiate the terms of adulthood within a more fragile relationship.

## Teen Birthrates

Some of the best kept records in the United States document teen birthrates—we know how many teenagers give birth in each state in any one year. We also know that birthrates reflect the interaction of three different parts of teens' experience: teens' level of sexual activity, their use of contraception, and the relative acceptability of giving birth as opposed to getting an abortion. Moreover, teen births—as opposed to sex, contraception, and abortion—are visible matters of public record. Accordingly, they not only indicate the birth circumstances of the next generation, but they also reflect communities' perceptions of accepted practices. Do communities support early marriages or discourage conceptions and births? Do they provide access to contraception or discourage abortion?

Teen birthrates are measured in terms of the number of births per 1,000 female teens in the population. In 2003, the five states with the lowest rates of teen births were New Hampshire, Vermont, Massachusetts, Connecticut, and Maine—all concentrated in the Northeast and all voting Democratic in 2004 and 2008. The five states with the highest teen birthrates were Texas, New Mexico, Mississippi, Arizona, and Arkansas.[2] These states are all in the South or Southwest and voted red in 2004, with all but New Mexico also voting Republican in 2008.

Examining patterns in teen birthrates as they have changed over time shows that the most telling change has been the drop in teen births in the Northeast. In 1988, the lowest teen birthrates included Minnesota, North Dakota, and Iowa. Since then, rates have dropped more dramatically in New England than in the upper Midwest, increasing the regional concentration. The five states with the highest rates in 1988 (Mississippi, New Mexico, Arkansas, Texas, and Arizona), in contrast, have not changed over time. While teen birthrates dropped for the country as a whole, the biggest declines were in New England, and teen birthrates in some parts of the South and Southwest hardly changed at all.

These patterns partially reflect racial composition. The states with low teen birthrates (New Hampshire, Vermont, Massachusetts, Connecticut, and Maine) are much less diverse than the states with larger numbers of teen births (Texas, New Mexico, Mississippi, Arizona, and Arkansas). (Indeed, New Hampshire, Vermont and Maine are more than 95% white, among the highest percentages in the country). Breaking down the statistics by race and looking at just whites, the states with the lowest teen rates in 2003 were New Jersey, Connecticut, Massachusetts, New York, and Rhode Island. The wealthy Mid-Atlantic states joined or surpassed New England, suggesting that the entire Northeast has embraced a new family model—and solidly pro-Democratic politics. In contrast, the highest white teen birthrates were concentrated in the very red border and southern states: Arkansas, Kentucky, Mississippi, Oklahoma, and Tennessee.[3] In these states, both African-Americans and whites contribute to the high teen birthrates,[4] while in the southwestern states of Texas, Arizona, and New Mexico, the large number of teen births reflects the concentration of Latinos.[5]

Controlling for race reinforces the connections between teen births and party affiliation. Perhaps most dramatic is the voting change from 2004 to 2008 in the states with the highest white teen birthrates. Only 22% of counties increased their Republican percentages from 2004 to 2008, while the rest of the country swung more heavily Democratic. The states with the heaviest concentrations of such counties were Arkansas, Tennessee, and Oklahoma, followed by Louisiana and Kentucky.[6] Four of them were in the top five for white teen births and Louisiana was not far behind.

### Marriage and Abortion

Teen birthrates reflect two factors: the number of teens who choose to start families and the much larger number of teens who become pregnant accidentally and give birth to the chlid rather then having an abortion. We know from national figures that a higher percentage of teens who marry give birth within eight months of the marriage than older brides, suggesting that the shotgun marriage continues to be the solution for improvident pregnancy in some parts of the country. We also suspect that communities more open to teen marriage may also be more open to early childbearing and that some of the pregnancies may be welcome.

A comparison of marital versus nonmarital teen births, while it cannot in itself tease out whether the marriage is the cause or the consequence of the pregnancy, should provide insight into the support for early marriage in different parts of the country. The lowest percentages of teen births to married mothers occurred in the states of Massachusetts (only 8% of teen births are marital); Delaware, Pennsylvania, and Rhode Island (9%); and Connecticut and Maryland (10%),[7] all blue states, all in the Northeast or Mid-Atlantic

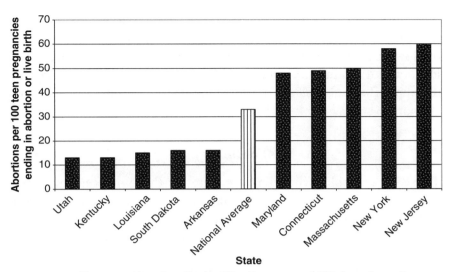

FIGURE 1.1: Teenage Abortion Ratio (Five Lowest and Highest States)
SOURCE: Guttmacher Institute, *U.S. Teen Pregnancy Statistics: National and State Trends by Race and Ethnicity* (Sept. 2006) *available at* http://www .guttmacher.org/pubs/2006/09/12/USTPstats.pdf.

regions, and all with relatively low teen birthrates, particularly by whites.[8] The states with the highest percentages of teen births taking place within marriage are Idaho, where 36% of teen births are marital; Utah (34%); Texas (27%); and Colorado, Kentucky, and Wyoming (each with 26%).[9] All of these states voted Republican in 2004, and all but Colorado did so again in 2008. Indeed, Utah, Wyoming, and Idaho produced the highest percentage of Republican votes in 2004 of any states in the union, and together with Oklahoma (one point behind Colorado, Kentucky, and Wyoming in the percentage of teen births within marriage) did so again in 2008.[10]

The final piece in the picture is abortion. The prevalence of abortion reflects access, acceptability, and need. It also indicates something about the support for teen childbearing. Abortion ratios, defined as the number of abortions for every 100 births, provide the telling data here. The higher the abortion ratio in a state, the more likely it is that a teen pregnancy will end in abortion rather than birth. Moreover, while overall state pregnancy and abortion rates reflect concentrations of racial minorities, with African-Americans and Latinas having significantly more teen pregnancies and abortions than whites, the ratios of abortions to live births are less skewed by race.[11] As shown in figure 1.1, the five states with the highest ratios for teens are New Jersey,

New York, Massachusetts, Connecticut, and Maryland, all solidly blue states from the Northeast and Mid-Atlantic regions.[12] The states with the lowest teen abortion ratios are Utah, Kentucky, Louisiana, South Dakota, and Arkansas. Utah is in the Mountain West, South Dakota in the upper Plains, Louisiana in the South, while Kentucky and Arkansas are border states.[13]

## *Summary*

These data establish that the blue states of the Northeast and Mid-Atlantic regions have lower teen birthrates, higher use of abortion, and lower percentages of teen births within marriage, while a set of red states mostly in the South and the southern border tend to have higher teen birthrates, fewer abortions, and a higher percentage of teen births occurring within marriage.[14] The first set of states effectively discourages teen childbearing, with abortion as an established fallback.[15] Those teens who do give birth in these states, however, may either feel little pressure, or have little opportunity, to marry. In the second set of states, where teen birthrates are higher and more of them are within marriage, family formation begins at an earlier age. The higher birthrates may thus reflect either more intentional births within marriage or greater reliance on shotgun marriages rather than on abortion to deal with accidental pregnancies.[16]

## *Temporal Distortions*

Regional variations in the relative age at marriage can be expected to complement the regional variations evident in the teen birth figures, and it does. The age of *legal* marriage in almost all states is 18. That is, until they are 18, teens need permission from someone else—a parent, a guardian, or a court—in order to get married. But the law today has little to do with the actual age at which most people get married. Most people do not marry until they are in their mid-20s. On the other hand, women and men who live in red families are more likely to tie the knot earlier than are women and men in blue families.

In the United States as a whole during the period from 2000 to 2003, the median age at marriage for women was 25.1, while for men it was 26.7.[17] According to the U.S. Census Bureau, these numbers are continuing to rise, reaching 26.0 for women and 27.7 for men in 2007 the highest ages ever recorded in the United States. These figures have changed dramatically since 1960, when the median age at first marriage was 20.3 for women and 22.8 for men.[18] As the median ages at marriage have increased, there has been a slight decrease in the age gap between men and women, which was 2.5 years in 1960 and to 1.7 years in 2007. While this difference may be small, it does show that people are becoming slightly more likely to marry their age peers.

The five states with the lowest median age at marriage in 2007 were red states: Utah (22.8 for women, 25.2 for men), Idaho (23.5, 25.5), Arkansas (24.0, 25.7), Oklahoma (24.5, 25.9), and Kansas (24.7, 26.3), states that also have relatively high teen birthrates and/or low abortion ratios.[19] Correspondingly, the states with the highest median age at marriage are blue: Massachusetts (28.5, 29.9), New York (28.0, 29.9), Rhode Island (28.1, 29.3), Connecticut (27.5, 29.4), and New Jersey (27.5, 29.4)—states with low teen birthrates and higher abortion ratios. Indeed, all of the states with above average ages of marriages voted blue in 2008, except for South Dakota.

The pattern for the woman's age at first birth corresponds with the pattern for marriage figures. If marriage is later, then we'd expect age at first birth to be later as well, given that the majority of births still occur within marriage. Table 1.1 provides information on the age at marriage and first birth for all 50 states and shows that this pattern is generally true. In 2007, the mean age of the mother at her first live birth for the country as a whole was 25; Massachusetts had the highest mean age, at 27.7, followed by Connecticut (27.2), New Jersey (27.2), New York (26.8), and New Hampshire (26.7). In contrast, Mississippi had the lowest (22.6), followed by Arkansas (23.0) and New Mexico (23.0), Oklahoma (23.1), and Louisiana (23.3).[20] Since the late 1970s, all states have experienced an increase in the mean age of mothers at the time of their first childs' birth, but the changes range from a 5.3-year increase in Massachusetts to a 1.9-year increase in Utah. With the highest rates of change concentrated in the Northeast and Mid-Atlantic states, and the smallest rates of change in the states with the lowest average ages at birth, the gap between the states is growing.[21]

Intriguingly, if we look at the *change* in the age at first birth over the last several decades, the areas with the biggest jumps were the District of Columbia, Massachusetts, Michigan, New Hampshire and New Jersey, North Carolina, and Virginia. New Hampshire has been leaning Democratic as the Boston suburbs move across the state border, and North Carolina and Virginia both changed from

TABLE I.I    Median Age at Marriage and Mean Age at First Birth

| | Median Age at Marriage | | Mean Age of Women at First Birth |
|---|---|---|---|
| | Men | Women | |
| United States | 27.7 | 26.0 | 25.0 |
| Alabama | 26.2 | 25.2 | 23.6 |
| Alaska | 26.3 | 25.2 | 24.3 |
| Arizona | 27.4 | 25.8 | 24.0 |
| Arkansas | 25.7 | 24.0 | 23.0 |
| California | 28.5 | 26.5 | 25.6 |
| Colorado | 27.0 | 25.5 | 25.7 |
| Connecticut | 29.4 | 27.5 | 27.2 |
| Delaware | 27.8 | 25.9 | 25.0 |
| District of Columbia | 30.0 | 29.9 | 26.5 |
| Florida | 28.3 | 26.6 | 25.0 |
| Georgia | 27.5 | 25.7 | 24.5 |
| Hawaii | 28.1 | 26.1 | 25.7 |
| Idaho | 25.5 | 23.5 | 23.8 |
| Illinois | 28.0 | 26.4 | 25.4 |
| Indiana | 26.7 | 25.3 | 24.0 |
| Iowa | 26.6 | 25.0 | 24.5 |
| Kansas | 26.3 | 24.7 | 24.2 |
| Kentucky | 26.5 | 24.8 | 23.8 |
| Louisiana | 27.0 | 25.8 | 23.3 |
| Maine | 27.1 | 25.6 | 25.6 |
| Maryland | 28.7 | 27.2 | 26.1 |
| Massachusetts | 29.9 | 28.5 | 27.7 |
| Michigan | 28.2 | 26.5 | 25.0 |
| Minnesota | 27.3 | 25.8 | 25.8 |
| Mississippi | 26.6 | 25.8 | 22.6 |
| Missouri | 26.6 | 25.5 | 24.1 |
| Montana | 28.3 | 25.8 | 24.5 |
| Nebraska | 26.6 | 25.4 | 24.7 |
| Nevada | 28.1 | 25.4 | 24.6 |
| New Hampshire | 28.4 | 26.9 | 26.7 |
| New Jersey | 29.4 | 27.5 | 27.2 |
| New Mexico | 28.1 | 25.7 | 23.0 |
| New York | 29.9 | 28.0 | 26.8 |
| North Carolina | 27.1 | 25.6 | 24.6 |
| North Dakota | 26.3 | 25.7 | 24.7 |

| | | | |
|---|---|---|---|
| Ohio | 27.2 | 26.2 | 24.7 |
| Oklahoma | 25.9 | 24.5 | 23.1 |
| Oregon | 27.7 | 25.8 | 25.4 |
| Pennsylvania | 28.5 | 26.6 | 25.5 |
| Rhode Island | 29.3 | 28.1 | 26.2 |
| South Carolina | 27.5 | 25.8 | 24.0 |
| South Dakota | 27.3 | 26.6 | 24.0 |
| Tennessee | 26.4 | 25.3 | 24.0 |
| Texas | 26.7 | 25.2 | 23.9 |
| Utah | 25.2 | 22.8 | 23.9 |
| Vermont | 27.4 | 26.5 | 26.5 |
| Virginia | 27.5 | 26.0 | 25.8 |
| Washington | 27.3 | 25.7 | 25.9 |
| West Virginia | 26.5 | 25.2 | 23.9 |
| Wisconsin | 28.0 | 26.1 | 25.3 |
| Wyoming | 26.5 | 24.1 | 23.7 |

*Sources: U.S. Census Bureau*, Median Age at First Marriage for Men, *2007;*
*U.S. Census Bureau*, Median Age at First Marriage for Women, *2007;*
*Centers for Disease Control*, Births: Final Data for 2006, *57 NAT'L VITAL STAT.*
*REP. (Jan. 7, 2009).*

the Republican to the Democratic column in 2008. All three states have benefited from the increasing wealth associated with the information economy.

Later ages at marriage and first birth, however, lower overall fertility. Unsurprisingly, then, the percentage of childless women is highest in the northeastern states and lowest in the southern states.[22] The 19 states with the highest fertility rates are red, while the 16 states with the lowest fertility rates are blue.[23]

Adult abortion ratios correspond with lower birthrates. The states with the highest abortion ratios—the number of abortions per 1,000 live births to women between the ages of 15 and 44—were New York, Delaware, Washington, Massachusetts, and Connecticut.[24] These five blue states each had a ratio of over 300. The states with the lowest abortion ratios, under 100, were Colorado, Utah, Idaho, and South Dakota. Kentucky was fifth with a ratio slightly over 100.[25] Similarly, the states with the lowest abortion rates, that is, the number of abortions per thousand women of childbearing age, were Colorado, Utah, Idaho, Kentucky, and South Dakota, while those with the highest abortion rates were New York, Delaware, Washington, New Jersey, and Rhode Island.[26]

The abortion rates show a slightly different regional emphasis from the birthrates discussed earlier, although the blue state tilt remains unchanged. The less-diverse upper New England states of Vermont and New Hampshire do not appear on the lists of states with the highest abortion rates, replaced by the West Coast's Washington[27] and more of the Mid-Atlantic states: New York, New Jersey, and Delaware. The states with the lowest abortion rates are largely from the less-diverse mountain states and upper Midwest (Colorado, Utah, Idaho, and South Dakota), largely excluding the South with the exception of Kentucky.[28] Abortion rates accordingly replicate red-blue, if not always Northeast-South, patterns of division.

The final issue in family patterns concerns the number of adults who are unmarried, either because they have never married or because they have gotten a divorce. Household composition again reflects a general, if less uniform, red-blue state division. The states with the highest rates of unmarried cohabiting partners are Maine (7.3), New Hampshire (7.2), Vermont (7.1), Alaska (6.6), and, tied for fifth, Arizona and Nevada (6.3). The states reporting the fewest unmarried partners are Alabama (3.0), Utah (3.4), Arkansas (3.6), Mississippi (3.8), with Kentucky and Kansas (4.0) tied for fifth.[29]

When it comes to divorce, early marriage is typically associated with more divorce, and that is certainly true in the states we are analyzing. The states with the highest divorce rates in 2004 were Nevada,[30] Arkansas, Wyoming, Idaho, and Kentucky, while four out of the five states with the lowest divorce rates were blue: Massachusetts, followed by Pennsylvania, North Dakota, Illinois, and Connecticut.[31] Of course, divorce rates vary with the number of people marrying, particularly as those most at risk for divorce become increasingly less likely to marry at all. We also recognize that census data reflect the place where the divorce occurs, thus overstating the instability of Nevada marriages, since Nevada's lax residency laws continue to make it a destination of choice for those seeking to tie or untie the knot. Nonetheless, divorce risk increases with younger age at marriage, lower economic status, and having a baby either prior to marriage or within the first seven months after marriage.[32] Conversely, marital stability improves with age and income.[33] Accordingly, family strategies that emphasize either marrying young or marriage as the solution to an improvident pregnancy are likely to increase rates of divorce, all other things being equal.

Before turning to further analyses of these data, note that not all issues in family formation are associated with red and blue paradigms. Nonmarital birthrates, for example, reflect race more than geography. With African-American and Latina birthrates higher than white rates, and the African-American nonmarital rates double the white rates (Latinas are in between), the states with the lowest birthrates to never-married mothers are among the least diverse racially: Utah (208 per 1,000 women of childbearing age), Vermont (213), Minnesota (234), North Dakota (241), and Idaho (247).[34] In addition, they are all states with relatively small populations, without large urban centers, in the northern part of the country. Looking just at white nonmarital birthrates also produces a complex geographic pattern. In 2004, for example, the highest white rates were in Nevada, Maine, West Virginia, Indiana, and Vermont, while the lowest rates were in the District of Columbia, Utah, New Jersey, Connecticut, Colorado, and Idaho.[35] We suspect that the social meaning of the births, however, varies considerably with high rates in West Virginia reflecting the relative poverty of whites in the state while the rates in Vermont may be an indication of the greater acceptability of cohabitation generally in that part of the country.

## A CULTURAL SNAPSHOT

The demographic data suggest that life patterns do differ regionally, that some of the differences—higher teen birthrates, for example—may be a source of concern, and that the differences are great enough to suggest that family policy and family law are likely to differ regionally. Moreover, the differences in the age at marriage and the incidence of teen births are relatively recent in origin. The entire country experienced a decline in age at marriage and an increase in the teen birthrate in the 1950s; the subsequent decline in fertility and increase in the age at marriage, in contrast, has been far more regionally concentrated, with the changes occurring more thoroughly and dramatically in the Northeast and more slowly in the South, the Mountain West, and the Plains.

The differences in family structure, of course, do not occur in a vacuum. We recognize, for example, that they strongly reflect wealth and that wealth plays a major role in reinforcing both the political and family patterns we describe. Moreover, we realize that family formation varies within the states. White Californians, for example, may experience patterns more like that of Massachusetts, while the large Latino population in California marries and bears children at younger ages, producing state totals distinctly different from those of the South or Northeast. We also make no statement about causation; we cannot say, for example, that a pregnant 19-year-old is choosing to conceive and bear a child *because* she lives in Mississippi rather than Massachusetts, or even that the Mississippi teen has become pregnant because of a lack of access to contraception, less optimism about her economic future, racial patterns that make early sexuality more common for blacks than whites, or religious patterns that discourage use of birth control or abortion, though we note that others have looked at these issues.[36]

Finally, we acknowledge that our red and blue family paradigms intersect with other cultural constructs. Mormon life in middle-class Utah, for example, may differ significantly from rural life in Baptist portions of Arkansas even as they both embrace portions of the social conservative family frame. Indeed, we suspect that while there may be one dominant blue pattern for the well-educated, there are at least two comparable red patterns. The poorer red areas, such as Arkansas and Oklahoma, combine high rates of early marriage with high teen birthrates. The somewhat better-off families in states such as Utah and Nebraska have high rates of marriage at younger ages with relatively lower levels of teen pregnancy.

Despite the differences within and between states, however, we believe that the cultural differences between regions of the country frame the world views voters bring to the ballot box and the milieus in which legal issues are decided. Issues related to marriage, contraception, abortion, and divorce take on different symbolic and practical meanings if young adults characteristically marry at 22 rather than at 29, and if teen pregnancy is a routine pathway to marriage rather than an inopportune event to be managed. Moreover, we suspect that political attitudes might well vary between states where over half the population lives in married-couple households versus those where household patterns are more diverse.

Causation, however, runs in multiple directions. Bill Bishop's book *The Big Sort* argues that the regions have become more distinct—and different from each other—as the like-minded have become more likely to move closer to each other. He maintains that the most dramatic movements have occurred in the country's technological centers (e.g., Silicon Valley in California or the high-tech corridor near Boston), which attract well-educated, ambitious—and overwhelmingly blue—

professionals. Steve Sailer, a columnist at the *American Conservative*, notes further that states where the costs are lower (cheaper housing and family-related expenses) are more likely to be Republican, suggesting that family-oriented Americans may be voting with their feet as they also seek out more family-friendly communities.[37] Moreover, even if diversity exists within each region, and even if regional differences reflect an amalgam of income, class, race, and the ethnic origins of the original European immigrants who settled there, they frame family law decision making. Other scholars are examining the correlations among these factors and finding statistically significant connections between family styles and voting patterns. Michigan political scientists Ron Lesthaeghe and Lisa Neidert, for example, have demonstrated that family characteristics showed a significant correlation with voting preferences in the last three presidential elections. They measured family factors in terms of a host of variables that include postponing marriage and childbearing, overall fertility, marriage, abortion, and cohabitation rates, which they describe as indicators of the second demographic transformation (SDT) and which we link to the blue family paradigm. The political scientists found that the weaker the state's score on the composite SDT measure, the more likely it is to vote Republican, which "is to our knowledge one of the highest spatial correlations between demographic and voting behavior on record."[38]

What we are doing in our analysis is both simpler *and* more complex than that of the political scientists. It is simpler in that we are not performing the type of statistical analysis they perform. Although we accept their more-sophisticated calculation of the strength of the correlation between family characteristics and voting patterns, we do not attempt to say whether each of the variables we discuss independently correlates with political preferences. Instead, we break down the components of their term, "second demographic transition," to examine the role of factors such as teen births or abortion rates in the construction of family understandings.

In the process, we have begun to unlock the factors that help determine the acceptability of legal innovations. Family life has changed in the United States, it has changed unevenly across the country, and it is a major factor determining the life chances of the next generation—and aggravating the increased inequality that characterizes our society. The critical question for us is understanding the legal frameworks that create and reinforce different pathways to family life, such as the variations between support for abstinence-only education or contraception, the restrictions on or broader availability of abortion, the creation of family-friendly workplaces, and the meaning of marriage or cohabiting relationships. Having observed substantial demographic variation between regions, this brief exercise convinced us to probe further. We wondered what accounts for these regional differences and whether they are reflected in the law. Finding some answers requires returning to the broader literature on the family to which both of us have contributed.

## CHAPTER 2

# Sexual History

WE THINK OF modern changes in the family—plunging fertility rates, high average ages at marriage, and the explosion in divorce and nonmarital births—as extraordinary. The combination of these changes in recent American history is certainly remarkable. Nonetheless, family composition and norms have varied throughout history. In seventeenth-century England, for example, the average age at marriage for women was 25.9 years, older than the average at the end of the twentieth century, and 17.5% of women did not marry at all. The percentage of upper-class children who remained unmarried was even higher. Historian Lawrence Stone reports that the ranks of unmarried males rose from 15% in the early part of the seventeenth century to more than 20% by the century's end, and unmarried females rose from 10% in the sixteenth century to 15% in the early part of the next century to 25% in the years between 1675 and 1799.[1] The stage was set for *Pride and Prejudice* and other English novels capturing women's longing for a groom.

Today's changes, though dramatic, take place on different terms. Higher numbers of unmarried people are producing higher rates of nonmarital births. Like the English precedents, the increasing number of people who remain unmarried corresponds to profound economic changes and new class-based strategies to adjust to them. In understanding how the American family has changed, and how these transformations might explain regional, class, and racial disparities, it is useful to compare today's developments with those of the nineteenth-century American family. In both cases, the middle classes championed delayed marriage, greater investment in children, and smaller families as the way to secure economic advantage. And, in both cases, these changes in family formation underlay moral transformations that enhanced class differences. The nineteenth-century version, however, allied the middle class with increased sexual restraint and greater celebration of women's (largely white, Protestant, middle-class women's) virtue. Today's family changes ally the prospering middle class with what many others see as a wholesale assault on the very idea of virtue.

## DEMOGRAPHIC TRANSFORMATIONS

The United States has experienced two "demographic transformations,"[2] each of which reflected worldwide technological shifts: the nineteenth-century change from a rural, agricultural economy to a more urban industrial one, and the late twentieth-century shift from the industrial era to an information economy. Both transformations redefined the relationship between home and market, and both produced greater investment in children by delaying childbearing and reducing overall fertility. Both did so, at least in part, by redefining gender roles and by moving to counter an overreliance on the shotgun marriage. Moreover, in both transformations, at least in the short term, changes in family organization exacerbated societal inequality as the wealthier middle class used the benefits of the new system to enhance its class standing.[3]

Demographers generally use the term "demographic transition" to mean the changes in a society as it moves from high birth and mortality rates to lower ones.[4] Since the 1980s, some demographers have distinguished between the first transition, which was characterized by declining fertility and mortality and which began in Europe in the eighteenth century, and the second transition, which reduced fertility even further in the latter half of the twentieth century. A large literature ties these family changes to changes in economic production, the rise of an expressive individualism that celebrates individual freedom and self-fulfillment rather than duty or obligation, and redefinitions of social norms and the law that make sense of and reinforce the reorganization of family life.[5]

We have each written about these events at greater length elsewhere. One of us, disagreeing with Nobel Prize–winner Gary Becker's work in economics, which claimed that the changes produced *less* specialization within the family, instead showed that these changes produced *more* specialization overall.[6] Thus, the first demographic transformation accompanied the rise of the industrial economy. That economy created greater demand for professionals and executives, rewarding greater investment—and longer periods of formal education and training—in the male children of the middle class. The information economy similarly created greater demand for highly educated women, rewarding greater investment in daughters as well as sons, and creating even greater pressures to delay the beginning of family formation. The other, disagreeing with the numerous theorists who have described the second transformation as producing a diminution or even a void in moral values, argued instead that the changes have produced a transition to a new set of values, more appropriate to men's and women's changing roles in the new social structure.[7] Our work intersects with that of other scholars who claim that with the economic transformation has come greater wealth and, with that greater wealth, societies less focused on the material terms of survival and more concerned with self-actualization and less material needs; some label this "post-materialist."[8] Both the economic changes (especially greater wealth) and the societal changes (fewer children, at later ages, and more support for individual expression) make possible greater diversity in family forms and values. While there are many ways we (and other scholars) can describe these changes, we will use the terms of the demographers (first and second demographic transitions or transformations) to describe the effects of these transformations on American culture and society.

The first transformation created a new middle class to staff the professions and the managerial ranks of the industrial economy.[9] Critical to its success was greater investment in boys' formal education, which required in turn postponing marriage and entry into the labor force.[10] An important vehicle in producing that result was an emphasis on women's purity and their greater agency in forging the new moral code.[11] As women become more able and willing to say no,[12] the number of brides who gave birth within eight and a half months of their weddings declined from 30% in 1800 to 10% by 1860, the average number of children per family fell from eight in 1800 to four by century's end, and the average age at marriage rose.[13]

Law professor Jane Larson provides a vivid description of the change in courtship patterns. She observes that a "modest girl's shyness and innocence were her excuses for sexual delay, allowing her a leisurely period of courtship during which she could observe her lover and judge his qualities as a future husband."[14] Ironically, while repressing women's sexuality, Victorian conventions of female modesty reinforced women's moral authority, allowing them to withstand men's sexual advances. Thus, female virtue secured strategic advantages in the competitive "marriage market." Victorian advice manuals reinforced these mores, suggesting that men might dally with permissive women, but they "married only modest ones." The new advice combined threats and incentives to inculcate sexual modesty in young women to protect them against the lures of lotharios who might derail otherwise promising futures.[15]

These changes affected the moral understandings of the country as a whole in spite of the fact that the urban middle class, the driving force behind the changes, constituted a tiny part of the population. Newly created women's magazines, which were only too happy to offer courtship suggestions, influenced the farm wives who would constitute the majority of women until the much greater urbanization of the twentieth century.[16] But class divisions ironically served to reinforce, rather than undermine, the new order. Social historian Mary Ryan emphasizes that the cultural divide in upstate New York involved the often-pejorative comparison of native-born Protestants with newly arriving Catholic immigrants. The Protestant middle class identified moral superiority with their emphasis on their daughters' chastity, their determination to keep their children away from the temptations of either employment or romance at too young an age, and their restriction of family size.[17] The opinion leaders in newspapers, legislatures, courts, and many pulpits heralded the new middle-class standards as the moral order of the day and the standard by which other classes might be found wanting.[18]

The second transformation began in similar fashion in the twentieth century as technology transformed the economy. The "post-industrial economy" in which we now live has moved away from heavy manufacturing to greater emphasis on the information economy and the service sector.[19] The result is even greater returns to education, this time for both men and women, as the new technologies have increased the opportunities for well-educated "knowledge" workers, and expanded demand for the types of services women historically performed, such as administrative and health services. Just as the nineteenth-century changes brought greater specialization among men, the twentieth- and twenty-first-century changes involve greater specialization among women. With growth in the number of working women, not only could women enter management and the professions alongside men, but new positions opened as women supervised other women in expanding hospital, restaurant, office, and retail settings, and the new class of high-income working mothers hires women from different economic classes to care for their children and to perform what were once viewed as mothers' domestic responsibilities.[20]

Moreover, just as the nineteenth century required a family reorganization and a new moral code for the middle class to reap the benefits of the new order, so too have the twentieth- and twenty-first-century changes required moral understandings that facilitate this greater investment in women—and even later childbearing and smaller family size. Unlike the first demographic transition, however, these new moral understandings are unlikely to rest on increased parental vigilance and celebration of women's virtue.

While conservatives continue to decry the sexual revolution of the 1960s, that era followed from the demographic changes of the '50s, which sounded the death knell of the old moral order.[21] Indeed, as historian Stephanie Coontz argues, the "traditional" family of the '50s was in fact a qualitatively new phenomenon that reversed the trends of the rest of the century.[22] By 1960, the number of pregnant brides rose to almost a third, a level not seen since 1800.[23] The average age at marriage fell to the lowest levels in the twentieth century.[24] And, of course, the postwar era produced the "baby boom"—and dramatic rises in fertility. Dating became an exercise in sexual brinkmanship, with marriage or adoption as the fallbacks for sexual experimentation. The changing mores of the postwar era and the needs of the new economy were on a collision course, and something had to give way.

## THE NEW MIDDLE-CLASS MORALITY

What gave way first was the old moral code. The sexual revolution and the women's movement that we now identify with the '60s remade middle-class morality from an emphasis on women's virtue to a concern for equality and responsibility.[25] The transformation began as the baby boomers reached their college years. The new demographic bridled at colleges' parietal rules and at sexual double standards. The "pill" galvanized the shift from abstinence to contraception as the hallmark of responsible behavior.[26] The emotionally agonizing choice of abortion also reinforced the conviction that childbearing should be reserved for the right partner at the right time in life. The media celebrated the new sexual freedom,[27] and by the '80s, the majority of Americans no longer condemned premarital sexuality. By 1997, a Gallup poll found that 55% of American adults agreed that premarital sex was not wrong, and among those most directly affected, viz, those aged 18–29, 75% agreed that "pre-marital sexual relations are not wrong."[28] Moreover, actions were reflecting attitudes: 2002 data indicate that, by age 20, 77% of respondents had experienced sex, and 75% had experienced premarital sex. By age 44, 95% of respondents (94% of women, 96% of men, and 97% of those who had ever had sex) had experienced pre-marital sex. Even among those who abstained until at least age 20, 81% had experienced premarital sex by age 44.[29]

The remaking of moral understandings produced a cycle of rein-forcing shifts in attitudes. As women gained greater ability to avoid unplanned pregnancies, men felt less obliged to marry the women they impregnated.[30] As nonmarital sexuality became more acceptable, so too did the children who resulted, making their mothers more willing to raise them without marrying.[31]

In a parallel fashion, the shotgun marriages of the '50s produced the divorces of the 1970s. Younger marriages and shotgun weddings corre-late with higher divorce rates, and the no-fault legislation enacted in the '70s unleashed the pent-up demand for divorce that had begun build-ing with the explosion of younger marriages. Divorce rates increased exponentially, peaking in the late '70s at roughly the point when the children born during the post-War baby boom were leaving home.[32]

More divorces fueled, in turn, greater wariness about marriage, and greater access to contraception and abortion made it easier to delay marriage and childbearing. During the "baby bust" years of the 1970s, fertility rates plummeted as younger couples invested more in men's and women's education and postponed marriage and childbear-ing. Starting in the '70s, men began postponing family formation in ever-larger numbers that spanned every measurable group.[33] While overall fertility has risen recently, the intervening quarter-century transformed pathways into adulthood. Teens were increasingly likely to have premarital sex at a younger age,[34] but people were getting mar-ried later. Indeed, the change in age at first marriage is striking. For women, the median age rose from 20 in 1961 to 25.3 in 2005. For men, it increased from 22 to 27 in the same time period.[35] The societal structure and support underlying more-traditional family formation (e.g., high school romances and unintended pregnancies that lead to early marriages) have atrophied.

Less-reliable marriages created greater incentives for women to invest in their own earning potential. As women gained experience and self-confidence, they won benefits that made work more attractive and rewarding; with longer work experience and greater educational equalization, they became freer to leave unhappy marriages; and as divorce became more of a possibility, women tended to hedge their bets by insisting on the right to work. Although very few researchers believe that women's employment has been a direct cause of the rising divorce rate, most agree that women's new employment options have made it easier for couples to separate if they are dissatisfied for other reasons. In turn, the fragility of marriage has joined economic pressures, income incentives, educational preparation, and dissatisfaction with domestic isolation as one of the reasons that modern women choose to work.[36] With greater independence, the consequences of divorce for women became less catastrophic, and unhappy partners felt less pressure to stay together. Increasing divorces made single parents more visible, which weakened even further the stigma associated with nonmarital births. Taken together, these changes undermined the economic and social coercion that had promoted family stability whatever the quality of the enduring unions.

Conservative writers decry these changes as signs of moral decay. Indeed, the shift away from marriage and two-parent families has undeniably had negative consequences for children.[37] It is a mistake, however, to see the transformation only in terms of family disintegration. Underlying the changes and less visible than the *Playboy* centerfolds that merit denunciation from the pulpit is a new middle-class ethic—with handsome rewards for those able to reap its benefits. The college-educated, who postpone childrearing until the parents achieve a measure of financial self-sufficiency and emotional maturity, have become more likely to marry and less likely to divorce than the rest of the population, with two-parent families that remain intact, replicating the statistics that existed before no-fault divorce, the pill, and legalized abortion.[38] As we saw in the demographic map of the first chapter, the rest of the country has seen skyrocketing rates of nonmarital births, divorce, and single-parent families, magnifying the effects of income inequality on children.[39] Almost the exact opposite set of circumstances typifies the new middle class. Among the top quartile of educated women, only 7% of children were born outside of marriage compared to 43% in the bottom educated quartile. Moreover, college-educated women have now become more likely to marry than they once were and less likely than other women to divorce. For couples who have four-year degrees, divorce rates peaked in the late '70s with roughly a quarter of marriages ending within ten years. The rates then

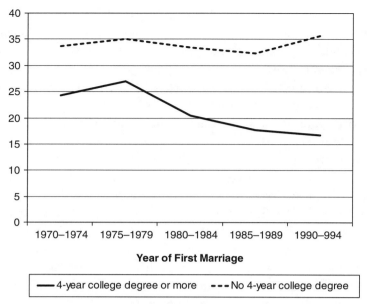

FIGURE 2.1: First Marriages Ending in Divorce within 10 Years as a Percentage of All First Marriages by Female Educational Attainment
SOURCE: Steven P. Martin, *Growing Evidence for a "Divorce Divide"? Education and Marital Dissolution Rates in the U.S. since the 1970s, available at* http://www.russellsage.org/publications/workingpapers/divorcedivide/document.

fell to 17% by the late 1980s. For couples without college degrees, divorce rates declined only slightly (to about 32%) by the late '80s.[40]

The hallmark of this new middle-class ethic is the later age at family formation, when adult behavior has stabilized. For the best-educated quartile of American women, mothers' median age at first birth rose from 26 in 1970 to 32 in 2000.[41] For mothers in the bottom quartile, it remained relatively flat in the early 20s.[42] For those who avoid early childbearing, conventional families with two married parents and a high degree of stability follow to a remarkable degree with a minimum of external coercion.[43] Those who have most unequivocally embraced the new patterns are those with college and postgraduate educations, who have tended to cluster to an even greater degree than in previous eras in urban areas, in economically prospering locales, and on the coasts—in short, in the regions we set out as politically and demographically blue in chapter 1.

If there is anything that represents the blue family morality, it is the bloggers who responded to news of Bristol Palin's pregnancy in late 2008, observing: "Ah, the naiveté of childhood. Who didn't want to marry their high school sweetheart? Pregnant and seventeen with no high school education isn't the way to begin life."[44] The sexuality is understandable and forgivable, but marriage is neither necessary nor sufficient. It is the decision to have the child that rankles, and it does so not in terms of overarching moral principles—thou shalt not have a child for whom one is not prepared to provide optimal circumstances—but in terms of instrumental values: waiting produces a better life.

## MORAL BACKLASH

This new middle-class ethic, unlike its nineteenth-century counterpart, is a direct affront to those who do not accept its premises. The nineteenth-century emphasis on purity, with its condemnation of those who could not live up to its principles, may have been hypocritical (and often racist), but it reaffirmed consensus-based standards of morality.[45] The new version, in contrast, is disdainful of traditional moral restraints, insistent on the rights of women and same-sex couples, and skeptical of once-venerated institutions such as marriage.[46]

Traditionalists have responded to the changes in family form, the negative consequences for children, and the class-based nature of the transformation with a sense of crisis.[47] If advocates of the new order are right that a promising future is the best contraceptive, this is disturbing news for poorer men and women who face less-hopeful prospects. Moreover, if investment in women opens new opportunities to prosper in a post-industrial world, it does little for the poorly educated men who have less to offer in a society in which the factories that once employed them have moved overseas and the farms of their youth have given way to mechanized agribusiness conglomerates. The advice to defer childbearing until financial independence just does not resonate for those who may never achieve it.

At the same time, the growing gap between the beginning of sexual activity and marriage creates much more dissonance for evangelicals and their parents than it does for those with more tolerant attitudes toward sexuality. In today's society, Protestant evangelical teens experience the biggest gap between beliefs and behavior. Both the teens and their parents hold more-conservative sexual attitudes than many others, but evangelically affiliated adolescents, for a variety of reasons that include class differences, lose their virginity at younger ages than the average for many other religious groups, and they are almost as likely to do so with someone other than the partner they will marry.[48] Sociologist Mark Regnerus reports:

> [Evangelical adolescents]...are urged to drink deeply from the waters of American individualism and its self-focused pleasure ethic, yet they are asked to value time-honored religious traditions like family and chastity. They attempt to do both (while other religious groups don't attempt this), and serving two masters is difficult. What results is a unique dialectic of sexual-conservatism-with-sexual-activity; a combination that breeds instability and the persistent suffering of consequences like elevated teen pregnancy rates.[49]

More than half of the weekly churchgoers, who constituted the most devout in Regnerus's sample, were no longer virgins by the age of 18, and well over 90% of all evangelical adults engage in sex before they marry; even those who delay sexual activity into their 20s nonetheless are likely to engage in premarital sex.[50]

This combination of sex and conservatism breeds (in addition to generational tensions) a set of reinforcing cycles. More sex prompts more sermons and more emphasis on abstinence. More religion may, in fact, delay the beginning of sexual activity, particularly for the devout, who constitute 20–25% of the evangelicals Regnerus studied.[51] It also, however, makes it more likely that teens who engage in sex will fail to use contraception, which in turn increases the likelihood of pregnancy. More pregnancy fuels parental concern and—as we will see in the next chapter—more forced marriages that raise the risk of divorce. Early marriage and childbearing, in addition to increasing instability, derails education and limits earning potential.[52] More-limited men's income compels women's greater workforce participation and, especially when it occurs because of the husband's limitations as a breadwinner, decreases family happiness, particularly among the most traditional families. The consequential sense of failure increases the demands to constrain the popular culture—and blue family practices such as contraception and abortion—that undermines parental efforts to instill the right moral values in children.[53]

The red analysis of our changing mores and its prescription for renewal have some validity. Greater religiosity does have a positive impact on sexual behavior and family commitment—but only for the most observant. Teachings that reinforce sexual restraint are most effective in the context of a network of the like-minded, who "teach and enable comprehensive religious perspectives about sexuality to compete more effectively against ubiquitous sexually permissive scripts" and provide supervised time and space that reinforce parental values and an orientation toward future goals, such as education.[54] The most significant effect of these teachings is delay—religiously devout teens do begin sexual activity a year later on average than less-devout teens who profess the same religious beliefs—but even the most devout overwhelmingly do not abstain until marriage.[55] Halfway measures that preach without providing supervision or support, or that restrict access to contraception without persuading teens to abstain, may be counterproductive. Moreover, such measures at their best may have an impact on the most-religious teens (a minority even among evangelicals), while increasing the risk that the relatively less-religious teens in these communities will become pregnant or suffer from preventable sexually transmitted diseases (STDs). Additionally, greater sexual restraint, even if it reduces the number of unintended pregnancies, does not entirely solve the matter of divorce. As we examine in greater detail in the next chapter, younger marriages provide a less-secure economic foundation for family life than they did in other eras, and lower income is a risk factor for divorce. That risk is compounded if the wife who would prefer a more-traditional division of family responsibilities has to work to support the family. Higher divorce rates, in turn, contribute to a sense of moral decay even in communities with more-stable family patterns than the country at large.

Central to the conservative calls to reinforce shared values, therefore, have been marriage promotion efforts. These efforts emphasize the special status of marriage as the institution that unites sex, procreation, and childrearing and the importance of permanence as a critical aspect of marital commitment. The Institute for American Values, in its statement *Marriage and the Law*, reasons: "The vast majority of human children are created through acts of passion between men and women. Connecting children to their mother and father requires a social and legal institution called 'marriage' with sufficient power, weight, and social support to influence the erotic behavior of young men and women."[56] Rather than ground family morality in investment in higher education and disciplined childbearing, these advocates continue to celebrate the unity of sex, marriage, and reproduction. The reward in this system, particularly for those who may never reach the enhanced status that comes with dual college-educated earners, is family life itself. For the traditional order to maintain its moral force, women must "save themselves" for marriage, men must have consistent sexual access to women exclusively through marriage, and marriage must remain a prerequisite for responsible parenthood.[57] By contrast, if men enjoy sex without responsibility and if women can construct parenthood on terms of their own choosing, why does anyone (and more particularly the 18- and 19-year-olds eager to get on with their lives) have reason to wait—or plan, invest, save, and prove themselves ready for adulthood?

The welfare reform legislation enacted in the mid-1990s reflects this reasoning. Congressional proponents characterized it as a measure intended to address "the crisis of out-of-wedlock childbearing,"[58] and the first three legislative findings state: "(1) Marriage is the foundation of a successful society. (2) Marriage is an essential institution of a successful society which promotes the interests of children. (3) Promotion of responsible fatherhood and motherhood is integral to successful child rearing and the well-being of children."[59] The fact that welfare reform did little to affect marriage rates among the population most likely to receive benefits did not affect the importance of the public reaffirmation of marriage for red family constituents. The conflicts between the competing world views had entered the political realm.

## CULTURAL CONFLICT

This clash of moral world views plays itself out in settings that have always involved a sizable degree of intensity, viz, the control of sexuality. Moreover, these competing world views depend on different mechanisms to instill their different visions of the "good life." The blue family morality is cast in the language of reason and instrumental values. It may be agnostic on the permissibility of nonmarital sexuality, but it is unequivocal in concluding that unprotected sex is unwise, and having a child that derails the life chances of mother, father, and baby is wrong. To instill these values, however, it prefers private discipline and internalized precepts to public sanction. Tolerance is the order of the day for the public square.

If there is internal tension in this vision, it lies with the importance of childbearing itself. For blue families, children follow career success and relationship stability. Critics, however, charge that, in such a world, children become an "add-on," lower in priority in their claims on parental time and attention than adult concerns and less central to family and society. Even those who would dispute this conclusion acknowledge a practical concern: deferred childbearing for many women may lead to no children, in part because of the age-related risks of infertility. These risks are greater for poorer women and for African-Americans, both of whom suffer from higher levels of infertility at younger ages and have less access to the kind of health care that might prevent or ameliorate difficulties with reproduction. Waiting, whatever its benefits for children, is hard to advocate on a universal basis; those societies, whether in Massachusetts or northern Europe, that have fully embraced the new values have seen fertility rates fall below replacement—and often in circumstances where the adults might ideally prefer more children.

For red families, the central irony is that the moralistic basis of family attitudes requires and generates even stronger pressures for reinforcement. Adherents see themselves as an embattled minority whose hold on their own children is endangered. In the era of the pill, red efforts to restrain sexuality take considerably more effort than blue efforts to restrain reproduction. Moreover, the most-effective means of doing so—community vigilance and reinforcement of the norms of chastity and family stability—have become much harder to produce in a society that disagrees in profound ways on family values.

The values of the blue paradigm therefore threaten adherents of the red paradigm at the same time that the blue script of financial independence before marriage leaves out younger and poorer families. These families have always required greater support. In today's world, however, where formal education has become increasingly important to economic success and where increased mobility both multiplies opportunities and undermines family and community networks, that support is harder to come by.

## CONCLUSION

The economic changes of the late twentieth and early twenty-first centuries reinforce the dominance of the blue family model in the wealthier and more urban areas of the country. Young adults who are able to realize the benefits of increased education and delayed childbearing attain greater socioeconomic and geographic mobility. College graduates are more than twice as likely as those who do not finish college to move across state lines, and when they move, they choose communities with more opportunities and more compatible forms of cultural expression. As like chooses like, the wealthier areas of the country become richer, and the dominance of the middle-class model increases within those regions, increasing in turn the support for controlled childbearing, two-career families, and egalitarian gender roles.

The rest of the country, and particularly the more rural, more traditional, and slower-growing communities, would like to reaffirm traditional values. The reaffirmation of traditional values, however, has become more difficult as economic conditions reserve greater rewards for the well-educated and undermine the traditional division of labor on which family stability previously rested. Moreover, the reaffirmation may prove to be counterproductive for the community as a whole if restricted access to contraception and abortion increases teen births, early marriages produce more divorces, and a changing family structure undermines the educational and employment prospects of parents and children.

These changes, which correspond to increasing economic inequality in the United States as the blue areas of the country have disproportionately benefited from the information economy, have understandably increased the sense of moral alarm in red states. The question of what can and should be done to address these issues, however, depends on both the diagnosis of the problem—moral decay or too-early family formation?—and the ability to garner the political will to address the underlying issues. We take up these issues in the next two chapters.

## CHAPTER 3

# The Age of Division

PSYCHOLOGIST ABIGAIL BAIRD asked a group of adults and teens to identify "good" and "bad" ideas. One of the ideas she asked about was the advisability of "swimming with sharks." While the adults responded instantly with a visceral "no way," the teens did not connect the image of sharks with palpable *feelings* of fear, danger, or instinctive caution. They had to think about whether swimming with sharks was a good or bad idea, and they did so without any corresponding "gut" reactions to process. It turns out that adults and teens use different parts of their brains to guide their responses. Adults use their amygdala—the evolutionarily older, emotion center of the brain. Teens use the frontal cortex, the evolutionarily newer, reason center of the brain, which is not as efficient. Imagine, then, that instead of swimming with sharks, the question becomes: "Should I take a ride in a stolen car with Rick, the coolest kid in school?"[1]

If the single biggest factor dividing red and blue families is age at family formation, then it becomes worthwhile to consider *how* age matters. In chapters 1 and 2, we showed that red and blue family patterns reflect different ideals about family formation. These understandings come from diverging attitudes toward sexuality, attitudes that reflect religious, cultural, class, and legal differences. In this chapter, we show that age at family formation matters, that red and blue family formation intersects the life cycle at different points with different consequences. Within the red family paradigm, with its higher teen birthrates and younger average age at marriage, couples enter adulthood to a greater degree through the assumption of family roles and require more help and support in doing so. With the later marriage of the blue family ideal, couples attain emotional maturity and financial independence *before* they enter into more-permanent commitments. As the parents of adolescents realize all too well, beginning a family at 19 is a very different matter from doing so at 31 or even 23. Changes in the economy have made younger marriages more perilous, and as larger portions of the population marry at later ages—or not at all—societal support for younger couples diminishes. Within the blue family paradigm, this simply reinforces support for greater delay; within the red family world, it increases the calls to instill moral fiber.

As people throughout history have known, young minds are more malleable than older ones. So, a traditional view has held, if marriages are to last, young people should be socialized into pro-marriage habits even before they enter adulthood. Let them enjoy independence too long, and they may never tolerate the deference and commitment to a mate that a good marriage requires. Marriage is seen as particularly important to "civilizing men, turning their attention away from dangerous, antisocial, or self-centered activities"; indeed, the various "norms, status rewards, and social support offered to men by marriage all combine to help men walk down the path to adult responsibility," according to an influential group of family scholars working with the Institute for American Values.[2]

Young people, however malleable, the blue view goes, are also immature. They are more likely to be impulsive, unfaithful, insensitive, and unreliable. Indeed, if evolutionary analysis makes any sense, young adults will be programmed to seek new mates, sire new offspring, and take too many risks—whether they are married or not. Let them acquire a measure of maturity, instead, and making marriage work will change from an uphill struggle to running downhill. After all, the conventional wisdom of yore also recognized that, after a period of sowing their wild oats, adults could be expected to settle down into patterns of greater stability. Families formed as youthful exuberance wanes are more likely to endure without external coercion.

Whatever the truth of these views, the choice between them must be made in a way that takes changing realities into account. Marriage and parenthood once served as important markers of the assumption of adult roles. Family formation was integrally bound to the transition to adulthood. Social support, supervision, and, in many cases, coercion shepherded the transition, assisting fragile families in acquiring stable foundations and helping them to navigate the difficult early years that precede full adult maturity. Gender roles further cemented the relationships. Young women, especially if they had children soon after marriage, depended on their husbands for economic support. If they were unhappy in their relationships, there was often no place to go.

Today, the pathways are different. When researchers ask what signifies the entry into adulthood, young Americans are inclined to reject both chronological age and the assumption of adult roles, such as full-time employment or marriage and parenthood. Instead, they choose individual factors as the top three criteria: accepting responsibility for oneself, making independent decisions and relating to parents on an equal footing, and becoming financially independent.[3] Family formation is neither necessary nor sufficient to mark the transition to adulthood; rather, today's young Americans look to qualities of mind and judgment. With experience and maturity, however, also comes independence, and independence for both men and women changes the marriage dynamic. Together, these factors pose a challenge to traditionalist models: to be successful, younger marriage and childbearing have to account both for youthful immaturity and the changing models for marital relationships.

In this chapter, we examine the clash between the red and blue paradigms in terms of the transition from younger to later marriages. As we indicated in the last two chapters, the changing economy has produced much later average ages at marriage for the country as whole. These changes produce a dilemma with red and blue answers. The blue paradigm suggests: embrace the transformation, teach young people to wait, and consider age-appropriate interventions to reconcile exploration with responsibility. The red paradigm retorts: what is necessary is to reinstill the right moral values, reasserting parental control over adolescents and commitment to marriage in early adulthood.

Accordingly, this chapter first examines the effects of the economic changes on prospects for marriage, the implications of new research on the transition to adulthood, and the prospects for success of new strategies to guide sexuality and marriage.

## THE NEW PATHWAYS TO ADULTHOOD

The intersection of family formation with mature brain development has varied over time. Psychologist Abigail Baird suggests that the first stage of puberty involves sexual maturity, and the shift in focus from parents to peers is an understandable first step in preparation for reproduction. In most societies, marriage—and the structure that marriage brings—has followed relatively quickly after full sexual maturity, at least for women. Some pre-industrial societies, for example, arrange marriages for prepubescent girls. Their entry into adult roles then takes place under their husbands' supervision. Most societies, of course, wait at least until the bride is physically of age, but any society that values virginity closely supervises the period between puberty and marriage.[4] Moreover, for women whose adult roles are tied to childbearing and housekeeping, why wait? Women's fertility—and, presumably, attractiveness to potential mates—peaks by the early 20s.

Over the past several centuries, women's socialization into adulthood has typically taken place within the context of courtship and marriage—experiences that place a premium on stereotypical gender roles. The big factor in women's socialization into marriage was the extent of women's economic and social dependence on their husbands. The marriage of a young woman right out of her father's home into her husband's has often been analyzed as a strategy designed to encourage women's acceptance of male authority. Moreover, whatever the initial relationship between husband and wife, the quick birth of children is likely to reinforce gendered roles and female dependence. Studies of power within relationships emphasize that women who have responsibility for the care of young children experience the least power in their marriages.[5] Early childbearing with or without the shotgun marriage thus locks women into relatively dependent roles. For women who marry young, therefore, their socialization into adulthood is socialization into a system of inequality. Some scholars even suggest that women's acceptance of these gendered understandings contributes to marital longevity and relationship quality.[6]

The picture for men is more varied. Males typically mature later than women (look at any group of seventh-grade boys and girls to see the differences) and marry later. In societies that emphasize financial independence as a precondition for marriage, many men marry late or not at all.[7] For those who marry later in life, habits and character are forged in contexts other than courtship and reproduction.

In many periods, classes, or societies, however, men have married much earlier, soon after sexual maturity. Nobel Laureate George Akerlof and economists Janet Yellen and Michael Katz took a comprehensive look at the relationship between shotgun marriages and the technological innovations of contraception and abortion. They contrast contemporary acceptance of single motherhood with the earlier stigma attached to the same behavior, at a time when a man was expected to marry a woman whom he had gotten pregnant. They describe courtship among working-class San Franciscans in the early '60s as "sexual" and "brief," and they quote a young man who explained, "If a girl gets pregnant, you married her. There wasn't no choice. So I married her."[8] Marriage in such circumstances then brought substantial pressure for the man to support his family and for the woman who was now economically dependent on him to stay with him so long as he did.[9] For these couples, the improvident pregnancy triggered the assumption of adult responsibilities the couple might have preferred to postpone.[10] The husband's employment setting then shaped much of his entry into adulthood, the demands of motherhood shaped hers, and family pressure and financial dependence kept them together in what was often a turbulent start to family life.

In those societies in which men marry at older ages, the most common reason for the delay is the time needed to establish financial self-sufficiency, but whether marriage occurs early or late, men's introduction to the workplace has tended to be an important aspect of socialization into adulthood. Women, in contrast, whether engaged in paid employment before or not, have rarely enjoyed the opportunity for independence: their socialization occurred in terms of expectations for marriage.

Over the last half-century, patterns of American family formation have been transformed, as we discussed in chapter 2. The relatively high-paying positions available to men without a high school diploma have moved overseas, the service sector positions traditionally held by women have expanded, and the payoff for investment in postsecondary education and training has dramatically increased, spurred in part by technological changes raising the demand for and value of more highly educated workers.[11] Women are now more likely than men to graduate from college (21.3% to 17.8%) and high school (61.5% to 59.8%).[12] Men's occupational status in the workplace is lower than women's with 40% of women aged 18–34 holding professional, technical, or white-collar positions compared to only a quarter of men.[13] Both hourly wages and employment figures have correspondingly decreased for men while increasing for women.[14] Racial inequality has also worsened with African-American men born in the '60s faring worse than African-American men born a decade earlier.[15] In addition, African-American women have outpaced African-American men's educational and employment prospects to an even greater degree than white women have gained on white men.[16]

Better-educated, more affluent, and more ambitious Americans spend the years between 16 and 24 in school or in temporary positions that add to their later employability. A high percentage of lower-income men in this age group, however, are neither in school nor employed on a regular basis. For the least-advantaged men, prison has become the single institution most likely to shape the transition to adulthood; yet, it discourages both human capital formation and marriage rates for those who are released.[17]

Moreover, even for those who secure full-time employment, the rate of employment turnover has increased in the economy as a whole, making the ability to acquire new skills, seek new employment, and manage the period in between jobs more critical for every social class. Henry Farber, an economics professor at Princeton University, finds: "By virtually any measure, more recent cohorts of workers have been with their current employers for less time at specific ages."[18] He concludes that the drop in long-term employment for men has been dramatic.[19] These factors, in turn, have changed the nature of the 20s: young people not only spend more time in school, but they also find it takes longer to get the experience and training that lead to economic security and long-term employability. These changes further increase the importance of two incomes, with each partner not only adding to the overall family income but also seeing each other through times of unemployment.

For the country as a whole, this has meant a shift in the relationship between family formation and adulthood. In 1960, for example, 77% of the men and 65% of the women had completed all of the major transitions (leaving home, finishing school, becoming financially independent, getting married, and having a child) by the age of 30. In 2000, in contrast, only 46% of women and 31% of men age 30 had done so.[20] Indeed, in 1960, 30% of the *20-year-old* women and 70% of the 25-year-olds had completed all of the major life events. In 2000, only 6% of the women had done so by 20 and 25% by age 25.[21]

With these changes, Americans have also shifted their attitudes toward the markers of adulthood. The majority of Americans believe that young adults *ought not* be ready to support a family before their mid-20s and that many will not be able to do so until their 30s.[22] The traits that now mark adulthood are those associated with full cognitive and emotional maturity and financial independence. Bristol Palin and Levi Johnston are not, in this perspective, fully adult.

## RISKY BUSINESS: YOUTHFUL BEHAVIOR

Nor can marriage today compensate for the lack of emotional maturity that has always marked adolescence. A growing literature addresses late adolescent development, and it almost seems as if young people, in their definitions of adulthood, have been reading the latest findings in neuro-science, which focus on the recognition that the brain may not reach full adult development until the early to mid-20s. Cognitive neuroscientists examine the development of brain structure and operation. While they are still a long way from charting the precise relationships between brain development and judgment, neuroscientists have established that, con-trary to earlier belief that the brain changed little after early childhood, brain structure and function continue to change into the 20s.[23] Law pro-fessor Elizabeth Scott and psychologist Laurence Steinberg suggest that adolescents may have the cognitive capacity for adult decision making, but they lack the skill and experience necessary for reliable judgments in stressful situations. Scott and Steinberg further agree, on the basis of psychological research, that psychosocial development proceeds more slowly than cognitive ability and that a stable sense of identity does not emerge until early adulthood.[24]

Psychologist Abigail Baird provides some of the most intriguing research on how teen brains differ from adult brains. Her studies use MRIs (magnetic resonance imaging) to peer into the brains of still-developing college students and to chart the regions involved in decision making. Through MRIs, scientists can scan the brain to get pictures of which parts are actively involved in decision making. Researchers have established, for example, that the last area of the brain to develop is the prefrontal cortex (the reasoning center of the brain), and the con-nections between the prefrontal cortex and the emotional or visceral centers of the brain take longer still to mature.[25] At the same time, the most profound differences between adult and adolescent behav-ior involve decision making, or executive-level processing. Teenagers and adults, for example, both perform the complex visual calculation necessary to determine when a car will enter an intersection in similar ways. They are more likely to differ in how they reach a decision about whether to attempt to beat the approaching car into the intersection or to wait[26]—or whether it is a good idea to swim with sharks.

Baird's examination of college freshmen, who are in their first year away from home, found continuing changes in five different brain regions associated with the conscious awareness of emotion, the inte-gration of sensory information into higher-order processes, and the formulation of strategies.[27] She found that the most accurate responses for a variety of tasks required the integration of reason and emotion; reason is much less efficient in the absence of emotion, and reason in turn makes the emotional parts of the brain more accurate.[28] Yet, the last parts of the brain to develop are the connections that more thoroughly integrate cognitive and emotional processing. Both Baird and Dr. Ruben Gur, who is the director of the University of Pennsylvania Medical Center, agree that there is strong and growing evidence that the brain continues to mature into the early 20s "in those relevant parts that govern impulsivity, judgment, planning for the future, foresight of consequences, and other characteristics."[29] Students going off to college, the military, and their first jobs after high school really do return as different people, with the brain reaching full maturity in the early 20s and the experiences in late adolescence shaping the specific pathways of brain development.

Scientists may not be able to precisely chart the effects of the late-developing neural connections between the brain's reasoning (prefrontal cortex) and emotional (amygdala) centers on behavior, and we know that individual adolescents vary in their experiences and maturity in ways that college lab MRIs may not exactly capture. Nonetheless, a large body of traditional research documents the roller coaster that describes many aspects of teen behavior, including teens' likelihood of engaging in risky, foolish, and shortsighted actions. Scott and Steinberg, in examining juvenile crime and behavior, use these data to distinguish between what they call "cognitive" capacity and "psycho-social" development.[30] Their insights parallel the newer findings on brain development.[31] They observe that, by mid-adolescence (around age 16), teens resemble adults in their cognitive capacity, that is, their ability to learn through education and experience; their information-processing skills, such as attention, short- and long-term memory, and organization; and their overall ability to understand and reason. In short, teens have the same ability as adults to judge the approach of that speeding car as it enters the intersection.[32] What develops more slowly than cognitive ability is psychosocial development, that is, the contextual judgment to determine whether it is worth the risk to attempt to enter the intersection before the approaching car. That judgment may involve weighing the small chance of an accident against long-term catastrophic consequences, the reaction of peers present in the car versus the impact on loved ones who are not physically present, and experience: those who drive regularly or have witnessed an accident may respond differently from those who have not.[33] This psychosocial analysis, which focuses more on observed behavior and less on neurological changes in brain development,[34] reiterates that, with respect to four factors critical to mature judgment (peer orientation, attitudes toward and perception of risk, temporal perspective, and capacity for self-management), teens cannot be expected to demonstrate the same capacities as adults.[35]

# IS OLDER BETTER?

What does this have to do with marriage and childbearing? While we can easily imagine how teen pregnancy differs from 30-something family planning, it also suggests that younger and older marriages will face different challenges. Ask a 40-year-old parent who is chasing around after a kindergartener: stamina and energy decrease with age. But older may be better, at least when it comes to child outcomes and marriage stability. Older parents can give their children very different benefits than can younger parents. The most immediate are the greater resources older parents bring to childrearing. Parents in their late 20s are better educated, psychologically more mature, and more likely to interact with and stimulate young children than are younger parents.[36] Moreover, they are almost certainly wealthier, with more material resources to spend on their children and more of a financial cushion to weather unexpected difficulties.[37]

Research indicates, moreover, that age is an independent factor in predicting children's outcomes, even controlling for the mother's circumstances. In a 30-year follow-up study that measured children's well-being in terms of educational attainment, financial independence between ages 27 and 33, and childbearing after 20, researchers found that inner-city mothers over the age of 25 had the best outcomes and teens the worst, after controlling for other factors.[38] John Mirowsky and Catherine E. Ross further reported that maternal depression is greater for women who have their first child before the age of 23 and falls to its lowest level for women experiencing a first birth around 30.[39] They observed that "[a]n early first birth suggests a poor start in life. It may reflect a disordered transition from adolescence into adulthood and may itself disrupt that transition, with lifelong consequences that influence emotional well-being."[40] They also indicated that the lesser depression that comes with greater parental age may correlate with later first marriages, higher educational attainment, lower risk of having had a prolonged period of needing a job but not being able to find one, lower risk of having had periods lacking the money for household necessities, and better current physical health.[41]

The more profound advantages, however, may have to do with partnership formation, and here we distinguish two different factors. Teen marriages have always been risky. Studies have long indicated that marriage before the bride turned 20 produced a dramatically greater likelihood of divorce.[42] The most comprehensive modern data, by the government's Centers for Disease Control, showed that the greatest gains in marital stability occurred when the woman's age at marriage increased from the late teens to the early 20s, while for cohabitants, stability was best achieved when the woman began the relationship in her mid-20s.[43] These data, which examined the likelihood of divorce for different cohorts in 1995, indicated that the risk of divorce declined from a very high rate of 59% within 15 years for those who married before the age of 18, to 49% for those marrying at 18 or 19, then fell to 36% for those marrying in their early 20s, and to 35% for those marrying over 25.

A new, more-intensive study of marital happiness, using more recent data, however, shows that the age factor has changed. Instead, of looking only at divorce, the researchers examined a series of factors, including marital happiness, interaction, conflict, and "divorce proneness." They found, as did the earlier studies, that marriage before the age of 20 strongly correlated with increased divorce risk. And their 1980 data, like the earlier studies, showed a decline in divorce risk after the age of 19, but very little further decline as the marriage age increased from 20–24 to 25–29 to 30–34 (though it did show substantial gains in marital quality with marriage over the age of 35). Their data from 2000, however, showed a strikingly different pattern. Those who married at age 19 or younger continued to be at much greater risk of divorce than those who married later. But the 2000 data also showed consistent gains in marital quality with each increase in age, so that the divorce proneness of the group dropped steadily from under 19 to over 20, from 20–24 to 25–29, from 25–29 to 30–34, and again over the age of 35.[44] The authors concluded that the "trend for young adults to postpone marriage to complete their education, become economically secure, find more suitable marriage partners, and ensure that they are psychologically ready appears to have benefited contemporary marital relationships."[45]

We believe two different factors are relevant here. With marriage before 21, relationship stability is likely to reflect a combination of immaturity—that still-developing adolescent brain—and selection factors that may make those with the least future orientation and impulse control more likely to marry young. These factors (both the immaturity and the selection effects) make the union less likely to last. Intriguing research suggests, for example, that the number of sexual partners declines with age, controlling for marital status,[46] and that infidelity is higher for younger spouses, just as evolutionary accounts predict.[47] Moreover, disruptive behavior, such as alcohol abuse and criminal conduct, also peaks in the late teens and early 20s and declines thereafter.[48] Teen marriages are not a good bet in any society that allows divorce.

Amato's findings, in contrast, show a new pattern. Unlike marriages studied in the '80s, today's marriages experience improvement in marital quality with a change in the age at marriage not only from the teens into the 20s, but from the early to late 20s, with further improvement into the 30s. We believe that the new pattern reflects a combination of selection factors (the well-off and well-educated have become much more likely to marry later and to marry each other) with greater economic and social support for later marriages.

## GUIDANCE ALONG THE PATH: YOUTHFUL ENERGY OR RUNNING DOWNHILL?

These factors underscore the importance of the institutions that guide the transition to adulthood. Family formation at later ages requires less societal energy to produce successful unions; intimate relationships as vehicles that steer the transition to adulthood—and the socialization of unruly young males—require considerably more. Historically, the institutions that would have managed the transition included the military; male education, training, and employment; oversight of female sexuality; churches and religious teachings that reinforced the stigmatization of fornication and adultery; and socialization into gendered family roles.[49] Today, for the middle class (male and female), it includes university and postgraduate education, a lengthier period of parent-subsidized acquisition of workplace experience—and the postponement of family responsibilities. For a substantial portion of the rest of the population, it may involve an unmooring from the institutions that once provided guidance without any ready replacements in sight.[50]

The change in male employment, for example, provides telling evidence.[51] Men without high school degrees lack stable employment, which may also contribute to a lack of socialization into responsible family roles. The blue-collar workforce settings in an era of widespread early marriage would, after all, have been dominated by husbands and fathers. Today's more marginal employment settings for lesser-skilled men may include fewer attractive family role models. The ideals, leisure activities, and expectations of unattached men may be quite different from those of husbands and involved fathers.

Similarly, for working-class women, the transition to adulthood once took place in the context of early childbearing that locked women into dependent roles. So long as their husbands provided support they could not acquire elsewhere, they might have felt obligated to put up with drunken, abusive, or simply inconsiderate behavior.[52] Today's women, of every social class, enjoy greater opportunities of their own that may make them less inclined to put up with what law professor Amy Wax has called "bad behavior by men." The results are mutually reinforcing: weaker employment opportunities for less-skilled men may make them less-attractive partners; women's greater independence may make them less inclined to put up with "poor catches"; women's lesser dependence may make men feel less compelled to stay in unsatisfying and poorly paying positions—or in unsatisfying relationships in which they may be unable or unwilling to live up to their partner's expectations; men's lesser employment and weaker family attachments may undermine the inculcation of more responsible behavior—all of which may in turn make successful marriage that much less likely.

It is easy to see why red America perceives a crisis in morals. Yet, as blue America recognizes, simply prescribing more prayer—or a return to tradition—cannot solve the problem. Instead, our exploration of the pathways to adulthood has framed two issues, which we believe should be kept distinct.

The first is the relationship between marriage and adulthood. We have shown in this chapter that the information economy has substantially undermined the foundation for young marriages, and in the twenty-first century, it is not just teen marriages, but the marriages of those in the early 20s that are at risk. Marriage promotion efforts, whether couched in the rhetoric of red or blue, have to ask what foundation offers the best prospects for relationship success. We will suggest in part III that the role of marriage as a device to channel sexuality cannot be separated from the task of reintegrating families into the larger economy.

The second, more difficult issue is the management of adolescence. Here, youthful risk taking, raging hormones, lack of judgment, and peer orientation complicate the task. Red families would like to take back teen socialization from the larger society. They wish to reassert parental authority and affirm the right values. Blue families see their objective as training for adult autonomy. They differ in their views of both "the right values" and the way to instill them. It is here that the differences between embracing and resisting the new world around us become most profound.

Our red versus blue differences in family formation thus have potentially far-reaching implications for family understandings. Nonetheless, differences in the age at marriage are not simply matters of culture or choice. They also reflect the foundation provided by the larger society. In 1960, regional variation did not result in major differences in the age at marriage. Today, it does. In earlier eras, moreover, such differences where they did exist did not necessarily give rise to political or legal controversies. To understand how family differences have inflamed a culture war requires consideration of the changing roles of personality, religion, and politics.

CHAPTER 4

# Personality, Politics, and Religion

T HE EVOLUTION OF family practices, even with the magnitude
of the changes we describe in this book, does not inevitably
involve political division; indeed, in many instances, family
values are not political issues at all. Demographic differences, such as
those in the age at family formation, could simply mean that family
law evolves at a different pace, in accordance with different needs, in
different parts of the country. Indeed, many potentially controversial
family law issues, such as the validity of premarital agreements, vary
widely and change within states without significant political controversy.[1] So why are family values so different?

Part of the answer is the nature of the subject. Changes in so basic
an institution as the family can be seriously threatening to the existing social order. Standards of sexual morality, designed to restrain
deeply rooted carnal instincts, require a coherent system of societal
reinforcement to be effective, and the evolution of these standards
almost inherently challenges the status quo. The transformation we
described in chapters 2 and 3, which at its start in the 1960s and
'70s was associated with self-styled radicals chanting "make love, not
war," is especially challenging. For those who have bristled at what
they see as antiquated and restrictive moral standards (and for those
who are open to the accompanying changes), these developments
may provide welcome opportunities for personal experimentation
and for the creation of families based on individual choice. For those

who fear change, however, or who see the changes dismantling critical parts of the moral order, the shift in moral standards can be deeply disturbing and lead to calls to reinstill the "right" values. These two groups may differ by region, ideology, religiosity, and, as a growing body of research suggests, personality type. They may also give rise to different political loyalties and legal agendas.

The Republican Party, starting with Ronald Reagan in the '80s and reaching a height with the reelection of George W. Bush in 2004, has directly addressed the cultural anxiety associated with the groups most opposed to family change. It has done so in ways that clash with some of the gains associated with women's greater independence and equality and with the desire of others for greater personal autonomy with respect to family formation. During the same period, the public has become increasingly more divided on the issue of moral values, and these differences continue to distinguish core Republican from core Democratic areas of the country. A growing body of research across a variety of disciplines examines the source of political divisions and suggests that the moral values issue falls on the dividing line between basic differences in personalities, values, and world views. In this chapter, we explore the literature that charts these differing world views, connects them to underlying personality differences, and considers their relationship to overlapping political and religious identifications. This research suggests that, to the extent that divisions between red and blue family perspectives correspond to ideological and personality differences, they are likely to be less tractable than more conventional political issues, such as the size of the deficit or rate cuts in the capital gains tax.

## DIFFERENCES IN WORLD VIEWS: TRADITIONALISTS V. MODERNISTS

Researchers have been examining differences in cultural orientations, values preferences, and attitudes toward risk without agreement on vocabulary. Some refer to conservatives versus liberals, others to hierarchs versus egalitarians, or communitarians versus individualists. Berkeley professor George Lakoff, in a much more colorful way, speaks in terms of "nurturant mothers" and "strict fathers." Although each of these terms has its own definition, and each has been extensively studied using distinct terminology, we examine these studies as a group to capture two different ways of looking at the world: (1) adherence to tradition, respect for authority, and desire for order, which we call "traditionalist" views; versus (2) flexible thinking, tolerance of diversity, openness to change, and greater emphasis on equality, which we call "modernist."[2]

Few people approach the world through an entirely modernist or traditionalist perspective, but the categories help to construct an individual's dominant world view. Researchers at this point cannot say why one person is a modernist and another person is a traditionalist. Perhaps the most intriguing and controversial study that attempts to distinguish between these two basic world views suggests that the differences may correspond to genetic predispositions toward change and authority. Religious and political identifications (Protestant v. Republican v. Democrat v. Jew) are often products of parental influence and upbringing.[3] The choice of a particular position within a given party or religion, however, is more likely to reflect individual preferences and personalities. George W. Bush may be a Republican, for example, because his parents were Republicans, but his identification with the social conservative base of the party that distrusted his father may say more about his personal values than about the family in which he was raised. In an innovative study that considered the relationship between genes and politics, three political scientists compared identical and fraternal twins to try to tease out the effects of nature versus nurture on the development of political attitudes.[4] They used surveys of the twins on 28 different issues, ranging from school prayer to federal housing, and then coded the responses as "conservative" or "liberal."[5] They looked at differences in approaches to out-groups, codes of behavior, and perspectives on human nature.

Conservatives were typified by "a yearning for in-group unity and strong leadership." They were suspicious of other groups and experienced "a desire for clear, unbending moral and behavioral codes" that also included a belief in the importance of punishing anyone who violated these codes, "a fondness for systematization (procedural due process), a willingness to tolerate inequality (opposition to redistributive policies), and an inherently pessimistic view of human nature (life is 'nasty, brutish, and short')."[6]

When confronted with the same issues, liberals were characterized by comparatively "tolerant attitudes toward out-groups, [and] a desire to take a more context-dependent rather than rule-based approach to proper behavior." They also demonstrated more empathy and less emphasis on strict punishment for violations of moral and behavioral rules, along with "an inherently optimistic view of human nature (people should be given the benefit of the doubt)," a "suspicion of hierarchy, certainty, and strong leadership (flip-flopping is not a character flaw)," and intolerance of inequality.[7]

The study hypothesized that to the extent identical twins differed from fraternal twins—each set of twins was raised in the same environment—then greater disparity between the fraternal twins would reflect genetic differences. The researchers found that genetics accounts "for approximately half of the variance in ideology, while shared environment including parental influence accounts for only 11%."[8] They concluded that while political issues and configurations vary considerably over time (e.g., Republican views on price controls in 1972 might be more liberal than Democratic views on price controls in 1996), basic divisions between liberal and conservative perspectives are remarkably persistent.[9]

The idea that political orientations are inherited is certainly controversial. Moreover, even where differences appear to be the product of innate differences (that is, the product of genetic predispositions), the expression of these traits may depend on conditions in the womb or early experiences that such studies cannot detect. We are intrigued not so much by the source of the differences (which may or may not be genetic), but by the indication that such characteristics influence perceptions and values and are relatively hard to change. A number of studies confirm the deep-seated nature of these personality-based preferences without passing judgment on the source of the differences.

The Cultural Cognition Project at Yale, for example, has surveyed attitudes toward a variety of controversial issues from gun control to global warming, and it has consistently found that perspectives on these issues are correlated with personality differences that generate different orientations toward risk. The cultural cognition researchers use what they term a "parsimonious framework for classifying individuals' cultural values," that is, rather than use the ten or more variables that characterize some personality studies,[10] they create two intersecting axes: "hierarchy-egalitarianism" and "individualism-communitarianism." The distinction between hierarchy and egalitarianism corresponds to many traits in the conservative versus liberal world views described in the study of twins' political attitudes. Hierarchs tend to favor the distribution of goods and benefits in accordance with a well-established system that may be based on wealth, gender, ethnicity, or lineage while egalitarians prefer equality in the distribution of rights and benefits. Communitarians, in addition to favoring societal interests over individual ones, believe that "society should secure the conditions of individual flourishing," while individualists believe that each person should be responsible for his or her own well-being without societal assistance or interference.

The cultural cognition researchers maintain that the critical part of these values differences is the perception of what creates risk. Asked, for example, the question of whether strict gun control laws would make university students safer, people tended to think differently about the risks of gun ownership: 68% of the egalitarians, compared to 41% of the hierarchs, said that students would be safer with gun control, and 64% of the communitarians agreed in contrast with 44% of the individualists. The hierarchs and the individualists thus perceived safety more in terms of their ability to own a gun with which they might defend themselves than in terms of society's ability to disarm a potentially violent student. The Cultural Cognition Project has shown over a number of studies that these perceptions of what conditions create the most risk better predict how a person will respond than his or her self-identification as liberal or conservative.[11]

Given such basic differences in orientation, the rhetoric and style of political debate have the potential to diffuse or inflame divisions. George Lakoff is a linguist, whose early writings included "Metaphors We Live By," before he wrote *Don't Think of an Elephant! Know Your Values and Frame the Debate* in 2004. He argues that liberals and conservatives view the world through different metaphors about the relationship between the state and its citizens and that these metaphors involve deeply rooted patterns of perception.[12] The language of political discourse then frames issues, consciously or unconsciously, in ways that trigger the metaphors, and the metaphors produce associated reactions that may have relatively little to do with the specific statement that triggered the response.[13]

Lakoff maintains that the contrasting metaphors track the paradigmatic roles of parents within the family, and he uses these roles as the basis for his categorization of world views.[14] Conservatives celebrate the "strict father," who enforces relatively fixed and hierarchical values, an identification that is similar to our notion of "traditionalists." Liberals prefer the "nurturing mother" who makes context-based decisions designed to promote individual well-being, a concept similar to our "modernists." Those who share the strict father mentality see the world as dangerous; children need to be protected, and it is the responsibility of the strict parent to impose discipline on the children.[15] Children are born bad and learn through punishment.[16] By contrast, the nurturing mother mentality views the world as basically safe, with parents responsible for nurturing their children with empathy and responsibility.[17]

**Birds of a feather get lost together**

FIGURE 4.1

SOURCE: http://sangrea.net/free-cartoons/polit_birds-feather.jpg.

Different ways of framing issues—including the calls for a reaffirmation of traditional values versus insistence on the need for greater acceptance of diverse family forms—appeal to different world views.

When political issues are framed in these terms, practically or metaphorically, they reinforce deeply held beliefs. Such beliefs are resistant to argument, logic, or facts. Indeed, cultural research suggests that when empirical data conflict with these beliefs, people reinterpret or deny the empirical findings rather than change their views.[18] Neuroscientists have even shown that different parts of the brain are activated by information that conforms to or challenges people's beliefs. Consequently, when many people are confronted with new scientific information on issues that are "culturally disputed...men and women in white lab coats speak with less authority than (mostly) men and women in black frocks."[19] Attitudes toward homosexuality provide a clear example of this phenomenon. Twice as many liberals as conservatives say that people are born homosexual; 73% of white committed evangelicals think homosexuals can change their sexual orientation in contrast with two-thirds (66%) of seculars of all races who state that homosexuality cannot be changed.[20] The relationship between politics and the pulpit, with Protestant fundamentalist clerics emphasizing the evils of homosexuality more than mainline Protestant ministers or clergy in other religions, may reinforce cultural predispositions that are relatively impervious to change.[21] New information on, for example, the genetic basis of homosexuality is thus likely to reinforce the beliefs of those predisposed to tolerance rather than to change the attitudes of those who see the conduct as an immoral choice.[22]

The fact that different personalities have different value preferences and different perceptions of risk does not in itself lead to political differences, nor do politicians and other leaders inevitably attempt to inflame divisions. The shared experiences of the Great Depression, World War II, and the Cold War brought a large degree of consensus to American life and generated claims that "ideology" or "history" had ended.[23] In the postwar era, the Democratic and Republican parties were "big tents" that tended toward the center of the political spectrum. Party loyalty often had to do more with economic issues (the Republicans as the party of big business, the Democrats as the party of the working class) than personality types or cultural differences. For example, Democrats and Republicans were almost equally likely to express support for the Vietnam War in the late 1960s.[24]

In the last decades of the twentieth century, however, as the United States became wealthier, Americans also acquired a greater ability to choose the neighborhoods in which they live, the churches they attend, and the views they hold. As they acquired that greater ability, they also became more likely to seek out those whose views are closer to their

SOLVING POLITICAL PROBLEMS
THROUGH REASONED DEBATE

FIGURE 4.2

SOURCE: http://sangrea.net/free-cartoons/polit_political-debate.jpg.

own. The process reinforces people's initial predispositions and sets the stage for greater divisions that reinforce each other. For example, in contrast to the almost equal support among Republicans and Democrats for the Vietnam War, Republicans were much more likely to support the Iraq war than were Democrats (in 2003, approximately 95% of Republicans and 55% of Democrats; in 2006, 80% of Republicans and less than 25% of Democrats).[25] Nonetheless, we recognize that, even in today's more polarized world, people fall on a continuum; for example, a study in 2004 found that just under half of all Republicans did not self-identify as conservative, and slightly more than one-third of Democrats described themselves as liberal.[26] While we can argue about whether the average citizen has become more partisan, all of the evidence suggests greater overlap among residential, party, religious, and ideological associations, increasing the significance and divisiveness of moral issues.[27]

## RELIGION, THE BIG SORT, AND THE COLLAPSE OF THE CENTER

Journalist Bill Bishop begins his book *The Big Sort* by describing his move from rural Kentucky to Austin, Texas. He and his wife looked for a house in a number of neighborhoods, picked an area in which they were comfortable, chose a house they really liked, and without knowing much else about the neighborhood, moved in. In a region that voted overwhelmingly for George Bush, they quickly discovered that all but one of their neighbors were Democrats. They had not thought about party affiliation when they bought the house. Instead, preferences for cities over suburbs, townhouses rather than large lawns, active community groups versus private clubs, and diverse rather than homogeneous residents seemed to predict party affiliation. The Bishops chose to live in a community that thought about the world in the same way they did, and they did so without explicitly basing their housing choice on their political preferences.

Bishop explains that his family's choices parallel those of a large part of the country and reflect the increased mobility of the nation as a whole and the college-educated in particular. He reports that, during the 1980s and '90s, "only 19% of young people with only a high school degree moved between states, but 45% of those with more than a college education" made such a move.[28] The process of "going off" for higher education separates students from their hometowns and not only prepares them for better jobs, but primes them psychologically to be willing to search for the communities with the opportunities and lifestyles that further their interests. As the ranks of the college-educated grow, from 17% in 1970 to 45% in 2004, the mobility of the young also increases.[29]

This mobility reinforces the regional identification with different political and family patterns. When Barack Obama completed Harvard Law School, he did not return to the Hawaii of his youth. Instead, he chose to live in Hyde Park, Illinois, a diverse neighborhood associated with the University of Chicago. He married another elite law school grad whom he met at a firm where both of them worked. And he chose a church (with a controversial pastor) far removed from the experiences of his youth. His journey is less unusual today than it would have been in the middle of the twentieth century. Fifty percent of highly educated "power" couples live in large cities, and the percentage of young adults with college degrees in the average city is now double that in rural areas. Moreover, the increase in the number of college graduates in some cities (e.g., Austin) is dramatically greater than in others (e.g., Cleveland). Since the college-educated are likely to form families later in life, this exacerbates the differences between largely rural and more urban states, between rapidly growing centers of the new information economy and more slowly developing rustbelt areas, and between more religious and more secular communities. More critically, it increases not just the actual differences between these groups, such as the age at marriage, but the perceived values that underlie the different regions—and these differences tend to reinforce each other.

Studies of group psychology show that, when people with similar views talk to one another, they end up at even more extreme positions.[30] And when people receive new information about social issues, they typically rely on leaders whom they trust to help them sort through the new claims. Not surprisingly, people trust leaders who share their perspectives.[31] To the extent, therefore, that changes in neighborhood, churches, and community groups embed Americans in more politically varied communities, they may moderate overall views. To the extent that the "big sort" that Bishop describes allows them to choose more homogeneous or insular communities, with leaders of strikingly different views, these groups may exacerbate divisions. The very ability to choose—neighborhoods, cable TV stations, Internet sites, churches—increases the risk that we will hear only those with whom we already agree.

One of the arenas where the big sort has produced the greatest polarization in world views has been with respect to religion. Just as we today choose to live in communities that reflect our individual values to a greater degree than our parents did, we are also more likely to choose synagogues, parishes, congregations, or no religion in ways that are more likely to express our individual differences. The result has been a "collapse of the middle" in American church life.[32] Bill Bishop observes that, historically, political loyalty did not correspond with church membership or attendance.[33] This began to change in the 1960s and '70s. Mainline Protestant churches, which tended to be more moderate and inclusive, started to lose membership to evangelical and fundamentalist congregations.[34] Where churches were once built around geographic communities, today they involve a much more deliberate "choice of a way of life,"[35] a way of life that has become more likely to integrate the choice of a congregation with the choice of a political party with the choice of family organization in ways that reinforce each other.[36] These trends have been particularly dramatic at the large-scale megachurches—the churches that have shown the greatest growth over the last several decades. Eight in ten of the megachurches are traditionalist; only 7% characterize themselves as moderate.[37] The shift from the center to the poles set the stage for the greater political salience of religion in contemporary American politics.

This religious divide has become much less one between religions, and much more a "devotional divide" between frequent versus less-frequent churchgoers. These differences played out in the most-recent presidential elections. In 2004, a significant portion of Bush voters asserted that their faith was "more or about as important as other factors in their voting decision,"[38] while "a majority of Kerry's religious constituencies reported that their faith was less important."[39] The Pew Forum on Religion and Public Life has found that, of people who attend religious services more than once per week, 38% voted Democratic and 60% voted Republican, a number that remained consistent in 2002, 2004, and 2006.[40] Among people who never attend religious services, 67% voted Democratic, compared to 30% who voted Republican.[41] Among white Protestants, 37% voted Democratic, 61% Republican in 2006, a gap that narrowed from 30% Democratic and 68% Republican in 2002.[42] The 2008 results, while showing some movement among Catholics back to the Democratic Party, narrowed but did not bridge the gap defined by religious participation.[43]

The devout, moreover, may differ from others in world views attributable to more than time spent in church or even intensity of beliefs.

The American National Election Survey identifies traditionalist versus modernist voting patterns, not in terms of church attendance, but in accordance with responses to four statements that emphasize openness to change and attitudes toward family values:

(1) The world is always changing and moral values should adjust to those changes.
(2) The newer lifestyles are contributing to the breakdown of our society.
(3) We should be more tolerant of people who choose to live according to their own moral standards, even if they are very different from our own.
(4) This country would have many fewer problems if there were more emphasis on traditional family ties.[44]

Responses to these statements reflect different world views, and these world views correspond to liberal versus conservative voting patterns. Political scientist David Campbell reports, for example, that in 2004, only 24% of the top quartile of modernists voted for Bush, compared to 84% of the highest quartile of traditionalists. When he compared the level of traditionalism with various religious traditions, he found that "it is clearly traditionalism that makes the difference." Campbell concludes that, looking at both evangelical and mainline Protestants, "eighty-nine percent who scored in the highest quartile of moral traditionalism voted for Bush," irrespective of denomination.[45]

These differences in beliefs, which exist in all regions of the country, skew regional patterns as well. In a study designed to test the correlation between religious and political beliefs, the researchers divided people into three categories:

• fundamentalists, who believe literally in the words of the Bible;
• modernists, who believe in the events in the Bible, but who do not believe literally in each word of it;
• and biblical minimalists, who don't believe that the Bible reflects the divine word at all.

In red states, almost half of the voters were fundamentalists, while in blue states, only 28% were fundamentalists. These divisions translated into opinions on political issues, for example, less than 14% of the fundamentalists compared to more than two-thirds of the biblical minimalists expressed support for same-sex marriage.[46]

Finally, framing political issues in terms that appeal to traditionalist or modernist world views can trigger different, deeply held beliefs.

This tendency to filter data through existing belief systems, which is true of most human convictions, may be particularly true of religious practices. One of the keys to understanding the role of religion is recognizing that religious belief requires taking "what is materially false to be true" and "what is materially true to be false."[47] Rituals are critical to reinforcing such beliefs. Anthropologist Richard Sosis maintains that, while both secular and religious rituals generate cooperation, religious rituals promote even greater commitment precisely because they depend on belief—and thus emotion—rather than logic or proof.[48] Emotional commitment, Sosis believes, is deeper and longer-lasting than reason.[49] It is also harder to question and, once instilled, harder to alter. These qualities, of course, make religion invaluable in instilling partisan loyalties. By providing a coherent moral structure, religion can also encourage responsible behavior.

These findings suggest that issues that fall on the dividing line between the devout and the secular and that evoke distinctions between more authoritarian and more flexible political orientations are likely to be among the more divisive topics on the political landscape.[50] These divisions will be even more intense if either group finds that a particular issue goes to the core of its belief system. The combination of teen sexuality, the changing family, and the growing secularization of American society is particularly combustible.

## FAMILY CRISIS AND THE THREAT TO TRADITION

Developments in the United States over the last several decades have exacerbated the division between those with different values preferences. These developments started with the '60s, a period of very public rebellion against what had been consensus traditions and included religious, cultural, and family changes. Fundamentalists in communities with larger numbers of nonbelievers experienced greater feelings of religious "threat" than did those residing in communities of believers,[51] perhaps leading to a bunker-type mentality. The personality studies show that traditionalists tend to rank security higher on their list of values and to be attracted to institutions and leaders that they believe can provide it.

At the same time, however, the growing prominence of religion in public life may have exacerbated the concerns of those who distrust religion and religious authorities. In 2002, two Berkeley sociologists pointed out that the number of adults who reported "no religion" in the '90s doubled. This did not necessarily mean an absence of religious belief, they suggested, and, indeed, the majority continued to believe in both God and an afterlife. Instead, the researchers concluded that this shift reflected the desire of many Americans to distance themselves from the increasingly close association between organized religion and conservative politics.[52] Younger people, aged 18–25, are increasingly likely to report that they do not have a religious affiliation.[53] In addition to this growing distrust of organized religion, public defense of atheism has become more vocal, with bestsellers including *The God Delusion*, *God Is Not Great: How Religion Poisons Everything*, *God: The Failed Hypothesis/How Science Shows That God Does Not Exist*, and *The End of Faith: Religion, Terror, and the Future of Reason*.[54] These works embrace reason in opposition to religion and, in doing so, appeal to the modernists over the traditionalists. The stridency of the opposition may in turn heighten the feeling of community among fundamentalist denominations. A pluralist society, ironically, can serve to strengthen more absolutist religious beliefs, and a period of growing public expressions of disbelief may accelerate the process. Christian Smith, a scholar of American evangelicalism concludes, "It is precisely evangelicalism's heavy...engagement with modern pluralism...which reinforces evangelical boundaries, identity, solidarity, mobilization, and membership retention."[55]

Corresponding to fundamentalists' reaction to an increasingly secular society has been an increased sense of the fragility of traditional values, particularly those that involve the family. Indeed, evangelical Protestants who attended church frequently were disproportionately concerned about the decline in the family during the last quarter of the twentieth century.[56] Since traditionalists are more drawn to absolute verities, and since they are more inclined to perceive change as a threat, the changes in family composition over the 1970s and '80s, with the unprecedented increases in nonmarital births and divorce should have been—and were—seen as a crisis. Traditionalists found increasing societal liberalization troubling and very much at odds with the values with which they had been raised.[57] Those raised within a modernist tradition who nonetheless felt overwhelmed by the multiplication of choices or the instability of their own relationships also sought out teachings, leaders, and groups who promised greater certainty. Berkeley sociologist Kristin Luker, who has done in-depth ethnographic studies of abortion and sex education, concludes that traditionalists might reasonably feel "that families are in dire straits and that their only hope of having a happy family life is to practice a clear commitment to the family based on an understanding that this is God's will as exemplified in church teachings."[58]

## CONCLUSION

The culture wars started with genuine differences in family structure, which, in an era of growing partisanship, intersected with class and ideological divisions. A higher percentage of families in blue states have embraced the new family paradigm of delayed family formation partly because such states are wealthier (and the college-educated have more to gain from delay) and partly because they are more modernist for reasons that may go back to the different groups that settled in different parts of the country. Blue states that had greater concentrations of education and wealth a half-century ago have become that much more attractive to the like-minded as economic disparities have increased, heightening the concentration of the better-educated. These groups as a whole, and in blue states in particular, tend to be more secular and more modernist. The political leadership in these states unsurprisingly reflects these views and therefore constructs both political platforms and policy proposals in blue terms.

Red states, in contrast, have more of what we might call "communities on the cusp." That is, they have a higher number of more-traditional communities in which almost everyone marries by the mid- to late 20s—and they have more communities threatened by the changes in family structure. One of us, for example, first really understood the differences when at the age of 25 she took a cross-country trip with her soon-to-be husband and stopped overnight with a friend in Lincoln, Nebraska. The evening featured a birthday party for one of her friend's children, everyone home by 9 P.M., and lots of discussions of square footage and lawn care. Yet, all of the adults at the party, who were overwhelmingly college graduates, were still under 30. At another party of people who were the same age in Arlington, Virginia, a week later, few of the author's friends were married, none had children, and no one talked about square footage in part because almost no one at the party could yet afford a house.

Today, the differences between these communities have grown (and the disparity in housing prices, which contributes to it, is out of sight). Divorce rates, which were beginning to rise at the time of the cross-country trip in the late 1970s, have leveled off near their historic highs, with the risks becoming systematically greater for those who marry young. Nonmarital birthrates, which were already high in the '70s for minority women, have now risen substantially for whites and affect communities where such births were virtually nonexistent 30 years ago.

While the college-educated in Lincoln, Nebraska, may be doing fine, they will have lost ground economically to those in Washington, D.C., and they will be surrounded to a greater degree today by lower middle-class and working-class families with high divorce and rising nonmarital birthrates. Perhaps as critically, the political leadership in the states has also changed. In red regions, the college-educated and higher-income voters are more likely to be religious and traditionalist than in blue states. The leaders in these states are more likely to craft their appeals in traditionalist terms. Lower-income voters, while they do not necessarily have different personality preferences than other classes, are more likely to have been raised in a traditionalist culture. At the same time, they may strongly feel, as legal scholar Joan Williams emphasizes, that adherence to traditional values is what continues to separate successful families still hanging on to middle-class life from their harder-living neighbors.

As these changes have played out in accordance with region, class, and ideology, they have also become increasingly political. The blue regions of the country, such as the Northeast and the West Coast, have over the last half-century become wealthier, more Democratic, more committed to a later age at family formation, and more tolerant of different family forms. The red states, as they have lost ground economically and socially, have become more Republican, more committed to traditionalist values, and more troubled by divorce and teen and nonmarital births. The conflict between red and blue is, at its core, a disagreement on how to rebuild family support on terms that can be applied to the nation as a whole. In the next section of the book, we accordingly examine how these conflicts have structured the legal issues that underlie family law and the prospects for a revitalized family agenda on a basis other than all-out warfare.

# PART II

# THE LEGAL MAP

## CHAPTER 5

# Contraception

## *Securing the Pathways to Blue Family Life*

*I went to the gyno when I was scared I was pregnant. We discussed protection
and how I can stay safe from sexual no-nos.*

—*Jocelyn, 15, Houghton, Michigan*

*I've been going to Planned Parenthood since I became sexually active. How long ago that was is
irrelevant! Jokes aside, PP has been kind of like my makeshift parent. I never got "the talk," so
I really have to give it up to them for schooling me in the ways of being a healthy, responsible
and informed individual in my...umm...activities.*

*Trish G., Los Angeles, California[1]*

FOR MANY YOUNG women, the first trip to Planned Parenthood,
a Title X clinic, or a gynecologist is an important rite of passage. Some go with a parent. Some go because they think they
*might* have sex. Many go for the first time because they think they are
already pregnant. Others go because they are married and not ready
for children—or don't want more than they already have.

Yet, access to contraception, which most Americans think of as an
everyday matter throughout the country, was once illegal—in some
states for everyone, in most states for the unmarried, and in all states

for minors. Of course, obtaining a condom—or a prescription for the pill—was possible. It just required access to the druggist's back room or a convenient lie. In the 1950s, these discrepancies between the formal law and informal availability magnified disparities between rich and poor, the sophisticated and the naïve, the more experienced and the young. The lack of readily available and reliable birth control also blocked the pathways to women's economic equality. This chapter explores the fight to legalize access to contraception for married women, single women, *and* teens, a fight that set the stage for the creation of the two distinct family paradigms.

## BE FRUITFUL?

Birth control devices, which were legally available during much of the nineteenth century, became victims of the Victorian quest for moral purity. In 1873, Anthony Comstock launched a crusade against obscenity. As a result of his broad-based campaign, he was able to persuade Congress to pass a law that restricted using the mail service to circulate obscene materials *and* that prohibited advertising, importing, transporting across state lines, or mailing contraceptives.[2] The states followed suit, with about half passing legislation that explicitly banned the distribution or sale of contraception and most of the rest passing less clearly worded laws that could be interpreted to do so.[3] Connecticut went the furthest, prohibiting any use of contraception, including by married couples in the privacy of their bedrooms.[4]

Scholars have developed numerous theories to explain the origins and popularity of the anti-obscenity campaign. For some, the anti-obscenity campaign represents a class-based attempt to return to a more traditional morality in the midst of a rapidly industrializing world; others see it as an attempt to punish women as they gained more autonomy; still others as an attempt to protect elite children from corruption.[5] Whatever the initial reasons for adoption, by the 1950s, court decisions allowed doctors to circumvent the law everywhere but in Massachusetts, Connecticut, and Mississippi, and a thriving black market developed. The result, however, was a segmented industry in which the wealthy and sophisticated had relatively easy access to contraceptives purchased discretely from catalogs or drugstores while poorer people, "who either didn't have the cash for such items or even the knowledge that they were available," were left out.[6]

Unmarried women, especially if they were below the age of majority (21 in most states), were among the many denied systematic access to birth control.

## MORAL CRISIS IN THE LAND OF OZZIE AND HARRIET

What set the stage for the greater legal and actual availability of contraceptives—and the emergence of the blue family paradigm—was the explosion of unplanned pregnancies in the '50s. During the period from 1947 to 1957, birthrates jumped for women aged 15–19 from 79.3 to 96.3 per 1,000.[7] During that same period, the adoption rate doubled, the average age at marriage fell to the lowest level in a century, and the percentage of brides who gave birth within eight months of marriage grew to 30%, figures not seen since the early 1800s. One of the casualties was women's educational attainment; women's degree of educational parity with men dropped sharply. Historian Stephanie Coontz in her account of the '50s, *The Way We Never Were*, describes it as an era of "sexual brinkmanship." Young women were expected to "draw the line" on sexual conduct, a line that was constantly changing. And when that line was crossed, young people were less expected to say no than in earlier eras; instead, they were "handed wedding rings."[8] The restraints on nonmarital sexuality, held in check by the threat of pregnancy, were threatening to give way.

By 1980, family patterns had been transformed—at least for the new class of baby boomers heading off to college. Of the women born in 1950 and entering college in the late '60s, half were married by the age of 23. For those born 7 years later, in 1957, and entering college in the mid- to late 1970s, fewer than 30% were married by 23, a year after the normal age of college graduation.[9] With the decline in birthrates, a new cadre of women not only secured university degrees but entered the professions. Between 1950 and 1970, the percentage of women in professional schools stayed flat, with no more than 1% in medicine (0.1), law (0.04), dentistry (0.01), and business administration (0.03). By 1980, however, the numbers had jumped to 30% in medicine, 36% in law, 19% in dentistry, and 28% in business.[10] What happened?

The explanation starts with an increase in the ranks of college graduates. Overall college attendance grew, and from 1960 to 1970, the rise in the number of college students "was nothing short of phenomenal," with enrollment growing from 3.8 million to 8.5 million,

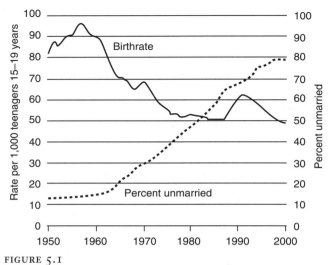

FIGURE 5.1

SOURCE: National Center for Health Statistics, *Births to Teenagers in the United States, 1940–2000*, 49 NAT'L VITAL STAT. REP. 10 (2001).

an increase of over 100%, which increased by another 42% in the '70s.[11] Women's attendance grew faster than men's, rising from 1.3 million in 1960 to more than 3 million in 1970. By 1980, women constituted more than half of all undergraduates. In 2003, 30.9% of the women aged 25–29 in the United States were college graduates compared to 26% of the men.[12]

The rise in women's educational attainment and career ambitions would have been difficult to reconcile with the family formation patterns of the 1950s, and the entire set of practices changed. The percentage of college graduates married by 23 decreased from 50% for those born in the mid-1940s to 30% for those born in the late '60s.[13] The increase in the ranks of unmarried young adults occurred with an increase in the sexual activity of younger women more generally, a dramatic drop in teen births, and changing expectations about fertility. Harvard economists Claudia Goldin and Lawrence Katz observe that, using a variety of data samples from the era, the percentage of women who reported engaging in sex before the age of 21 grew from about 40% of those born in 1945 to more than 70% of those born a decade later. Those reporting sexual activity before the age of 18 grew even more dramatically, from about 15% of those born in 1945 to more than 40% of those born in 1955.[14] Moreover, while in the '60s, half of the women who engaged in premarital sex did so only with their fiancés, by the mid-1980s, less than 25% of the women who reported having premarital sex did so only with men they expected to marry.[15]

Despite the increase in sexual activity, birthrates dropped. Whereas the birthrate crested in 1957 at 97 births per 1,000 teens between the ages of 15 and 19, by 1983 the rate fell almost in half to 52 births per 1,000 young women (see figure 5.1).[16] Adoption rates between unrelated individuals also changed markedly. They peaked at all-time highs in 1970, but dropped in half by 1975.[17] During this same period, expectations about fertility changed. In 1963, 80% of non-Catholic female college students wanted three or more children, and 44% wanted at least four. By 1973, just 29% wanted three or more (and the group had fewer children than even those lower numbers)—an extraordinary shift in a ten-year period.[18]

The traditional emphases on sexuality only within marriage, on early marriage as the means of containing the sexual urges of the young, and on shotgun weddings or adoption as the fallback to hold the line on unsanctioned pregnancy were giving way, and giving way dramatically for the most advantaged part of the population. To explain so far-reaching a transformation within so short a period requires exploration of the social and legal changes that introduced the pill into American life.

## THE BIRTH CONTROL PILL, THE LAW, AND THE REMAKING OF WOMEN'S LIVES

Research on the possibility of a birth control pill may have begun as early as 1921, but legal restrictions on development discouraged the effort until the 1950s. Then, Katharine Dexter McCormick, the widow of Stanley McCormick, heir to the International Harvester Company fortune, funded private research on the use of progesterone to prevent ovulation.[19] The clinical trials were conducted in Puerto Rico and Haiti, which unlike most American states, had no laws interfering with the tests, and the Food and Drug Administration approved the first commercial birth control pill in 1957 as a treatment for "gynecological disorders" and in 1959 as a contraceptive.[20] By the time the manufacturer Searle secured the 1959 approval, 500,000 women were already using the pill as a contraceptive. Those numbers increased to a million by 1961, 1.75 million in 1963, and 10 million in 1973. More than 80% of American women born after 1945 have been on the pill at some point in their lives.[21]

Legal changes—brought about through a series of test cases engineered by birth control activists and lawyers—facilitated the pill's greater availability. The landmark case of *Griswold v. Connecticut* brought the issue to public attention in 1965.[22] Connecticut had the strictest birth control law in the country, an act passed in the nineteenth century that banned the use of contraceptives, even by married couples. The courts had rejected early efforts to test the legality of the statute, concluding in 1961 that doctors did not have standing to challenge the law.[23] Estelle Griswold, the executive director of Planned Parenthood in Connecticut, and Dr. Charles Buxton, the chief of obstetrics and gynecology at Yale University's School of Medicine, sought to force the issue by opening a birth control clinic in New Haven. Three days after the clinic opened, local detectives raided the operation. The clinic did not attempt to conceal its provision of contraceptives; indeed, Harold Berg, one of the New Haven detectives, told the *New York Times*, "They gave us everything we were looking for."[24] The trial court convicted Griswold and Buxton, and the appeal went to the U.S. Supreme Court, with Thomas Emerson of the Yale Law School faculty arguing the case. In a 7–2 decision, the Court found the statute to be unconstitutional, thereby allowing contraceptives to be distributed to married couples. The most controversial aspect of the decision was not the invalidation of the law, which many viewed as archaic and which was rarely enforced, but the recognition of a right to privacy grounded in the "penumbra" of other constitutional guarantees.

The Supreme Court extended contraception to single individuals in 1972. *Griswold*'s guarantee of contraception only to married couples prompted Planned Parenthood (which had helped to bring the 1965 case) to provide the following advice in 1967: "Medical consultation and services may be provided to minors who are married or engaged or have been pregnant or are accompanied by a parent or guardian or are referred by a recognized social or health agency, a doctor or a clergyman."[25] While broader than the law allowed in many states, these limitations were too conservative for Bill Baird, a 1960s activist who wished to ensure access to everyone, and particularly to poorer and less-privileged women. Massachusetts had one of the most conservative remaining laws on birth control, which the legislature had refused to change, that punished unlawful dissemination as a felony with up to a five-year prison sentence.

In an effort to test the law, Baird gave an unmarried 19-year-old a condom during a speech on the Boston University campus in front of several thousand people and was arrested in April 1967.[26] The Supreme

Court reversed his conviction, holding: "If the right of privacy means anything, it is the right of the individual, married or single, to be free from unwanted governmental intrusion into matters so fundamentally affecting a person as the decision whether to bear or beget a child."[27] In 1972, however, the age of majority was still 21 in many states, so even a right to contraception for single adults did not necessarily extend to the growing ranks of college students. Five years after Baird won the right to distribute contraceptives to the unmarried, the Supreme Court concluded that the same rights extended to minors. The Court explained: "Read in light of its progeny [*Eisenstadt v. Baird* and *Roe v. Wade*], the teaching of *Griswold* is that the Constitution protects individual decisions in matters of childbearing from unjustified intrusion by the State."[28] The Court observed that an unwanted pregnancy should not be imposed as the punishment for improvident sexual activity. The Supreme Court thus swept away the remaining barriers to the widespread dissemination of contraception.

The effective availability of contraception, however, changed at different times in different parts of the country. Some states began to relax their birth control laws after the *Griswold* decision in 1965. Still, most states limited distribution to minors without parental consent until the *Carey* case in 1977. In between, however, with ratification in 1971 of the 26th Amendment, the Vietnam era amendment that lowered the voting age to 18, the vast majority of states changed the age of majority from 21 to 18 as well. Although the state legislatures that lowered the age of adulthood rarely considered the potential effect on the ability to get contraception, the legal changes had the effect of increasing access to the pill for students of college age. These changes also made it possible for universities to offer comprehensive family-planning assistance. Only 12 institutions of higher learning, for example, would prescribe the pill to unmarried students in 1966; yet, by 1973, 42% of university students had access to such services.

Goldin and Katz used the uneven pace of these changes to test the effects of the law on birth control use and on the changing attitudes toward women's careers, marriage, and fertility plans. They observed that the earliest states to lower the age of majority and thus provide college-age students access to birth control without parental consent were a seemingly random group: California and Georgia in 1968; Mississippi in 1969; Arkansas in 1970; Colorado, the District of Columbia, Illinois, Michigan, New Hampshire, New York, Oregon, and Tennessee in 1971. Controlling for other factors, they discovered that the timing of state liberalization of access to contraception had a small but statistically significant effect in decreasing the likelihood that a college graduate would marry before the age of 23.[29] Abortion, of course, complemented and enhanced the effect of contraception, and the economists found further that the legalization of abortion also contributed to a drop in the ranks of college graduates who married at earlier ages. They then used statistical techniques to attempt to separate the effects of abortion from those caused by greater access to birth control and concluded that legalization of access to birth control for minors had "a substantial and significant effect," while the effect of the availability of abortion became "small and insignificant" once they teased apart the combined effects.[30] Goldin and Katz concluded that legal changes in the access minors had to the pill in a given state generated "24–27%" of the large decline in the number of college graduates married by age 23.[31] While the economists recognized that many minors obtained the pill even in the states that restricted access, legalization appears to have played a substantial role in the dramatic changes in family practices. They emphasize that "a virtually foolproof, easy-to-use, and female-controlled contraceptive having low health risks, little pain, and few annoyances" made possible widespread usage and a wholesale change in the marriage norms of the newly expanded class of college graduates.

The increase in the age at marriage that followed also produced a cascade of other changes. Goldin and Katz argue that the effect of the pill was magnified by the fact that the ranks of college-educated men and women increased so rapidly, from about 10% of the earlier generation to approximately a quarter of the baby boom generation. The growth of a large group delaying marriage meant that those women who had not found a spouse by 23 were not left out of the marriage market; instead, the men waited alongside of them and remained available when the new college graduates were ready to marry. Although marriage rates have dropped substantially since the highs of the '50s, the one group for whom marriage rates have increased is college-educated women.

These trends have also enhanced the inequality generated by assortative mating. We have a much better sense of who will be successful and who will not, who will outgrow teen partying and who will be an alcoholic, who will pursue career ambitions and who will give up by the age of 30, then at 20. At the same time, men and women with poorer labor market prospects may not do as well in the marriage market either. Demonstrated failure may depress marriageability, particularly male attractiveness, in the same ways that demonstrated success enhances it. If, as Goldin and Katz demonstrate, college and professional women have been the biggest winners, the pill—and the blue family paradigm to which it contributed—created a new set of losers as well.

## CONTRACEPTION FOR THE MASSES

The advent of birth control did more, of course, than simply enhance the careers and marriage prospects of college-educated women. It changed the norms and attitudes of society as a whole toward sexual activity. The laws supporting greater availability of birth control reinforced the social processes through which premarital sexuality was becoming increasingly acceptable. Today, 75% of the population will have had premarital sex by the age of 20. By the age of 44, 95% of the entire population will have had sex outside of marriage, and they will overwhelmingly have done so with someone other than a person they will eventually marry.[32] Public attitudes toward nonmarital sexuality have shifted with the cultural and legal changes; 61% of adults aged 18–29 approve of premarital sex today compared with 21% of the same group in a Gallup poll in 1969.[33]

Acceptance of nonmarital sexuality also meant, at least for a brief period, a willingness to consider its consequences. Political proposals for greater family-planning assistance date back many decades. In the '50s, however, President Dwight D. Eisenhower dismissed them, observing that he could not "imagine anything more emphatically a subject that is not a proper political or governmental activity or function or responsibility.... This government will not, as long as I am here, have a positive political doctrine in its program that has to do with this problem of birth control. That is not our business."[34] By the mid-1960s, however, the discourse on contraception more generally came together with greater concern about poverty and a racialized discourse about fertility.

Perhaps the most influential study of fertility in the '60s indicated that, while poor women had dramatically higher fertility rates than the affluent (one report compared the birthrates of the Chicago urban poor to those in India), poor women and minority women actually wanted fewer children than the affluent, and twice as many of the children born to the poor were unwanted in comparison with the children born to better-off mothers. The study found, for example, that 17% of whites and 31% of blacks had not wanted the last child born to them. For those women who had not completed high school, the figures were even higher, with 31% of whites and 43% of blacks stating that their last child had not been wanted.[35] The two-tiered system that had been produced by the Comstock laws, in which the sophisticated secured effective birth control while the less-advantaged did not, continued to have a palpable effect on fertility rates.

Increasing discussion of fertility came as President Lyndon B. Johnson was launching the War on Poverty and as the Supreme Court was eliminating the last vestiges of the moral regulations that excluded poor women from welfare eligibility. When Congress authorized the Aid to Dependent Children program (later, Aid to Families with Dependent Children, or AFDC) in the 1930s, it had designed the program primarily for widows and allowed the states to bar nonmarital children from benefits. By the '60s, the federal agency charged with oversight of the program had eliminated most of the formal prohibitions, but it continued to deem the income of males present in the home available to the family making them ineligible for benefits. To check up on the presence of such unreported cohabitants, welfare authorities conducted midnight visits to the homes of female welfare recipients, dubbed Operation Bedcheck, to determine continued eligibility. In 1968, the Supreme Court ruled that such practices were inconsistent with the statutory scheme. It explained, "Congress has determined that immorality and illegitimacy should be dealt with through rehabilitative measures rather than measures that punish dependent children." The Court found it "simply inconceivable" that any state would be free "to discourage immorality and illegitimacy by the device of absolute disqualification of needy children."[36]

As a result of active outreach as part of the War on Poverty and the relaxation of the restrictions, welfare ranks swelled. In the early to mid-1960s, only half of those who were eligible received welfare benefits.[37] Over the next decade, the number of families participating in the welfare program increased from less than a million in 1964 to 3.5 million by 1976, more than tripling the size of the program.[38] While the majority of welfare recipients have always been white, African-Americans are dramatically more likely than whites to be poor. The percentage of African-American beneficiaries increased steadily through the 1960s and early '70s, peaking in 1976 with blacks at 46% of the caseload, even though they constituted only 11% of the population.[39] During the same period, concern grew about the changing composition of the African-American family, with nonmarital births growing from 25% of the total in 1965 (the time of the Moynihan

Report, *The Negro Family*, which touched off a political firestorm by calling attention to the high numbers) to 60% by 1975.[40]

In this context, calls for increased access to family-planning services won bipartisan support. Kristin Luker reports: "When poor women were having unwanted, out-of-wedlock births in such large numbers (out-of-wedlock births were assumed to be unwanted births), and when unwanted babies seemed to [be] swelling the AFDC roles [*sic*], an archaic birth control policy that kept contraceptives out of the hands of the poor seemed ludicrous, if not tragic."[41] It probably did not hurt politically that the Supreme Court's birth control decision in *Griswold* had drawn little protest nor that the major skeptics of the new proposals were black nationalists who saw the emphasis on birth control for poor black women as a form of genocide.

In 1966—a year after the Moynihan Report, six years before the Supreme Court's decision in *Eisenstadt* extending the right to contraception to single women and a decade before the Court's decision providing access to adolescents—a bipartisan congressional committee recommended that publicly funded birth control be made available to any AFDC recipient over the age of 15, regardless of whether she was married. Congress also made contraception a special emphasis of the War on Poverty, appropriating specific funds for family-planning efforts. In 1970, Congress passed and President Richard Nixon signed Title X of the Public Health Service Act, which created "a comprehensive federal program devoted entirely to the provision of family-planning services on a national basis." The vote was unanimous in the Senate and overwhelming in the House (298–32).[42] Two years later, at the insistence of the Nixon administration, Congress amended the Medicaid statute to add family planning to the list of "mandated services" that health care organizations must provide in order to remain eligible for federal Medicaid funds. Even more remarkably, by the late '70s, Congress agreed that adolescent sexuality was an important concern and, in 1978, the year following the Supreme Court's insistence that teen access to contraception could not be conditioned on parental consent, Congress amended Title X to make it clear that recipients of Title X family-planning funds were *required* to provide services to adolescents.[43] Family planning had become central to Democratic *and* Republican anti-poverty efforts and been transformed, in the words of one historian, from "private vice to public virtue."[44] It was not the partisan, morality-laden issue that it has become in the twenty-first century, but a matter of consensus.

# BLUE PRINCIPLES TRIUMPHANT

The emergence of what we are calling the blue family paradigm was neither partisan nor ideological, though parts of it were certainly controversial. It reflected the convergence of the interests of a favored group—middle-class college students—with concerns about the "excess fertility" of a disfavored group: the urban poor. Moreover, the strongest assertion of the new paradigm—support for contraception—was intensely pragmatic. Middle-class women, whether married or single, had embraced the pill in overwhelming numbers, and opposition was politically perilous. At the same time, making the same means available for poorer women simply made sense, whether the support was motivated by concern for reproductive autonomy or for reducing the numbers of a group viewed as a drain on societal resources.

At the center of these developments, however, were important principles that allowed a reformulation of family practices. Critical among them was the idea that childbirth should be chosen, rather than be an inevitable or punitive consequence of sexual activity. This idea commanded overwhelming support both in the congressional votes for family planning and in the Supreme Court cases that extended the right to privacy to single adults and teens. The idea was both substantive (at its core is a commitment to reproductive autonomy) and pragmatic (the alternatives were proven failures as the numbers of unwanted pregnancies attested).

The Supreme Court, in the series of cases from *Griswold* to *Carey*, articulated the central tenets of the new paradigm. *Griswold* recognized a right to privacy extending into the marital bedroom. *Eisenstadt* extended that right to single individuals, remaking the meaning of privacy in the process. Before these cases, the law had long recognized a concept of marital privacy that rested on a recognition of marriage as privileged space in which the law did not peer too closely at what took place therein. The *Griswold* case, in invalidating the potential intrusion into the marital bedroom implicit in a ban on the use of contraception, could be reconciled with that tradition. *Eisenstadt* could not. Yet, the Court in *Eisenstadt* declared:

> If under *Griswold* the distribution of contraceptives to married persons cannot be prohibited, a ban on distribution to unmarried persons would be equally impermissible. It is true that in *Griswold* the right of privacy in question inhered in the marital relationship. Yet the marital couple is not an independent entity with a mind and heart of its own,

but an association of two individuals each with a separate intellectual and emotional makeup. If the right of privacy means anything, it is the right of the *individual*, married or single, to be free from unwarranted governmental intrusion into matters so fundamentally affecting a person as the decision whether to bear or beget a child.[45]

The Supreme Court thus affirmed the individual right to reproductive autonomy, and not just sexual relations within marriage, as entitled to the protection of the state.

The Court in both *Eisenstadt* and *Carey v. Population Services*, the case that invalidated the New York law restricting the distribution of contraceptives to minors, further rejected the asserted state interest in pregnancy as a deterrent to sexual activity as a legitimate basis of state regulation. In *Carey*, the state had argued that the availability of birth control would "lead to increased sexual activity among the young."[46] The Court dismissed the suggestion that it is appropriate to deter sexual activity by "increasing the hazards attendant on it," observing that "no court or commentator has taken the argument seriously." The reason, which the *Eisenstadt* Court had also recognized, was: "It would be plainly unreasonable to assume that the [State] has prescribed pregnancy and the birth of an unwanted child as punishment for fornication. We remain reluctant to attribute any such 'scheme of values' to the State."[47] With that declaration, the shotgun marriage as official state policy was at an end—at least until the next decade brought it back.

## RED BACKLASH AND THE NEW WAR
## ON CONTRACEPTION

The bipartisan support for contraception did not last. The Reagan administration cut funding by more than a quarter shortly after taking office and attempted to divert family-planning efforts from birth control to abstinence efforts, adoption counseling, and other practices more acceptable to its social conservative base.[48] In particular, the administration tried to undermine *Carey*; the Department of Health and Human Services promulgated new regulations requiring Title X recipients to notify their parents within ten working days and disqualified them from further treatment if they failed to do so. The courts struck down the regulations as inconsistent with the statute.[49] Nonetheless, by the time President Bill Clinton took office in 1992, teen pregnancy rates were back to the levels of the early 1970s.

While pregnancy prevention efforts received renewed attention under Clinton, federal funding, adjusted for inflation, never again reached the 1980 levels for Title X. In the later years of the George W. Bush administration, the levels remained stalled at 61% (in inflation-adjusted dollars) of the 1980 levels. Nor have the efforts to undermine adolescent access disappeared. Utah and Texas have passed laws that prohibit state funds from being used to support minors' access to confidential contraceptive services. And bills in other states, such as Maine (2009), sought to require parental consent for all prescriptions issued to a minor. Moreover, a number of states that use Medicaid funds to extend family-planning efforts now limit their programs to women over the age of 19. Even the Obama administration, early in its term, bowed to Republican pressure and removed expanded funding for family-planning efforts from its stimulus package.[50]

In the meantime, the unequal access to reproductive autonomy that motivated Congress in the '70s remains. In 2006, half of all pregnancies in the United States were unplanned. The rates varied by socioeconomic status. For those with incomes at 200% of the poverty line, there were 29 unplanned pregnancies per 1,000 women aged 15–44; for those with incomes at 100% of the poverty line, there were 81 unplanned pregnancies per 1,000 women in that age group; and those below the poverty line had 112 unplanned pregnancies per 1,000 women, almost four times the rate of the most affluent. The disparities have increased further in recent years, with poor women's unplanned pregnancy rates increasing by 29% while the rate dropped for the better-off. And the unplanned pregnancies produce even greater disparities in unplanned births: 11 per 1,000 women for the most affluent group; 35 per 1,000 for those women at 100% of the poverty line; and 58 per 1,000 for those in poverty, more than five times the rate of the wealthiest group.[51]

In the twenty-first century in the United States, birth control is readily available for those with the means and discipline to use it. Political divisions over its use, therefore, primarily affect the poor, the unsophisticated, and the vulnerable. The newer developmental studies we discussed in chapter 3 underscore that adolescence is a time when peer relationships are critical and when the inclination to consult parents about anything, particularly sexual behavior, is at a low point. Within the blue paradigm, universal access to contraception is an important rite in the transition to adulthood, and the test for political acceptability is effectiveness: if teens are unlikely to talk to their parents about anything so intimate, access without parental involvement becomes that much more important. Within the red paradigm, in contrast, the availability of contraception to unmarried adolescents, particularly if promoted too prominently by school or state, is an affront to traditional values and parental authority. One of the battlegrounds in the culture wars is therefore the ease of access to birth control. Despite the changes described in this chapter, three in ten of female American teenagers still become pregnant before they turn 20, and four-fifths of the pregnancies are unplanned.[52] In the next chapter, we examine the links between parental authority and reproductive control in the context of the far more divisive issue of abortion, an issue that has become the rallying cry for a return to traditional values. We argue that the far greater challenge to women's reproductive autonomy is the effort to make abortion rather than contraception the symbolic center of family planning—and to tag an ever-greater part of family-planning efforts with the abortion label.

## CHAPTER 6

# Abortion, Law, and the Cognitive Map

C ONTRACEPTION IS THE indispensable element of the blue family paradigm; abortion, in contrast, is the regrettable but necessary fallback. Yet, within the red family paradigm, abortion is the issue that has galvanized the reassertion of traditional values. The issue is intrinsically divisive. Either the fetus is a human life, as certain religious teachings maintain it is, and abortion is therefore murder, or the fetus is potential life, deserving perhaps of enhanced respect, but subject to the same balancing tests of advantages and disadvantages as other more prosaic decisions. Yet, the divisions over abortion have not always been *political*. The issue emerged as an emblem of cultural conflict only when religious opposition combined with anxiety about changing family mores to crystallize resentment about the perceived societal indifference to the loss of traditional family values. In that context, the very difficulty of crafting a middle ground on the permissibility of terminating a pregnancy has contributed to its political potency.

A growing literature describes the emergence of abortion as a defining political issue with the creation of the Reagan coalition. Before the 1980s, Catholics led the opposition to abortion. The Catholic Church staked out a strict position on conception as the beginning of life, and Catholic churches then and now have made the subject a frequent topic of Sunday sermons. Protestant churches, in contrast, paid less attention to the issue. Indeed, Harold O. J. Brown, editor of *Christianity Today*, observed: "At that point, a lot of Protestants reacted almost automatically—'If the Catholics are for it, we should be against it.' . . . The fact that Catholics were out in front caused many Protestants to keep a very low profile."[1]

What changed, according to Yale law professors Robert Post and Reva Siegel, was the identification of the abortion issue with feminism and the perceived threat to traditional family values. They observe that, by the end of the '70s, "conservatives mobilized against abortion in order to protect traditional family roles."[2] The *Christian Harvest Times* in 1980, for example, denounced abortion as part of a parade of secular evils. In "A Special Report on Secular Humanism vs. Christianity," it explained, "To understand humanism is to understand women's liberation, the ERA [Equal Rights Amendment], gay rights, children's rights, abortion, sex education, the 'new' morality, evolution, values clarification, situational ethics, the loss of patriotism, and many of the other problems that are tearing America apart today."[3] Ronald Reagan ran for the presidency in 1980 on a Republican Party platform that pledged to "work for the appointment of judges at all levels of the judiciary who respect traditional family values and the sanctity of innocent human life."[4] The attack on "activist judges" merged with the protection of traditional gender roles as the basis for family stability and with opposition to abortion not just as a violation of religious teachings, but also as a symbol of public condoning of nonmarital sexuality.

Since the 1980s, the identification of the Republican Party with traditionalist values and forms of expression has deepened. Moreover, the partisan identification with family values has also been couched in language designed to appeal to those who prefer more absolutist to more contextualist expression. Drew Westen, echoing linguist George Lakoff, observes that, as a matter of political strategy, the Republicans have been "unequivocal" in conflating abortion and murder, setting out "an uncompromising stance as the only *moral* stance one could take, get[ting] the 30 percent of Americans with the least tolerance for ambiguity on moral questions to the polls," and allowing the Democrats to splinter in their approach to the issue.[5] Aligning opposition to abortion and more general support for the right kind of family values reinforces the political nature of the red-blue division.

First, to the extent that political views reflect personality types, the abortion debate is likely to divide along absolutist-contextualist lines. Thus, the researchers who found a genetic basis for conservative views distinguished between those who have "a desire for clear, unbending moral and behavioral codes (strict constructionists) [and] a fondness for swift and severe punishment for violations of this code" versus those who prefer "a context-dependent rather than rule-based approach to proper behavior" and have "a distaste for preset punishments (mitigating circumstances)."[6] Moreover, other studies indicate that, over the three presidential elections from 1996 to 2004, personality factors that predict ideological orientation strongly correlated with the state-level support for the two parties, even controlling for other factors such as population density, income, minority composition, and the percentage of the vote cast for the same party's candidate in the previous election.[7]

Second, the discussion of abortion in all-or-nothing terms can thus be expected to reinforce identification of the abortion issue with the underlying cultural orientation, whether the values preferences derive from innate personality differences or differences in regional cultural expression. Lakoff, for example, emphasizes that, within a conservative world view, abortion for the purpose of ending an inopportune pregnancy may not be appropriate for reasons independent of religious views on the beginning of life. He observes: "According to Strict Father morality, an unmarried teenage girl should not be having sex at all.... She has to be responsible for the consequences of her actions if she is to learn from her mistakes. An abortion would simply sanction her immoral behavior."[8]

Third, abortion views replicate the devotional divide. Of white evangelical Protestants who attend church at least once a week, 71% believe that abortion should be illegal in most or all cases compared to less than half of white evangelicals who attend church less often and 22% of mainline Protestants who attend church less than once a week. Catholics are in between. Among those who claim no religious affiliation, 7% believe that abortions should be illegal in all cases, and 16% in most cases for a total of 23%.[9]

Fourth, views on abortion, at least in recent years, correspond with political preferences more generally. Thus, 60% of liberal Democrats believe that abortion should be widely available in comparison with only 17% of conservative Republicans, while 50% of conservative Republicans believe that abortions should be illegal with few exceptions compared to only 13% of liberal Democrats.[10]

Voters tend overall to be more moderate in their views than party activists, and the majority of Americans continue to prefer a middle ground on abortion, one in which abortion would continue to be legal in at least some circumstances. Nonetheless, when the question is framed to give voters an opportunity to identify themselves as "strongly pro-life," "strongly pro-choice," or something in between, those choosing the "strong" positions make up 70% of the electorate.[11]

Given the power of the issue, political strategists have worked to keep abortion in the forefront of the public mind. Both in Congress and in state legislatures, anti-abortion activists have introduced ever more conservative measures, the Republican Party platform has moved ever further to the right—calling in 2008, for example, for a ban on somatic cell nuclear transfer, a form of stem cell research—and anti-abortion legislators have scheduled as many as 80 votes a year on the subject. These efforts have hardened positions over time. In 1980, there was relatively little divergence between Republicans and Democrats on the issue, with both groups rating their support for abortion at approximately 2.8 out of a 4.0 scale. After 1990, Democratic support for abortion rights moved up (closer to 3.0), and Republican support moved down (toward 2.5).[12] The percentage of the public describing themselves as "pro-life" has increased from approximately 32% in 1994, to 44% in 2008, to 51% in 2009.[13] And "pro-life" advocates are much more likely to say that a political candidate must share their views, though much more so in 2004 than 2008.[14] Moreover, while the majority of Americans favor intermediate positions on the issue, two-thirds of those who think abortion should always be illegal oppose any possible compromise.[15]

Abortion has long been a polarizing debate where neither side accepts the legitimacy of the other's position. This division, between those who equate abortion to murder and those who see traditionalist religious beliefs as hostile to women's equality, undermines protection for the most-vulnerable groups (poor women and minors). Legislators vie to prove their bona fides on the issue rather than to craft workable solutions. This chapter focuses on the issue of mandated parental involvement in teen abortion decisions because it goes to the heart of the symbolic divisions between the family paradigms and to the fracturing of the legal regulation of abortion rights. The marital and motherhood expectations of young women speak volumes about the lives their communities expect them to lead.

## PARENTAL AUTHORITY OR TEEN AUTONOMY?

The continuing fight over abortion focuses on the validity of both *Roe v. Wade*,[16] the 1970s Supreme Court decision that guaranteed a woman's right, under at least some circumstances, to elect termination of her pregnancy, and on the privacy cases that established a constitutional basis for the rights recognized in *Roe*. This line of cases, as discussed in chapter 5, began with *Griswold* and the recognition of a right to use contraception. *Roe* extended this right so that it included a woman's ability to choose to terminate her pregnancy, recognizing that the birth of an unwanted child may force upon a woman "a distressful life and future."[17] The 7–2 decision was not a partisan one. The two dissenters were a Republican (William Rehnquist) and a Democrat (Byron White). The majority included justices appointed by Republican presidents (Harry Blackmun, Warren Burger, Lewis Powell, Potter Stewart) and Democratic (Thurgood Marshall, William Douglas, William Brennan) ones.

In *Casey*, decided in 1992, the Supreme Court reaffirmed *Roe*, albeit somewhat more narrowly defining the rights at stake. *Casey* emphasized a mother's unique role in carrying a child to term and specifically rejected a state's ability "to insist...upon its own vision of the woman's role, however dominant that vision has been in the course of our history and our culture."[18] Justice Sandra Day O'Connor's opinion for the Court acknowledged that *Roe*, the 1973 decision legalizing abortion, and earlier Supreme Court opinions regarding contraception are "of the same character." Indeed, her description of the differences underlying the positions on abortion captures the divisions between the two family paradigms we have described in this book. O'Connor observed that both the cases on contraception and those on abortion "involve personal decisions concerning not only the meaning of procreation but also human responsibility and respect for it." She described one view as "based on such reverence for the wonder of creation that any pregnancy ought to be welcomed and carried to full term no matter how difficult it will be to provide for the child and ensure its well-being." The other view "is that the inability to provide for the nurture and care of the infant is a cruelty to the child and anguish to the parent."[19] She thus identified the pro-choice position with the idea of responsibility, linking *readiness* for pregnancy and childbearing with the ability to provide for the child. She described the pro-life position in terms similar to Luker's description of sex as "sacred." In accordance with this world view, a person should not engage in sex unless she is willing to accept the child that might result, and thus the obligation to provide for the child follows from the nature of that child as a gift from God. In *Casey*, O'Connor concluded that the choice between these two visions (which clearly echo red and blue world views) must be that of the individual.

The division between these positions is particularly acute on the question of whether states can require parental involvement in the form of either notification or consent for teen abortion decisions, bringing to the fore the issue of parental authority over teen sexuality. To be sure, much of the political activity surrounding the parental notification issue is a subterfuge for the larger fight about the acceptability of abortion, but the issue also has independent significance for understandings about family formation. Indeed, a majority of those who favor abortion rights also supports some form of parental involvement, and each state has had to address the issue of what type of involvement to mandate. To a greater degree than the larger question of abortion, therefore, parental involvement laws provide a window on the construction of family law paradigms, with particular salience in the cultural conflict between family systems.

The idea that parents should be involved in a medical decision concerning a minor child has, after all, intuitive appeal and a long history. Advocates emphasize the benefits of improved parent-teen communication,[20] including the protection of sexually active teens from predatory partners. New Hampshire, for example, justified its parental notification statute as serving "several compelling state interests, including protecting the emotional and physical health of the pregnant mother, vindicating the importance of the parent-child relationship, and promoting the family unit."[21] Senators who proposed the Child Interstate Abortion Notification Act (also called the Teen Endangerment Act) in 2006 "conjured up images of lascivious older men ferrying off their sexual prey to out-of-state abortion clinics"[22] and emphasized the importance of parent-child communication.[23] At the core of the issue—as both a cultural and constitutional matter—is deference to parental authority.[24] Interestingly, in an example of how rhetoric can be turned around, pro-choice advocates in Missouri appealed to parental authority in an effort to defeat a bill providing penalties for anyone who coerces a woman into an abortion: one member of the Missouri legislature argued that "parents of minors who are raped by a friend or family member would be criminalized for suggesting that their daughters have abortions."[25]

At the same time, empirical studies show that teens overwhelmingly *do* consult their parents when they are considering abortion.[26] Opposition to mandatory parental involvement focuses on the reasons a minority of teens does not consult, and the potential effect on this requirement on the timing of abortions. An early study by Planned Parenthood found that, of those minors who did not inform their parents of their abortions, 30% had histories of violence in their families, feared the occurrence of violence, or were afraid of being kicked out of their homes.[27] Other studies have found that parental notification laws delay medical treatment, turning otherwise routine abortions into riskier procedures.[28] Moreover, opponents maintain that, in the polarized climate of abortion politics, such laws are often intended to frustrate access to abortion services altogether.[29]

## JUDICIAL ABDICATION

In the period immediately following *Roe v. Wade*, parental involvement laws swept the country.[30] By 1988, over 20 states had enacted legislation, though about half were subject to court orders enjoining their enforcement.[31] Relatively liberal Massachusetts enacted one of the first (and strictest) statutes in 1974.[32] Forty-three states have at one time or another enacted such laws, and 36 states have them in force as of 2009.[33] Politically, such legislation seems like a good compromise because politicians can claim that, while they may support the right to abortion, they are also pro-life and pro-family. Although initially neither abortion nor parental notification laws split the states along lines of red state–blue state polarization, more recent developments echo this split as positions and political lines have hardened.[34]

The litigation over the constitutionality of the laws captures some of the shift. In 1976, the Supreme Court first considered parental involvement laws, striking down a Missouri statute that required parental consent unless the abortion was necessary to save the life of the pregnant child.[35] In subsequent cases, the Court has upheld statutes requiring parental consent, so long as they include a judicial bypass procedure that would allow a mature minor to make her own abortion decision or that would permit an abortion to occur if it were in the pregnant child's best interest.[36] These early cases balanced protection of the constitutional right to abortion with the recognition ordinarily granted to parents' interest in supervising their teens. In the Court's 1979 decision in *Bellotti v. Baird*,[37] for example, which struck down the Massachusetts statute, Justice Powell observed that the abortion decision was crucial to a minor's future and that the state must have important interests when seeking to restrict a minor's choice.[38] In contrast to later decisions, the Court in *Bellotti* focused on the right to an abortion, the potential impact of parental notification on deterring abortion, and what it clearly viewed as the negative consequences, "grave and indelible," of "unwanted motherhood" balanced against the parents' interest in supervising their children.[39] While the justices disagreed about the reasoning for the opinion, eight of the nine found the Massachusetts statute as written to be wanting. The Court suggested that, for such restrictions to pass constitutional muster, the state must provide for a judicial bypass procedure that could "be completed with anonymity and sufficient expedition to provide an effective opportunity for an abortion to be obtained."[40]

By 1990, however, the Court had become warier of overturning state decisions, and it fractured badly in *Hodgson v. Minnesota*.[41] The decision addressed a law that Justice John Paul Stevens described as "the most intrusive in the Nation" because it was the only one of the 38 state laws at the time to specifically mandate that both parents be notified and that the notification occur whether or not each parent wished to be notified or had participated in the girl's upbringing.[42] The trial court in *Hodgson*, after lengthy hearings on the effects of the legislation, had found that the two-parent notification requirement served no rational state purpose, the bypass procedures were terrifying to the petitioners, and many of the judges presiding over them had concluded that they were pointless. The court held further that the two-parent requirement was "particularly harmful" for a family "when the parents were divorced or separated, especially in the context of an abusive or dysfunctional family," and the requirement would have a negative effect even on an intact family where domestic violence was a serious problem.

Despite the strength of the trial court's findings, the justices could agree neither on methodology nor result. The Court accordingly issued five different opinions, with the justices variously concurring, dissenting, and joining parts of the other opinions. Taken together, four of the justices found the two-parent notification unconstitutional in any circumstances, though for differing reasons; four found it constitutional with or without judicial bypass; and one, Justice O'Connor, split the difference by finding it constitutional so long as judicial bypass provided sufficient protection. Six of the justices in contrast upheld single-parent notification with judicial bypass, though again without agreement on the reasoning and with significant dissent.[43] Later courts would find the result "impenetrable,"[44] and Justice Antonin Scalia used what he termed the "random and unpredictable results of our consequently unchanneled individual views" to "dissent from this enterprise of devising an Abortion Code, and from the illusion that we have authority to do so."[45] The Supreme Court could no longer reach agreement either on the substance of the parental involvement issue or on the judicial role in managing the litigation it produced.

By 2006, the Court withdrew from the field. In *Ayotte v. Planned Parenthood of New England*,[46] a unanimous Court declined to invalidate a New Hampshire statute that required parental notification without a judicial bypass, a law that seemed to stand in clear violation of earlier Supreme Court precedents. Instead, the Court emphasized that relatively few applications of the statute would raise constitutional issues, and the Court should "try not to nullify more of a legislature's work than is necessary, for we know that '[a] ruling of unconstitutionality frustrates the intent of the elected representatives of the people.'"[47] In the *Roe* era, legislatures often passed abortion measures of dubious constitutional validity, relying on the courts to take the political heat of striking down the laws and defusing the political pressure to adopt more-aggressive legislation.[48] As partisanship intensified around the issue of abortion, however, the Court signaled that the issue is better left to the political branches of government.

## STATE OF DIVISION

Within the U.S. federalist system, states have experimented with various approaches to parental involvement in the teen abortion decision. Enforcement of parental notification laws bears more relationship to the red-blue split we have documented than to the earlier importance of Catholic voters. Six states, all of which voted Democratic in 2004 and 2008—Connecticut, Hawaii, New York, Oregon, Vermont, and Washington—do not require any form of parental involvement in minors' abortion decisions.[49] New Hampshire, the battleground New England state, became the first state to repeal a parental notification act (during the summer of 2007).[50] The 2007 repeal came after Democrats swept into office in the 2006 election, replacing the Republican legislature that had passed strict—and arguably unconstitutional—parental notification laws only a few years before.[51] West Coast blue California and Oregon had passed parental involvement laws in earlier eras. The California legislation had been struck down on the basis of the California constitution in 1997, and the legislature has not acted since. Oregon had a relatively mild provision, mandating parental involvement only for those under the age of 15. Disgruntled conservatives in both states placed initiatives on the ballot that would have mandated parental notification. California voters defeated the initiative in a special election in 2005 and again in the regular elections of 2006 and 2008,[52] and Oregon did so in 2006 with 54% opposed.[53]

Some states, while mandating notification or consent, are quite liberal in making exceptions in appropriate cases. The majority of these states are blue. Maine, for example, allows a physician to override the parental involvement requirement and permits other family members to be notified in lieu of a parent.[54] Other states have relatively broad waiver provisions. Delaware, a blue state, allows notice to be given to a grandparent or a mental health professional, while Maryland, another blue state, and West Virginia, a red state, are like Maine in allowing a physician to waive parental notice in the best interests of the pregnant child.[55] A few states, blue and red, have also broadened the class of adults who can consent or to whom notice must be given in lieu of a parent.[56] Finally, some states have taken no state action in the wake of older decisions invalidating parental notification statutes.[57]

Taking these developments together, the blue states as a whole look different from the red states. Of the 19 states that voted for Kerry in 2004, almost a third (6) have no parental involvement statutes.[58] A seventh, New Hampshire, repealed its law, the only state to do so. Three others have had their state statutes declared unconstitutional and have declined to enact alternative measures (with California having defeated propositions that would do so three election cycles in a row), for a total of 10 with no enforcement whatsoever.[59] Four additional states have adopted more workable parental involvement statutes through physician waivers or an expansion of the adults who can act in place of parents.[60] This leaves 5 of the 19 states with relatively strict laws intact: Massachusetts,[61] Minnesota,[62] Rhode Island,[63] Pennsylvania,[64] and Michigan.[65] None of these more-restrictive statutes, however, has been enacted since 2000.

All of the 31 states that were red in 2004, in contrast, have at some point enacted parental notification statutes. Twenty-five of these states have strict parental notification or consent statutes, while 6 have less-stringent laws.[66] Moreover, 2 red states, Mississippi[67] and North Dakota,[68] mandate that *both* parents consent.[69] Oklahoma, Texas, Utah, and Wyoming require both parental notification and consent.[70]

## CYNICISM IN ACTION

Parental notification statutes—and the fight to enact or repeal them—reinforce the symbolic distinctions between the two paradigmatic family systems, but their implementation often bears little relationship to the legislation's stated objectives. Law professor Carol Sanger suggests that "parental involvement statutes, while often couched in the language of family togetherness and child protection, are less concerned with developing sound or nuanced family policies in the area of adolescent reproduction than with securing a set of political goals aimed at thwarting access to abortion, restoring parental authority, and punishing girls for having sex."[71] Empirical research, while imperfect, concurs that parental involvement laws are more important in discouraging abortion or increasing the number of pregnant teens who obtain abortions outside of their home states than in promoting individual teen health or family communications.[72] The symbolic fight, however, often obscures the law's practical effects. The bypass is difficult to navigate, even for the most mature and well-resourced teens, and operates in ways that further marginalize poor, very young, and geographically isolated minors.

First, parental involvement that occurs when a teen voluntarily initiates it is a very different matter from parental involvement imposed by law. Adolescents by and large tell their parents about their abortion decisions; when they do not or cannot, the consequences of mandating parental involvement may be severe. Parental consent laws, accordingly, have the harshest consequences on those who may be victimized (1) inside their families, where, because of domestic violence or other problems, they have a bad relationship with their parents; and (2) outside of their families, where the lack of ready access to abortion may persuade them to delay, try riskier alternatives, or give birth to a child they would prefer not to have. The law is out of step with the recommendations of health providers; indeed, in the less politically charged arenas of prenatal care and sexually transmitted disease testing, most states provide medical services without mandating parental notification or consent.

Second, judicial bypass, the Supreme Court's preferred safety valve for those who cannot realistically rely on parental support, has been largely ineffective in either protecting teens or encouraging more reflective abortion decisions. While teens often find such procedures to be terrifying, punitive, costly, and difficult to navigate, the courts also dislike overseeing the requests. The result presents two unsatisfying alternatives. In some jurisdictions, the judges are either highly likely to grant the requests, believing that any teen who opposes the pregnancy enough to request a hearing should not be required to bear an unwanted child, or they routinely oppose approval, trying to make it as difficult as possible to secure an abortion.[73] In other jurisdictions, the courts enter into fairly detailed factual findings that proceed from intrusive inquiry into the teen's circumstances, resulting in a process that is much more unpleasant for the teen and time-consuming for the court. Individual judges have enormous discretion to determine whether a pregnant teen satisfies the maturity or best interests standard, making it very hard to predict what the bypass will look like in any particular courthouse without knowing the predilections of the sitting judge. The bypass procedures place a strain on the judiciary's resources, reduce the availability of abortion for the teen who may be most burdened by an unwanted pregnancy, and make access less predictable, especially in rural areas where securing a bypass hearing is more difficult.[74]

Third, the statutes that appear to be more effective at protecting teens while also ensuring effective communication have allowed for alternative decision makers, such as grandparents or doctors. If an adolescent can substitute a trusted adult or seek counseling from a neutral third party such as a doctor, then the adult can help to provide support for the ultimate decision, including advice about abortion providers, information about adoption or other alternatives, or assistance in establishing constructive lines of communication with the parents.

So long as voters have more interest in affirming restrictions on adolescent sexuality than in teen well-being, however, legislatures and courts have little incentive to seek compromise solutions. The states that have moved toward these pragmatic measures, such as Maine and West Virginia, remain relatively few. In the meantime, however, parental involvement laws disproportionately affect the most vulnerable adolescents in ways that may affect the rest of their lives.

## CYNICISM MAGNIFIED

The availability of abortion, for both teens or adults, magnifies the consequences of lack of access to contraception. It therefore has a particularly critical impact on the life chances of poor and minority women, the victims of sexual assault, and those from abusive and dysfunctional families. The Guttmacher Institute reports that between 1994 and 2001, the "unintended pregnancy rate rose 29% among women living below the poverty level and 26% among women living between 100% and 200% of the poverty level, but fell 20% among more affluent women."[75] It increased as well for high school dropouts and women between the ages of 19 and 24, while declining for adolescents and college graduates. The poorest 30% of women of reproductive age in the United States obtained 57% of the abortions in 2000. During this period, white women had the lowest abortion rates (1.3%) while black women had the highest (4.9%). For whites, only 18% of conceptions ended in abortion compared to 43% of black conceptions and 25% of Latina conceptions.[76] Even when they are able to obtain abortions, two-thirds of poor women report that they would have liked to have undergone the procedure at an earlier point.[77] Abortion has accordingly become increasingly important for poor and minority women's reproductive autonomy even as it recedes in importance for affluent whites.

Yet, poor women are disproportionately affected by the practicalities of obtaining an abortion. New legal restrictions, which unnecessarily complicate the provision of abortion services, also make them more expensive and emotionally trying. When the *New York Times* reported in early 2009 that abortion was "safe, legal, and inexpensive," the directors of the Abortion Access Project and the National Latina Institute for Reproductive Health wrote in to protest: "An abortion at 10 weeks' gestation costs $523 on average, often out of pocket. To term this 'inexpensive,' especially in the current economy, is ludicrous."[78] For minors, cost further exacerbates their difficulties with access to abortion; they are often too young to have jobs, and if they are trying to avoid parental involvement, they cannot ask their parents for money.

Medicaid, the federal program which provides funding for health care for very poor Americans, provides no funding for abortion except, according to the 1977 Hyde Amendment, in cases of rape, incest, or life endangerment to the mother. The Supreme Court has repeatedly upheld indirect restrictions on poor women's ability to obtain abortions, first deciding in 1977 that a state need not pay for medically necessary abortions and then upholding the Hyde Amendment three years later.[79] Somewhere around one-fifth to one-third of women on Medicaid who want an abortion cannot afford to obtain one.[80] Some of these women are, however, more fortunate than others, if they live in one of the 13 states that covers medically necessary abortions with state funds: Arizona, California, Connecticut, Hawaii, Illinois, Maryland, Massachusetts, Minnesota, Montana, New Jersey, New Mexico, New York, and Oregon. Leaving aside the battleground state of New Mexico, the only red states on this list are Arizona and Montana.

# BLURRING THE DISTINCTIONS

Ultimately, restrictions on abortion access for teens and poor women are cynical attempts to "do something" about abortion by picking on constituencies who have little voice in the public policy debates. Because of the difficulties of reversing *Roe* entirely, anti-abortion advocates have pursued an incrementalist strategy of making abortion more difficult to obtain. For example, three states (all red) now require doctors to do ultrasounds on women seeking abortion, and then offer women the opportunity to view the images of the fetus before the abortion; eight states (all red except for Minnesota) require that a woman receive information on the ability of the fetus to feel pain; and five states (all red) prohibit private insurers from covering abortion, except in cases of life endangerment, rape, or incest.[81] A full assault on *Roe* has yet to be successful, and the election of Barack Obama means that the Supreme Court is unlikely—for the moment—to add another anti-abortion justice to its members. Nonetheless, abortion politics retains its ability to rally the red paradigm base.[82] Conservatives can't stop talking about abortion; abortion is "their meal ticket."[83] It remains the family values issue least amenable to compromise.

## CHAPTER 7

# The Irrationality of Adolescence

*What the Adults Are* Really *Fighting Over*

I n *17 AGAIN*, a 2009 teen movie, the main plot revolves around heartthrob Zac Efron, who marries his high school girlfriend when she gets pregnant, and, many years later, as they are going through a divorce, he becomes a teen again. In a pivotal scene, he lectures a class of high school seniors, including one of his own children, about the value of abstinence.[1] The movie, however, is full of ironies. The most critical is that Zac's perspective as an adult, in at least one respect, is almost exactly the same as his perspective at 17: his life begins and ends in high school. Of course, abstinence is a good idea *in* high school, especially for Zac's adolescent children. But what happens if Zac or his children get that college scholarship and move on with their lives? The movie's answer (spoiler alert!) is that Zac finds true happiness by reuniting with his high school sweetheart and taking a new job as the high school basketball coach. In the movies, high school need never end.

The world outside of high school is much more complicated than the world of *17 Again*. Yet, the most basic division between the red and blue family systems involves the transmission of values to the next generation. For traditionalists—and the core red family constituency—the critical need is to affirm the right values, and programs that even suggest that sex outside of marriage is permissible conflict with those values. For modernists—and the core blue family constituency—public policy should encourage programs that work, particularly in deterring childbirth and securing the right pathways to a prosperous adulthood. Both groups agree that getting your high school sweetheart pregnant is a bad idea. They differ on whether Zac's abstinence-only speech is likely to do any good, or whether public schools should prepare students to make their own choices through comprehensive sex education. Unsurprisingly, the issue of how to transmit such contested values is a flashpoint for cultural conflict, and sex education in public schools has become an issue of national controversy.

In this chapter, we describe the effort to make abstinence-only instruction a national priority. Abstinence-only education, spurred by the availability of federal funds, permits no mixed messages. It teaches public school students that abstinence until marriage is the only acceptable course and the only sure way to prevent pregnancy and sexually transmitted diseases (STDs). Comprehensive sex education, or "abstinence-plus,"[2] provides both comprehensive, medically accurate information about sexuality, pregnancy, contraception, and disease *and* information on the virtues of abstinence until marriage. Congress initially provided funding for abstinence-only efforts during the Clinton administration, the Bush administration expanded the funding, and the Democratic Congress under Obama, together with many of the states, is rethinking the wisdom of the efforts. This issue, while clearly a subject of intense debate, takes more twists and turns than the abortion issue.

## CULTURE CLASH DEFINED

Sociologist Kristin Luker of UCLA spent almost 20 years studying the controversy over sex education. In her fascinating examination of the approaches of several communities to sex education, she found a "chasm, wide and getting wider, between the *sexual* right and left."[3] She was trying to understand why people raised in the same general cultural environments become sexual liberals or sexual conservatives.[4] She characterizes sexual conservatives, who typically oppose sex education other than abstinence education, as dogmatists who "believe in a moral code derived from God, not man," while sexual liberals, who favor more comprehensive forms of sex education, "have a more forgiving view of morality."[5] She emphasizes that, for liberals, sex is "natural," while for conservatives, it is "sacred."[6] Within the blue paradigm, sexuality is to be managed, and morality is associated with responsibility. Use of contraception accordingly transforms a blameworthy act—unprotected sex—into an accepted one. In the red model, where sex is sacred, marriage is the institution that sanctifies the act. Within marriage, contraception is invisible: most Protestant denominations leave the decision to use or not to use artificial means of restricting conception to individual choice, and most American Catholics ignore church teachings. Outside of marriage, however, contraception cannot transform the profane, and it becomes controversial when it is associated with implied approval of premarital sexuality or a determination to escape the consequences of prohibited conduct.

Most religions, and particularly fundamentalist ones, tend to preach against nonmarital sexuality.[7] And if nonmarital sexuality is wrong, absolutists believe that the public schools should take a consistent position against it. Indeed, evangelicals are three times as likely as non-evangelicals to believe that sex education should not be taught in the schools,[8] and they cannot reconcile teaching abstinence with providing information about birth control. As Mark Regnerus found in his comprehensive study of sex education, parents who are "more devoutly religious" are worried that discussing contraception will encourage their children to engage in sexual activities.[9] Moreover, they emphasize the importance of adherence to authority and reinforcement of the moral order. Sexual liberals, in contrast, emphasize individual autonomy and fulfillment. They see sexual practices along a continuum of possibilities and support education designed to assist the responsible exercise of choice.[10]

A national poll documents these two different ways of thinking about responsible sexuality:

> Respondents were asked to choose which of two statements was closer to their belief: (1) "When it comes to sex, teenagers need to have limits set; they must be told what is acceptable and what is not," or (2) "ultimately teenagers need to make their own decisions, so their education needs to be more in the form of providing information and guidance." Forty-seven percent selected the first statement; 51 percent selected the second. Conservatives were much more likely to choose the first statement over the second (64 percent to 32 percent), as were evangelical or born-again Christians (61 percent to 35 percent). Liberals and moderates were more likely to choose the second statement over the first (61 percent to 37 percent for liberals and 56 percent to 42 percent for moderates).[11]

The content of public school instruction is thus an important practical and symbolic divide.

# THE FEDERALIZATION OF
# ABSTINENCE-ONLY FUNDING

At one time, these differences would have played out solely in local decisions about the content of public schools' curriculum. Starting as far back as 1981, however, when Congress enacted the Adolescent Family Life Act (AFLA), federal support has increased the prevalence of abstinence-only instruction.[12] The AFLA-related programs, which received $29.8 million in appropriations in 2008, focus generally on adolescent sexuality issues, including pregnancy and parenting.[13] The AFLA explicitly authorizes the involvement of religious organizations in its programs on teen sexuality.[14] Since 1997, all prevention programs funded through AFLA have centered on abstinence education.[15] Abstinence education also receives funding through Title V of the Social Security Act, which was enacted as part of the 1996 Welfare Reform Act. The legislation has a very specific and clear definition of abstinence education that strongly supports red family values. Abstinence education is a program that

(A) has as its exclusive purpose, teaching the social, psychological, and health gains to be realized by abstaining from sexual activity;

(B) teaches abstinence from sexual activity outside marriage as the expected standard for all school age children;

(C) teaches that abstinence from sexual activity is the only certain way to avoid out-of-wedlock pregnancy, sexually transmitted diseases, and other associated health problems;

(D) teaches that a mutually faithful monogamous relationship in [the] context of marriage is the expected standard of human sexual activity;

(E) teaches that sexual activity outside of the context of marriage is likely to have harmful psychological and physical effects;

(F) teaches that bearing children out-of-wedlock is likely to have harmful consequences for the child, the child's parents, and society;

(G) teaches young people how to reject sexual advances and how alcohol and drug use increases vulnerability to sexual advances; and

(H) teaches the importance of attaining self-sufficiency before engaging in sexual activity.[16]

The amount of government funding for abstinence education increased from $10 million in 1997[17] to $177 million in 2007.[18] During his first year in office, President Obama reduced the budget allocation for abstinence programs.[19] In the interim, adolescents have become far more likely to receive abstinence-only instruction.[20] In 1988, fewer than 2% of junior and senior high school students had abstinence-only education; less than 20 years later, abstinence education was the predominant approach in more than one-third of American schools.[21]

## THE RETURN ON TAXPAYER DOLLARS

Abstinence-only education might not be controversial if it were effective, but most studies conclude that it is not. Bristol Palin provided a cryptic summary, in a true teen voice, of what's wrong with the abstinence focus: "Everyone should be abstinent or whatever, but it's not realistic at all."[22] Her one-time fiancé, Levi Johnston, noted on *Larry King Live* that "all teens, or most of them, are sexually active" and that abstinence is unrealistic.[23] They're right. First, there is no evidence that abstinence-only education makes abstinence until marriage more likely, nor that it produces a decline in either teen or nonmarital births.[24] Some studies show that abstinence-only education leaves teens less prepared for the sexual relations they later develop, with a corresponding increase in unplanned pregnancies and STDs.[25] Teens who participate in abstinence-only education appear to begin sexual activity at roughly the same ages as teens who do not participate in the programs. In 2005, the American Psychological Association reviewed the existing scientific literature and concluded that abstinence-only education programs have limited effectiveness in encouraging abstinence and unintended consequences. Based on 15 years of research, the APA report concluded that comprehensive sex education programs that included abstinence education with information about birth control were at least as effective in discouraging early sexual activity and were more effective in reducing pregnancies and STDs.[26] Similarly, a study from the Centers for Disease Control indicated that five of the government-funded comprehensive sex education programs appeared to produce successful results compared to none of the abstinence-only programs.[27] Congressman Henry Waxman, in a report examining the federally funded programs, concluded that more than 80% of federal grants go to providing abstinence-only curriculums that "contain false, misleading, or distorted information about reproductive health."[28]

In April 2007, a comprehensive, congressionally authorized review of Title V programs found that youths who participated in abstinence-only education programs were *no more nor less likely* to have abstained from sex than those in a control group who had not participated in the abstinence-only education programs.[29] The study randomly assigned more than 2,000 youths to an abstinence-only education program group or to a control group that received no special programming: four to six years after the study began, the researchers found virtually no differences between the age of first sexual intercourse and the number of sexual partners between those who had received abstinence-only education and those in the control group.[30] The authors reported: "Findings from this study provide no evidence that abstinence programs implemented in upper elementary and middle schools are effective at reducing the rate of teen sexual activity several years later," although, as the authors noted, the study provided no evidence concerning programs implemented at earlier or later ages.[31]

Second, abstinence-only programs disproportionately disadvantage low-income women, who are more likely to be dependent on school and public services for information and support. A study during the Clinton years indicated that, by 2000, the number of young black and Latina women receiving abstinence-only instruction in lieu of other forms of sex education had significantly increased and exceeded the proportion of white women receiving such instruction. In addition, young women living below 200% of the poverty level were more likely to receive abstinence-only instruction (or no sex education at all) than were higher-income women. Two-thirds of white women had received instruction about contraception prior to their first sexual encounter, compared with fewer than half of their black peers.[32] The population

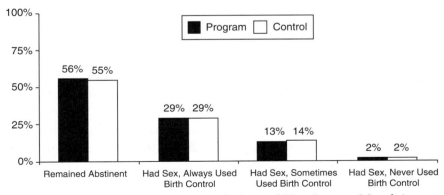

FIGURE 7.1: Estimated Impacts on Birth Control Use (Last 12 Months)
SOURCE: CHRISTOPHER TRENHOLM ET AL., IMPACTS OF FOUR TITLE V, SECTION 510 ABSTINENCE EDUCATION PROGRAMS 35 (Apr. 2007).

most at risk for unintended pregnancies and sexually transmitted diseases is thus offered the least preparation and assistance.

## THE VALUES OF ABSTINENCE-ONLY EDUCATION

Abstinence-only programs reflect the values and life choices of one side, and only one side, of a cultural divide. In the effort to renew abstinence-only funding in 2007, for example, one supporter rued the "seeming reluctance on the part of Christians to speak out about premarital, extramarital and other sexual sins."[33] Representative John Boehner, the House Republican minority leader, used a letter from the U.S. Conference of Catholic Bishops to rally support for the funding.[34] Conversely, the National Abortion and Reproductive Rights Action League rallied opponents of abstinence education to fight "ideology over science."[35]

It is accordingly unsurprising that implementation varies by region. In Title V of the Social Security Act, one of the dedicated abstinence education earmarks, states decide whether to participate, and the first five states that refused potential federal funding for abstinence education pursuant to this program[36] were California, Maine, New Jersey, Pennsylvania, and Wisconsin,[37] all blue. Since then, almost half of the states have followed suit.[38] Those opting out of the abstinence-only emphasis, while not entirely blue, are heavily concentrated in the Northeast, the upper Midwest, and the West. Notably absent are any of the states of the Deep South.[39]

Those who oppose these programs make two arguments. First, as we noted above, they point out that abstinence-only programs do not work and are arguably counterproductive. This argument, though unpersuasive to those who favor the programs because they teach morally "correct" values, may ultimately carry the day in many parts of the country.

Second, opponents have questioned the use of religious groups to implement some of the programs, giving rise to legal challenges. In the leading case to attack the allocation of federal funds to faith-based grantees, the Supreme Court split 5–4 in upholding the legislation.[40] The majority held that the purpose of the statute was secular, and religious organizations could comply with the statutory mandate without religious indoctrination. In a strong dissent, Justice Blackmun (joined by Justices Brennan, Marshall, and Stevens) wrote that "the religious significance in the counseling provided by some grantees... is a dimension that Congress specifically sought to capture by enlisting the aid of religious organizations."[41] As the dissent emphasized, various religious organizations will provide differing answers to questions of how an adolescent should handle her pregnancy.[42] Further, although the Court had previously upheld providing aid to religious organizations that were administering social welfare programs, in this case, the dissent noted:

> There is a very real and important difference between running a soup kitchen or a hospital, and counseling pregnant teenagers on how to make the difficult decisions facing them. The risk of advancing religion at public expense, and of creating an appearance that the government is endorsing the medium and the message, is much greater when the religious organization is directly engaged in pedagogy, with the express intent of shaping belief and changing behavior, than where it is neutrally dispensing medication, food, or shelter.[43]

In two subsequent cases brought by the American Civil Liberties Union against specific service providers alleging that the abstinence education programs promote religion, the parties have entered into consent decrees that carefully establish the boundaries of acceptable language and religious messages. In 2002, the ACLU sued the Louisiana Governor's Program on Abstinence, claiming that, in a variety of ways, it promoted religion through its own programs and that it funded organizations which transmitted religious messages and which were primarily sectarian, rather than secular.[44] Louisiana supported "programs that were going out and saying, you know, 'get saved by Jesus,' sponsored by the governor's program on abstinence."[45] Two months after the suit was filed, the court entered a preliminary injunction that prohibited the state from funding any religious activities and "pervasively sectarian institutions" and required the state to develop a monitoring mechanism to guarantee that abstinence education funds were not used for religious purposes.[46] Shortly thereafter, the state and the ACLU entered into a settlement agreement in which the state promised to clarify that government-sponsored abstinence programs could not include religious messages nor promote religion in any way.[47] The state also agreed to investigate any allegation that abstinence programs had religious content.[48] The ACLU returned to court in 2005, claiming violations of the settlement agreement because "the governor's program continues to feature religious materials on its official Web site, AbstinenceEdu.com. State-appointed experts advise readers, for example, that 'abstaining from sex until entering a loving marriage will...[make you] really, truly, "cool" in God's eyes' and that 'God is standing beside you the whole way' if you commit to abstinence."[49] This time, the judge upheld the religious content of the state's Web site, finding no excessive entanglement.[50]

A second suit, filed three years later, concerned funds appropriated to the Silver Ring Thing (SRT)[51] as part of a special congressional earmark. The Silver Ring Thing is designed to encourage adolescents to follow a "lifestyle of Christ-centered abstinence education until marriage."[52] It does this by holding live events for large groups, and, for smaller groups, there is a four-week program, available as a four-DVD set, to be facilitated by a group leader. During the program, students have sessions on "Temptation," "How Far Can I Go?" "Consequences," and "Where Does God Fit In?"[53] Teens can only wear the rings after they have attended a live event or completed the four-week program; parents can buy their own rings to indicate their support for their children.

The ACLU of Massachusetts sued the federal government, arguing that funding of SRT programs provided a "direct government grant to a pervasively sectarian institution in violation of the First Amendment."[54] Among other allegations, the ACLU asserted that each silver ring was inscribed with a verse from the New Testament and was accompanied by an SRT Bible; the SRT 12-step follow-up program included the SRT student acknowledging that "God has a plan for his or her life, and a plan for his or her sexuality";[55] and the SRT newsletter included information such as "more people are becoming part of this abstinence phenomenon. And ultimately, they are developing a relationship with Jesus Christ. This is such good news."[56] Three months after the filing of the SRT lawsuit, the Department of Health and Human Services withheld the remaining $75,000 of the SRT's $1.2 million funding.[57]

The parties entered into a settlement agreement pursuant to which SRT agreed that, if it sought further funding, it would certify its compliance with applicable federal regulations, which prohibit using federal funds to support "inherently religious activities."[58] The Department of Health and Human Services sent a list of "safeguards required" if SRT sought additional federal money; the safeguards included a requirement that abstinence education programs with religious content constitute separate and distinct programs from those funded by federal money, including a requirement that each program have a distinct name.[59] As Professors Ira Lupu and Robert Tuttle point out, the settlement agreement establishes a distinction between the religious activities that the government can support and those that are "inherently religious activities" in "terms that are constitutionally accurate, unambiguous, and detailed."[60]

These cases, however, which address the direct use of these programs to promote religion, miss the larger issue of the promotion of cultural issues integrated with religious views at a time when the majority of Americans do not share the same religious—or social—views. Repeatedly, in surveys of the public's attitude toward abstinence education, researchers find broad support for comprehensive information. The level of support for comprehensive sex education programs, however, varies depending on the respondents' frequency of attendance at a religious institution.[61] For example, in one survey of 1,000 people in late 2005, among people who attend religious services more frequently than once per week, 31.3% opposed abstinence-only education, while among those who never attend religious services, 57% opposed abstinence-only.[62]

Abstinence-only education is appealing to one side of the culture war. Comprehensive sex education programs provide information about and support for abstinence; abstinence-only programs do not provide similar information about contraception, abortion, or nonreproductive sexuality. If the programs were effective in the religiously and culturally neutral objectives of delaying the beginning of sexual activity, slowing the spread of STDs, and preventing unwanted pregnancies, the efforts would be applauded on both sides of the cultural divide. But in the face of convincing evidence that they are both ineffective and counterproductive, they become little more than a vehicle for the partisan promotion of religiously identified cultural views.[63]

## CONCLUSION

Contraception is essential to the blue family paradigm. Stopping abortion has been and is likely to remain the rallying cry for the red family model. Abstinence-only education, while a product of the same division over values, is a far more ironic flashpoint for cultural conflict. First, greater abstinence, at least in the sense of a later start to sexual activity and fewer partners, wins broad support. The irony is that belief in the importance of abstinence is not a terribly good predictor of its incidence. According to Regnerus, those most likely to still be virgins in their teens are Jews, Mormons, Catholics, and mainline Protestants. Evangelical teens, who are far more likely than most of the other groups to embrace the importance of abstinence until marriage, in fact begin sexual activity earlier and are no more likely to wait until marriage than members of other religions.[64] Although deep religiosity may delay the beginning of sexual activity for some, for the public as a whole, the willingness to defer intimate relationships has more to do with the inclination to defer gratification, with a focus on promising careers and interests, and with family support than with conviction alone.[65] Abstinence-only education, to the extent that it makes pregnancy more likely at younger ages, has a significant negative impact on the communities that have been its most enthusiastic supporters.

Moreover, while abstinence during the teen years has increased, it did so *before* the expansion in abstinence education funding, and it has declined as the funding has grown.[66] The emphasis on abstinence efforts thus says more about ideology than effectiveness.

The true cultural collision underlying abstinence education, as Mark Regnerus observes, may be that taking place within communities, rather than between them.[67] This collision involves what we have termed communities on the cusp. Marriage is more important to these locales than elsewhere in the country, childbearing rates remain high, and religion permeates community life. Yet, nonmarital sexuality has risen just as much in these regions as it has in other parts of the country, and it has been accompanied by more unplanned pregnancies and, to a greater degree than elsewhere, early marriage and divorce. What may ultimately change the dynamic of rising family instability, moral panic, and counterproductive responses is the rise in nonmarital births. Since the mid-1980s, they have grown more dramatically for whites than for minorities, they have grown most rapidly for women in their early 20s, and they now constitute more than 40% of all births in the country as a whole. The cycle of early marriage and divorce, while often destructive for the individuals involved, does not necessarily threaten the social life of communities based on marriage. Young single mothers raising children on their own does. Marriage, not abstinence, should be the real battleground in the culture wars.

## CHAPTER 8

# The Marrying Laws

*The primary and most important of the domestic relations is that of husband and wife. It has its foundations in nature, and is the only lawful relation by which Providence has permitted the continuance of the human race. . . . It is one of the chief foundations of the moral order.*[1]

—Chancellor James Kent, Chancery Court of New York,
Commentaries on American Law *(1830)*

AMERICANS REMAIN THE marrying kind. Television shows, ranging from *The Newlywed Game* in the 1960s to *Makeover Bride* and *A Wedding Story* in the twenty-first century, celebrate the central role of marriage in American culture. Since the late 1980s, the number of Americans who affirm the lifelong nature of the marital obligation and object to the ease of divorce has *increased*.[2] Indeed, Americans continue to believe in marriage to a greater degree than most of the industrialized world. Eighty-five percent of Americans can be expected to enter the institution at some time in their lives compared to less than 70% of Europeans. Only 10% of Americans agree that marriage is "an out-dated institution" compared to 26% in the United Kingdom and 36% in France.[3]

Nonetheless, the American institution of marriage is undergoing a transformation. What has changed demographically over the past half-century is *when* people marry and *who* is most likely to marry and stay married. There have also been heightened calls for legal reform to address who can marry whom, when people can end their marriages, and what difference marriage makes. For some parts of the country, marriage remains the foundation of family life; for others, it has almost disappeared. Moreover, the ability to marry has become an even greater marker of class. Consider the following:

- about 18% of men aged 40–44 with less than four years of college had not married in 2000 in comparison with 6% in the same group 20 years earlier.[4] For women, the likelihood of marriage had historically declined with more education; today, it is the reverse, and the college-educated are becoming *more* likely to marry than women without four-year degrees.[5]
- The tendency to marry a spouse with a similar income has also accelerated since 1980, compounding the advantages of marriage for the best-educated.
- The likelihood of divorce also varies with education, with 34% of the marriages of women without high school degrees breaking up within five years, compared to 23% of high school graduates, 25% of those with some college, and 13% of college graduates.[6] Divorce levels vary by race, and African-Americans have significantly higher rates than do whites.[7]
- Nonmarital births have risen to approximately 40% of total births and 70% for African-Americans. Teen nonmarital births, as a percentage of the total, are decreasing, while births to unmarried women in their early 20s is increasing. Slightly less than half (about 40%) of nonmarital births are to cohabiting couples.[8]
- Marriage also varies geographically. For example, in 2005, 31% of men over the age of 15 had never been married. That percentage, however, falls substantially in West Virginia (25.4), Arkansas (25.5), Wyoming (25.7) and Oklahoma (26.4) and rises in the District of Columbia (50.4), New York (35.2), California (34.6), Hawaii (33.9), Massachusetts (33.9), and Alaska (33.6). In 2005, the national average was 41 marriages taking place for every 1,000 single women. There were, however, a lot more weddings in some parts of the country, with the highest marriage rates concentrated in Arkansas (77), Idaho (66), Wyoming (60), Utah (58), and Alabama (54), while the lowest rates were all in the Northeast and Mid-Atlantic: Pennsylvania (24), New Jersey (27), Delaware (28), and Connecticut (28). In contrast, in the Northeast and the Pacific Northwest,

cohabitation is more common, especially in Vermont (14% of couples), Maine (13%), Oregon (12%), and Washington (12%), compared to a national rate of 10%. It is the least common in Alabama (6%), Mississippi (8%), Kansas (8%), and Arkansas (8%)—states that continue to have very high marriage rates and relatively higher divorce rates.[9]

No wonder, then, that the trilogy of family woes—divorce, cohabitation, single-parenthood—causes such consternation to traditionalists. In earlier American eras, marriage was close to universal with more than 90% of adults marrying, almost all births occurring within sanctioned unions, divorce unthinkable and rare (even if the frontier facilitated separation), and participation in many of the benefits of society dependent on marital legitimacy.[10] Moreover, at the turn of the twentieth century, today's class and race relationships were reversed. Well-educated women in that era were the least likely women to marry, and African-American women were more likely to marry, and to marry at younger ages, than whites.[11]

Today, the change in family structure has been most dramatic for the poorest Americans—who increasingly raise their children in single-parent families—and the communities that most revolve around marriage, where divorce has consequences not just for individual well-being but, as Chancellor Kent suggested in the epigraph to this chapter, for the foundation of shared notions of morality. The far-reaching nature of the changes in the marriage rate is widely acknowledged; what these changes mean and how to respond to them are contested territory. Nonetheless, what is most surprising is that the marriage laws differ much less along polarized lines than other topics in this book—with the notable exception of same-sex marriage.

## IS MARRIAGE A MOVING TARGET? RED AND BLUE PERSPECTIVES

Within the red paradigm, those who call for a "marriage movement" emphasize the mandatory nature of marriage. That is, they continue to insist on the unity of sex, marriage, and procreation; the complementary nature of the relationship between men and women; and the importance of commitment (and, indeed, acceptance of the "authority of marriage") to marital stability.[12] The social science researchers who support these views find that shared religious participation, the internalization of norms of sexual restraint, a gendered division of family responsibilities, and belief in the importance of marriage increase marital satisfaction and reduce the likelihood of divorce.[13]

Those who see marriage in crisis bemoan what they term "the withering away of marriage"[14] and argue that the legal regulation of the relationship has changed it from a publicly defined status to "a private relationship which the law has no right to regulate and whose consequences affect only the parties to the marriage, not the general public, not even their own children." Some rue this transformation, suggesting a strong "need or reinvigoration in law of the traditional understanding of marriage" because this "may be the only way Americans can resist other ideas inimical to and destructive of the institution of marriage."[15] They believe that Americans fail to internalize appropriate marital norms and would like to see the law reinforce the importance of doing so.

The blue paradigm, however, which emphasizes autonomy and responsibility, supports the deregulation of adult relationships and is more likely to recognize the continuum of relationship possibilities. Changing adult roles has increased the likelihood that even the individuals most committed to marriage will spend larger portions of their lifetimes outside of marital unions. Moreover, researchers have found no magic prescription to promote marriage, and there is thus no one way for the law to respond.

Consider the issue of gender roles. The latest research finds that the most stable couples are those who either share a commitment

FIGURE 8.1
SOURCE: http://
sangrea.net/free-
cartoons/social_
civil-union.jpg.

to egalitarian values and reap the benefit of dual careers OR those who share traditional values, and realize a gendered division of family responsibilities. Least satisfied are traditionalist women, who prize traditional gender roles, but who must work because of their husbands' lack of income. They, are among the least happy with both their labor force participation and their marriages.[16]

Conversely, studies of poor women show that higher education and earnings boost the likelihood of marriage *because* of the independence they bring.[17] Qualitative studies confirm the effect, indicating that single mothers in Chicago, Illinois, Camden, New Jersey, and Charleston, South Carolina insist that they will not marry if it means they must rely on a man's earnings. The poorest women, who exhibit greater concern about male fidelity and behavior, feel that only earnings of their own can guarantee equality and independence in a relationship.[18]

Given that relationship quality depends to some extent on external circumstances, some argue for recognition of all families. This would entail governmental recognition and support not only of marriage (including same-sex marriage), but also of "the many other ways in which people actually construct their families, kinship networks, households, and relationships," such as single-parent households, senior citizens living together and serving as each other's caregivers, adult children living with and caring for their parents, and children being raised in multiple households or by unmarried parents.[19] The Canadian government agrees, and even before it recognized same-sex marriage, it issued a report, called *Beyond Conjugality*, that called for much broader recognition of family relationships.[20]

These differing approaches to the recognition of relationships, of course, each contain a measure of truth. As supporters of marriage promotion recognize, spouses who share the same religious affiliation and commitment to traditional values often are happier than the average couple, especially once socioeconomic factors are taken into account. And societal reinforcement of shared norms can contribute to family stability. Nonetheless, it may be harder to realize traditional gender roles in a society that pays less of a premium for male labor and often requires two incomes to meet basic expenses.[21] Moreover, mobility, whatever its cause, often disrupts family and community networks,[22] and younger couples, especially if they marry because of an unplanned pregnancy or other forms of social pressure, may be less well matched for lifelong relationships.

Conversely, couples who share a similar commitment to egalitarian values, and who have achieved emotional maturity and a measure of financial success at the time of marriage have excellent prospects for marital happiness within any system. The greater difficulty is in extending the benefits of stable relationships to couples who lack either financial security or mature behavior. More direct insistence on adherence to community and family norms may provide the greatest assistance to those with a realistic chance of making marriage work. At the same time, marshaling greater support for a variety of family relationships would provide more benefits to those least able to realize the security of traditional marriage. Acknowledging that these patterns exist therefore does not in itself determine any particular policy approach, and, indeed, even those determined to address these issues have not proposed draconian legal changes.

Yet, they could. The law in Chancellor Kent's era in the nineteenth century systematically regulated the family by treating marriage as a bright-line status. The law drew clear lines between marital and non-marital children, limited family benefits to those married in the eyes of the law, and kept a close eye on exit—making divorce a complex and expensive process once it became possible at all. Those in nonmarital relationships were entirely shut out of any of the rights that attached to marriage.

The same legal revolution that dismantled restrictions on contraception and abortion dismantled the distinctions based on legitimacy—with remarkably little opposition. In the line of cases that started in the early 1970s with *Stanley v. Illinois*, for example, the Supreme Court struck down state laws that conditioned recognition of the father's parental status on marriage.[23] The Supreme Court fractured, however, in 1989 on the more divisive issue of the constitutionality of the marital presumption of paternity, which declares the mother's husband to be the father of her child. Justice Scalia's plurality opinion, which garnered the support of only three other of the justices, upheld the constitutionality of a California statute that recognized the mother's husband rather than the biological father as the child's sole male parent despite the fact that the biological father had obtained blood tests that established a high likelihood of biological paternity, lived with the mother and child, and had a relationship with the little girl.[24] In concluding that the biological father was legally "unable to act as father of the child he has adulterously begotten," the Supreme Court nonetheless left the issue to the states to regulate as they chose.[25] The Supreme Court split could be described in liberal versus conservative terms, with the most-conservative justices at the time (Rehnquist, O'Connor, and Anthony Kennedy) joining in the opinion and the more-liberal justices in dissent (Marshall, Brennan, Blackmun, and White). Justice Stevens cast the fifth vote to uphold the constitutionality of the statute, but he did so based on an idio-syncratic interpretation of the California statute with which no other justice agreed.

In the years since, however, the states have adopted no consistent or politically predictable approach to the continued validity of the marital presumption. This variation among the states shows not only the federalist nature of family law, in which each state makes its own decisions, but also that red-blue ideological divisions often dissolve in the face of the needs of large numbers of constituents. Thus, under their state constitutions, Iowa, Texas, Colorado, and West Virginia have gone further than the conservative Supreme Court justices and recognized unmarried, biological fathers as having a right to a relationship with their children.[26] Arkansas, Idaho, Indiana, and Mississippi enacted state statutes granting those who claim to be fathers legal standing to seek blood tests and establish paternity.[27] Conversely, states as diverse as Louisiana, California, Oklahoma, and Connecticut have continued to apply the marital presumption.[28] Implementation of these provisions has been even more complex, defying any easy political characterization.[29]

Perhaps even more surprisingly, states have undertaken no large-scale efforts to restrict divorce. While liberal versus conservative splits once dominated discussions of no-fault divorce, state laws have become more uniform since Ronald Reagan signed California's landmark no-fault divorce law in 1969. The differences that remain (Maryland, for example, has more-restrictive divorce laws than Louisiana) reflect an earlier era's divisions rather than today's, and empirical research demonstrates that the laws make little difference in state divorce rates. Indeed, even religious groups that continue to publicly decry divorce nonetheless counsel their congregants individually rather than trying to bring back stigma or denunciation.[30]

Nonetheless, alongside the demographic changes in marriage are two potentially divisive legal issues. One is a clash of ideals—which plays out more in laws that represent symbolic values associated with marriage than in the practical provisions that govern the majority of marriages and divorces. The second is whether to bring greater recognition to nonmarital relationships that would traditionally have received no legal protection or recognition. These relationships run the gamut from long-term same-sex unions to one-night stands that produce children. The states have begun to grant increasing recognition to domestic partnerships, "palimony" contracts, functional parents, nonfamily medical decision makers, and a host of other voluntary arrangements that would have been forbidden or unnecessary in another era.[31] Indeed, the American Law Institute would dissolve many of the financial distinctions between married and unmarried couples.[32] This greater legal recognition is symptomatic of the shift away from marriage as a bright-line status that provides the exclusive legal governance of adult relationships. Yet, while the results are often controversial, the disputes involve little of the intense, partisan conflict that characterizes the movement toward recognition of gay and lesbian relationships. Instead, the more intense conflicts address provisions that affect relatively small numbers of people.

## RED MARRIAGE PROMOTION:
## LET'S PREACH TO THE CONVERTED

To the extent that the United States can be said to have ever had a national family policy, it would be the insistence on marriage, between a man and a woman, as the sole legitimate locus for childrearing. Many of us have read *The Scarlet Letter*, the 1850 novel by Nathaniel Hawthorne that dramatically portrays the stigma of having a child outside of marriage, and many of us also know of the long and contentious history of efforts to ban polygamy. Yet, with respect to long-term changes in American society, there may be very little that government can do to affect marriage rates directly. Accordingly, much of the focus has been on symbolic measures—not quite extending to a scarlet letter—that reaffirm the importance of marriage.

At the federal level, the most significant initiative was "welfare reform." A generation of scholars had debated the role of welfare availability in poor mothers' declining marriage rates, and President Bill Clinton vowed to "end welfare as we know it."[33] Although congressional proponents emphasized that the 1996 Personal Responsibility and Work Opportunity Reconciliation Act (PRWORA) sought to promote marriage as a means of ending the dependence of needy parents on government benefits, welfare reform's principal effect was to push poor women into the workplace, not the marriage market. At the state level, there have been campaigns, proclamations celebrating the role of marriage in society, and commissions studying how to develop policies to strengthen marriage. Both red and blue states have considered legislation designed, for example, to make divorce harder, but little legislation has passed. The notable exception is covenant marriage, first enacted in Louisiana in 1997, which allows couples to opt into a marriage with strict limitations on when they can divorce. Even this reform, however, affects no more than a tiny percentage of marriages.

## Covenant Marriages

Three states, Arkansas, Arizona, and Louisiana, have responded to the marriage crisis by making divorce harder—but only if the couple chooses a covenant marriage. In these states, marrying couples elect either traditional or covenant marriage. If they choose the latter, the couple opts into three provisions that distinguish their marriage from others: (1) mandatory premarital counseling by a religious cleric or professional marriage counselor about the seriousness of marriage; (2) the execution of a Declaration of Intent, which includes a legal obligation to take reasonable steps to preserve the marriage if difficulties arise; and (3) limited grounds for divorce, consisting of serious fault on the part of one spouse or, in the absence of such fault, a significant period of time living separately and apart.[34]

Mike Huckabee, a 2008 Republican presidential candidate and former Arkansas governor, set up a public ceremony on Valentine's Day 2005, as part of Arkansas's first-ever "Celebration of Marriage," to convert his marriage into a covenant marriage. The conversion occurred in a sports arena in front of hundreds of other couples cheering them on. The actual ceremony was brief, without the romance that typically attends marriage celebrations: Governor Huckabee and his wife, Janet, were asked if they had sought counseling and if they had the appropriate paperwork. Once the covenant marriage affidavit was stamped, the crowd burst into applause.[35] Through this public event, he hoped to encourage other couples to make similar commitments to their marriages, a move endorsed by numerous Christian organizations. To date, his example has won over relatively few followers. The number of couples choosing covenant marriages is quite small—no more than 2% of new marriages in Louisiana and even fewer in Arizona and Arkansas.[36] One of the problems is that most people don't know about the possibility of a covenant marriage; others may simply not want to covenant themselves into one.

On the other hand, covenant marriage may be succeeding in giving expression to the conviction that marriage should be a special (and, for many, a sacred) status. As part of his lifelong study of marriage (including the marital happiness research discussed earlier in the chapter), Steven Nock and two of his colleagues conducted an in-depth study of covenant marriages, publishing their results in 2008. They surveyed all covenant marriages and an equivalent number of "standard" marriages from approximately one-third of all parishes in Louisiana. They conducted focus groups, interviewed both lay and religious marriage officiants, and even sent tester couples to see how court clerks were actually implementing the covenant marriage law.[37] This comprehensive study showed that the divorce rate, five years after the wedding, for covenant married couples (8.6%) is slightly more than half the rate for other couples (15.4%).[38] The researchers found, however, that the success of covenant marriages is not necessarily due to the institution itself. Instead, the lower divorce rate results from the characteristics of the individuals who choose these marriages. These characteristics include the wife's religiosity and her level of education, together with community support—factors that produce lower divorce rates even without covenant marriage.[39]

### Healthy Marriages, Courtesy of the Taxpayers

The most-recent national marriage promotion initiative began with Clinton's 1996 welfare reform legislation. Under the act, the federal government offered incentives to the states to increase marriage and reduce nonmarital childbearing. The Bush administration continued to fund marriage promotion through a Healthy Marriage Initiative that provides money to educate couples on more-effective communication and problem solving. It also encourages advertising on the benefits of a good marriage.[40] For the blue paradigm, marriage promotion efforts are targeted at the wrong problem. As William and Mary law professor Vivian Hamilton points out, although marriage promotion has been touted as an anti-poverty strategy, poor people already believe in marriage. What they lack are the economic opportunities to create stable marriages.[41] It is a fallacy, she suggests, to believe that promoting marriage will end poverty; instead, ending poverty is more likely to promote successful marriages.[42]

Researcher Steve Martin emphasizes that nonmarital births may be a function of the relationship between class and the timing of family formation. He argues that most women want children *and* marriage— and well-educated women, by waiting, are likely to end up with both. For less-educated women, however, delay significantly increases the risk of childlessness without increasing the probability of marriage.[43]

Covenant marriage and federal marriage promotion efforts are red paradigm strategies that seek to rearticulate marriage as an ideal, to emphasize its importance as the necessary institution designed to order intimacy and childrearing, and to reinforce habits that increase the number of marriages and that decrease single-parenthood and divorce. The principal effect of welfare reform, however, has been to move more of the healthy single mothers into employment and more of the children of the less-healthy mothers deeper into poverty. Increased marriage rates do not appear to be part of the equation for either set of programs.

## BLUE MARRIAGE PROMOTION: OPEN THE GATES TO THOSE WHO WANT IN

Few family values issues—other than abortion—are more polarizing than same-sex marriage. Indeed, it is difficult to think of another issue where opposing advocates so completely talk past each other. Those who support same-sex marriage simply do not get the opposition. Steve Blow wrote an op-ed in the *Dallas Morning News* titled "Gay Marriage: Why Would It Affect Me?" He observed:

> When opponents talk about the "defense of marriage," they lose me. James Dobson's Focus on the Family just sent out a mailer to 2.5 million homes saying: "The homosexual activists' movement is poised to administer a devastating and potentially fatal blow to the traditional family." And I say, "Huh? How does anyone's pledge of love and commitment turn into a fatal blow to families?"[44]

Dobson responded, referring to Genesis and explaining:

> The legalization of homosexual marriage will quickly destroy the traditional family.... [W]hen the State sanctions homosexual relationships and gives them its blessing, the younger generation becomes confused about sexual identity and quickly loses its understanding of lifelong commitments, emotional bonding, sexual purity, the role of children in a family, and from a spiritual perspective, the "sanctity" of marriage.[45]

The explanation for these divisions, like the explanation for divisions on abortion, involves the intersection of real anxiety about family structure and stability with radically different world views about the source of family regularity.[46] When we look at the sources of these divisions, we see the same issues that underlie the culture wars more generally, centering on the defining importance of marriage as the pathway to adulthood.

## Marriage as Moral Mooring

Within the red paradigm, marriage is the optimal basis for childrearing, and it is an eternal institution, rooted "in creation itself," for the purpose of ordering sexual relations and uniting mothers, fathers, and their biological children. Consequently, if the meaning of marriage is subject to change, if it is simply a matter of government policy or utilitarian reasoning, then, on this perspective, the foundation of the family is at risk. As Maggie Gallagher observes, the sanctity of marriage comes from "the intrinsic sacredness of bringing together male and female in the service of making the future happen"; in contrast, "officially endorsing gay unions as marriages...discards as false this once honored and honorable ideal, now considered stigmatized, backwards, and discriminatory [because it excludes gays and lesbians]."[47]

The blue family paradigm, in contrast, arose with the separation of sex and childbearing and with the identification of responsibility to children with preparation and maturity. In this context, marriage no longer serves to channel sexuality, though it is still about childrearing, and committed love and companionship have become the defining feature of the institution. With greater emphasis on autonomy and equality, the blue paradigm equates effective parenting with responsible choice—and there is no intrinsic reason that two people of the same sex cannot be either committed partners or capable parents. At a more practical level, as family formation occurs later in life, sexual orientation is both visible and more set: fewer people are uncertain about the nature of their sexual attractions at 29 than at 21, and fewer people are able or willing to hide it. Moreover, as we argued in chapter 4, more of those who identify with the blue paradigm are contextualists rather than traditionalists: they see a more-flexible world that is the creation of human choice rather than one that is either fixed or divinely ordained. Recognition of same-sex relationships thus becomes a matter of basic equality and fairness.

The red family paradigm, however, continues to identify the well-being of children with the unity of sex, procreation, and childrearing. It places greater importance for relationship stability on the presence of a *biological* father and mother, their modeling of complementary masculine and feminine roles, and the exclusivity of their relationship. Within the blue family paradigm, the various components of childrearing—genetic parentage, birth, parental love and guidance, and adult partnerships—can be separated from each other with their own norms, understandings, and responsibilities. Within a traditional family system, however, these different components are united, and the whole—built on the sacred institution of marriage—is greater than the sum of its parts.

Of course, a diversity of views exists among both proponents and opponents of same-sex marriage on the meaning of marriage; indeed, neither side even holds uniform views with respect to the basis for their opposition to each other. Opponents of same-sex marriage, to the extent they focus on sexuality, often express a combination of objections to same-sex conduct per se as unacceptable, an opposition to linking marriage and same-sex unions because of the impossibility of homosexual procreation, and an opposition to same-sex norms, which many see as placing less emphasis on exclusivity than do traditional heterosexual norms.

### Sexual Fidelity

The most fundamental of these objections is the one that links opposition to same-sex marriage to the more general policing of sexuality. Linguist George Lakoff suggests that the meaning of marriage is still "about sex. When you say 'gay marriage,' it becomes about gay sex, and approving of gay marriage becomes implicitly about approving of gay sex."[48] Philosopher Martha Nussbaum links bias against homosexuality to feelings of disgust and argues that it offers an inappropriate and unreliable basis for law.[49] Yet, the regulation of sexuality per se no longer commands widespread public support, and the Supreme Court, in *Lawrence v. Texas*, rejected criminalization of gay sex as a legitimate state objective.

Putting the acceptability of homosexuality aside, some opponents of same-sex marriage argue that same-sex couples, who do not have to deal with the possibility of pregnancy, place less of a premium on fidelity, changing the nature of the marital commitment. The Religious Coalition for Marriage, for example, finds same-sex marriage particularly threatening to the concept of faithfulness in marriage because gay men are less likely to value sexual fidelity than are lesbians or married people.[50] Indeed, writer Andrew Sullivan wrote in the first edition of his book in defense of marriage, *Virtually Normal*: "There is more likely to be greater understanding of the need for extramarital outlets between two men than between a man and a woman."[51] One study of civil unions and marriages in Vermont suggests this is a very real concern. More than 79% of heterosexual married men and women, along with lesbians in civil unions, reported that they strongly valued sexual fidelity. Only about 50% of gay men in civil unions, in contrast, valued sexual fidelity.[52] Yet, the public generally continues to emphasize fidelity in marriage with 93% rating it as important to a successful marriage,[53] and many proponents of same-sex marriage arguing that part of its value for same-sex couples *is* the societal reinforcement of the value of fidelity.[54]

## Marriage and Procreation

The far more central argument, however, for all opponents of same-sex marriage is the relationship between marriage and procreation.[55] The National Marriage Project, which provides research and education about American marriages, charges that the country has become less child-centered and that this has contributed to the decline in marriage.[56] In explaining opposition to a 2009 compromise proposal on recognition of gay relationships, an article in *Public Discourse* argued that marriage is "a community of husband and wife founded on a bodily union whose natural fulfillment is the conception of a child."[57] The Religious Coalition for Marriage argues that marriage provides the optimal setting for childrearing, as children do best with a mother and a father. Consequently, if the role of marriage changes so that it becomes easier both to get married and to get divorced, if marriage "is no longer the boundary of sexual activity," then the consequences are dire: "a host of personal and civic ills can be expected to follow."[58]

The New York Court of Appeals, without accepting the emphasis on policing the boundary of sexual activity, nonetheless emphasized that the legislature, in refusing to authorize same-sex marriage, could take reproduction into account. It explained:

> Heterosexual intercourse has a natural tendency to lead to the birth of children; homosexual intercourse does not. Despite the advances of science, it remains true that the vast majority of children are born as a result of a sexual relationship between a man and a woman, and the Legislature could find that this will continue to be true. The Legislature could also find that such relationships are all too often casual or temporary. It could find that an important function of marriage is to create more stability and permanence in the relationships that cause children to be born. It thus could choose to offer an inducement—in the form of marriage and its attendant benefits—to opposite-sex couples who make a solemn, long-term commitment to each other.[59]

Yet, the emphasis on reproduction, as opposed to adult companionship, is no longer consistent with many people's views of marriage. In a 2007 public opinion poll, the Pew Research Center found that only 41% of Americans find children important to making a marriage work, compared to 55% in 1993. By contrast, sharing household chores and having a happy sexual relationship have become more important, with 62% and 70%, respectively, citing those factors as important to a successful marriage.[60] When asked, "Which is closer to your views about the main purpose of marriage? Forming a lifetime union between two adults for mutual happiness and fulfillment or for bearing and raising children?" 65% chose mutual happiness and fulfillment, 23% chose bearing and raising children, and 7% said both. The study did not provide a regional breakdown, but it did find Latinos more likely than whites to rank children more highly as a purpose of marriage. Sixty-nine percent of Latinos ranked children "very important" to a successful marriage compared to 35% of whites and 49% of blacks. Nonetheless, even Latinos chose companionship over children as the "main purpose" of marriage, albeit by smaller margins (51% to 38% as opposed to 67% to 21% for whites and 63% to 23% for blacks). Regular churchgoers chose companionship over raising children by 58% to 25%, while those attending less regularly or not at all chose companionship over children by 74% to 18%.[61]

### Marriage and Gender

Related to the argument that children need a biological mother and father is the argument that children benefit from the gender relationships in a traditional marriage, and these relationships are important to children's own discovery of what it means to be a man or a woman. In an article in the online magazine Slate.com, Professor Richard Thompson Ford suggests that many people may be opposed to same-sex marriage because they "long for the kind of meaningful gender identities that traditional marriage seems to offer," which provide certainty at a time of changing gender roles.[62]

Empirical studies are mixed in their conclusions of whether gay and lesbian parents produce any differences in gender behavior in their children. The studies, which are generally small in size and not necessarily representative (openly gay and lesbian parents, for example, tend to be better educated than the general population), find that children raised by gay and lesbian parents do at least as well as those raised by heterosexuals in cognitive ability, behavior, and mental health, and they may even do somewhat better in some areas. The studies find that the ways that parents divide household tasks and parenting responsibilities do differ (same-sex relationships tend to be more egalitarian), but whether the differences matter tends to be a matter of opinion. Thus, some studies find, for example, that the children of lesbian parents are more accepting and open in their attitudes toward sexual identity, and the daughters may be more willing to question their own sexuality. Researchers conducting a meta-analysis concluded, "Where conservatives may see lax or immoral sexual standards, liberals may see commendably open-minded attitudes."[63]

The New York Court of Appeals, in determining that the legislature was not compelled by the state constitution to permit same-sex couples to marry, found that the legislature could legitimately decide that children benefited from the presence of a man and a woman. It wrote:

> Intuition and experience suggest that a child benefits from having before his or her eyes, every day, living models of what both a man and a woman are like....Plaintiffs, and *amici* supporting them, argue that the proposition asserted is simply untrue: that a home with two parents of different sexes has no advantage, from the point of view of raising children, over a home with two parents of the same sex. Perhaps they are right, but the Legislature could rationally think otherwise.[64]

### Equality

Despite the defeat of same-sex marriage in New York and the passage of Proposition 8 in California, which amended the state constitution to define marriage as a relationship between a man and a woman, the embrace of same-sex marriage has increasingly become a matter of basic equality within the blue paradigm.[65] With the separation of sex and procreation that became possible with the pill, sexual intercourse is no longer viewed as an appropriate matter of public regulation, and increasing majorities in the country as a whole disapprove of the criminalization of consenting sexual activity between adults.[66] Moreover, despite the association of parenting with the roles of mother and father, marriage itself is no longer associated with hierarchal authority or a gendered assignment of family roles.[67] Indeed, the variety of family arrangements has increased dramatically, with fewer children born within marriage, more born outside of marriage, and married couples using a variety of methods, including adoption and the use of donor eggs and gametes, to bear children.[68] Within these changing parameters, marriage becomes a matter of choice designed to express love and commitment.[69] The Massachusetts Supreme Judicial Court, in reaching the conclusion that the restrictions in that state on the ability of same-sex couples to marry were not rationally related to any legitimate state purpose, observed that "it is the exclusive and permanent commitment of the married partners to one another, not the begetting of children, that is the sine qua non of civil marriage."[70]

In other blue states, at least some of the judicial disagreement is more about process than content. Thus, in the 4–3 split on the California Supreme Court, the majority ruled that providing civil unions, but not marriages, for same-sex couples constituted a form of discrimination, reminiscent of the "separate but equal" laws that separated whites and blacks. The three justices who dissented said relatively little about same-sex marriage; they dissented because they did not believe that the *court* should decide the issue. In New York, where the state's high court refused to compel same-sex marriage, the majority framed the issue in terms of the ability of the legislature to choose not to extend marriage to same-sex couples. The court's emphasis, as we suggested above, was on the rationality of the legislative motives, leaving open the possibility of a future legislative shift—or, as New York has done since the *Hernandez* decision, of recognition of same-sex marriages performed in other jurisdictions.

Today, although the divisions on same-sex marriage and civil unions remain, the center of the country is shifting. Thirty percent of the country as a whole favored same-sex marriage in June 2008, up from 21% in November 2004. Twenty-eight percent favored civil unions (for a total of 58% supporting some recognition), and 36% opposed all state recognition for same-sex couples, down from 44% four years earlier. The public divided along ideology (56% of conservatives favored no recognition compared to 30% of moderates and 25% of liberals), political party (50% of Republicans opposed recognition compared to 31% of independents and 32% of Democrats), religion (67% of white evangelicals opposed recognition compared to 29% of Catholics; 57% of those who attended church once a week or more opposed any recognition compared to 22% of those who never or rarely attended), and region (the least opposition was in the Northeast and the West Coast; the most opposition was in the South). Nonetheless, even in the South, the public was almost evenly divided between those who would provide some recognition and those who would not. In the country as a whole, fewer than 30% of those under 30 or those with college degrees opposed all recognition.[71]

Columbia University political scientists Jeffrey Lax and Justin Phillips have tested empirically how strongly state laws/policies correspond to public sentiment in each state about those policies. They draw two notable conclusions. (Their conclusions are shown graphically in figure 8.2.) First, they observe that the laws generally, and with respect to same-sex marriage in particular, closely correspond to public opinion in each state. Their list of states, based on public opinion polls, largely follows the order we constructed in chapter 1 based on demographic factors, with the greatest opposition rooted in the Deep South (Alabama and Mississippi), the border states (Oklahoma and Arkansas), Utah, and then the Plains, and the greatest support in the Northeast and the West Coast. They conclude that the blue states we identify as having the strongest protections for same-sex relationships are also

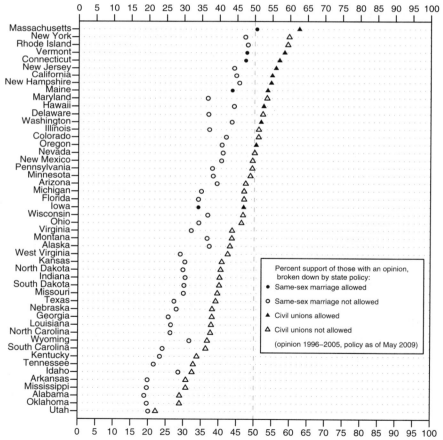

FIGURE 8.2: Same-Sex Marriage and Civil Unions: Policy and Public Opinion in the States

those with the greatest public support for extending such recognition; the courts have not been ahead of the public in doing so.

Second, they find that, to the extent that the law and public opinion diverge, the law lags behind, not ahead of public opinion. The law does so, in particular, with respect to equal rights in housing and employment, where the public increasingly favors stronger protections.[72] The law is more in sync with public opinion on the issues of marriage and adoption.

Politics, however, may inflame or ameliorate these divisions. Given the intensity of the positions on these issues, and especially the evangelical opposition to recognition of same-sex relationships, the Republicans in 2004 and 2008 placed a number of anti-same-sex-marriage initiatives on the ballot as a way of increasing the fundamentalist turnout.[73] These initiatives increased the visibility of same-sex issues within the political system,[74] further cementing opposition to same-sex marriage as central to the conservative family values coalition—even as opposition has faded in states as diverse as Iowa and Vermont.

## RED AND BLUE LAWS

These wars have played out dramatically in the states. Nationally, recognition of same-sex relationships follows greater tolerance toward homosexuality more generally, and the states listed in table 8.1 are among the most tolerant. Massachusetts, the bluest of blue states, was the first to recognize same-sex marriage; California was the second (although, after the 2008 election, this recognition was short-lived); and Connecticut the third.[75] Vermont, as the result of legislation, and Iowa, through a state supreme court ruling, have joined the list. The legislatures in Maine and New Hamphire have also voted to permit same-sex marriage, though the Maine legislation is subject to a vote at the polls.[76] Some states and the District of Columbia—all blue— recognize civil unions or domestic partnerships that are the equivalent of marriage.[77] A few states—all blue—provide some statewide rights to same-sex couples falling short of marriage.[78] The states with the most extensive recognition, such as Connecticut and Vermont, have moved toward full marriage rights, while Maryland and Hawaii offer somewhat less-expansive rights. Although its highest court has refused to compel the state to permit same-sex marriage, New York will recognize such marriages when the spouses were legally married in another state or country. Rhode Island has followed suit. Altogether, 15 of the

TABLE 8.1

| States That Recognize Same-Sex Marriages Performed under Their Own Laws | States That Recognize Same-Sex Marriages Performed under the Laws of Other States | States That Accord State-Level Spousal Rights to Civil Unions and Domestic Partners | States That Accord Some State-Level Spousal Rights to Civil Unions and Domestic Partners |
|---|---|---|---|
| Connecticut | New York | California | Hawaii |
| Massachusetts | Rhode Island | Vermont | Maine |
| Vermont | District of Columbia | New Hampshire | Washington |
| Iowa | | New Jersey | Maryland |
| New Hampshire (?) | | Oregon | |

*Source*: See *Human Rights Campaign*, Relationship Recognition in the U.S., *available at www.hrc.org/maps (updated 2009).*

states voting blue in 2008—and none of the red states—extend at least some form of recognition to same-sex couples.

At the other end of the spectrum, 44 states have some type of legal ban on marriage for same-sex couples—overwhelmingly as a result of propositions placed on the ballot between 2004 and 2008.[79] Three (Alaska, Nebraska, and Nevada) had constitutional provisions that limited marriage to a relationship between a man and a woman before 2004.[80] Two (Louisiana and Missouri) adopted this kind of amendment in early 2004.[81] Eleven more states adopted such amendments on November 2, 2004: Arkansas, Georgia, Kentucky, Michigan, Mississippi, Montana, North Dakota, Ohio, Oklahoma, Oregon, and Utah.[82] Kansas and Texas added such amendments in 2005.[83] Alabama did so in early 2006. Colorado, Idaho, South Carolina, South Dakota, Tennessee, Virginia, and Wisconsin passed amendments banning same-sex marriage in November 2006. Arizona voters considered such amendments in both 2006 and 2008; while Arizona rejected the language in 2006, thereby becoming the only state ever to reject such an amendment, the state's voters turned around and approved it in 2008.[84] Florida and California, which both voted for Obama, joined Arizona in 2008 when they amended their constitutions to define marriage as occurring between one man and one woman. California continues, however, to give some of the most expansive benefits to same-sex couples in the country. All told, more than half the states have both a constitutional and a statutory bar to recognition; as one commentator said, they're "so successful that, like potato chips, no state can pass just one."[85]

The amendments in Alabama, Arkansas, Georgia, Idaho, Kentucky, Louisiana, Michigan, Nebraska, North Dakota, Ohio, Oklahoma, South Carolina, South Dakota, Texas, Utah, Virginia, and Wisconsin go beyond marriage definition and include language that may limit civil unions or domestic partnerships.[86] Twenty-four of the 26 states with such amendments are red, and 6 of the 7 remaining red states (as well as 12 of the blue states) have statutes limiting marriage to a relationship between a man and a woman.[87] A number of the blue states, including California, Oregon, Hawaii, Maine, New Hampshire, Vermont, and Washington, provide recognition to domestic partnerships, civil unions, or reciprocal beneficiaries whether or not they recognize same-sex marriage. None of the red states do.

The only state that voted for Bush in 2004 not to ban same-sex marriage through either a constitutional amendment or legislation is New Mexico (and it went blue in 2008). Its legislature has repeatedly refused to enact such provisions.[88] Studies of attitudes toward homosexuality generally indicate that Latinos are more tolerant than whites or blacks and that Catholics are more tolerant than Protestants. In contrast, Catholic priests place greater emphasis in the pulpit on abortion than do Protestant ministers.[89]

Of the blue states, only Rhode Island has neither banned same-sex marriage nor adopted some recognition for same-sex couples, though it now recognizes same-sex marriages performed elsewhere. The other states without effective statutory prohibitions are blue: Massachusetts, New Jersey, New York, Connecticut, Rhode Island, and Vermont.[90]

## CONCLUSION

Lost in the battle over same-sex marriage is the larger fight between marriage promotion and the recognition of a wider variety of relationships. Allowing gays and lesbians to marry has become part of the national debate on the meaning of the institution. Indeed, the obstacles to letting gays and lesbians marry has energized the very developments that marriage proponents say they don't want: a proliferation of statuses short of marriage that address different aspects of family life. Thus, heterosexuals register as domestic partners to get medical care rights for their live-in partners, and states like Oklahoma and Virginia are required to give full faith and credit to gay and lesbian adoptions that took place in other states. In the meantime, the so-called marriage promotion efforts have been more notable for their impact on election turnout than for any effect on the frequency of either marriage or divorce.[91] In contrast, as we will develop at greater length in the next chapter, the family law that affects the public more generally has continued to evolve largely untouched by the maelstrom surrounding same-sex marriage.

## CHAPTER 9

# Custody and Compromise

I F CONFLICTS OVER abortion and same-sex marriage are the most obvious battles in the culture wars, custody is the skirmish most fail to notice. To the extent that the culture wars are about the legitimacy of continued policing of sexual mores, then custody standards, especially when a parent is "living in sin," should be a contested arena. And sometimes, particularly in high-profile disputes about lesbian parents and in men's fights to be recognized as co-equal parents, child custody disputes provide a forum for fights over appropriate sexual behavior. The much more remarkable story of this chapter, however, is how custody standards have adapted to cultural changes at different rates in different parts of the country with different regional nuances, yet without becoming much of a battle at all.

In this arena, courts have generally succeeded in defusing the conflicts. Unlike high-profile constitutional decisions, custody cases take place in state courts, their outcomes can be tailored to individual cases and regional sensibilities, and the participants continue to command a measure of deference. The determination of which of two fit parents is to receive custody may be too important and concrete an issue to be left to political maneuvering. Family law cases comprise a substantial portion of state court dockets, and custody disputes are an everyday occurrence that directly affects the parents and children who appear in the courtroom.[1] Judges can apply flexible standards designed to evaluate each family's individual circumstances.

Nonetheless, custody cases that pass judgment on sex and gender can and do fall on some of the same fault lines as abortion and gay and lesbian relationships. In the context of a family system that has largely deregulated the dissolution of adult relationships, child custody decisions at divorce have become "ground zero in the gender wars."[2] That is, while divorces granted on no-fault grounds do not necessarily pass judgment about the circumstances that produced the split,[3] custody decisions, which evaluate the quality of parenting, often rest, implicitly or explicitly, on moral views of parenting behavior.[4] For family systems that continue to celebrate marriage and to draw clear lines between marital and nonmarital sexuality, cohabitation with an unmarried partner should be a matter relevant to the child's interests. At the same time, in those states that have deregulated consensual adult behavior, nonmarital cohabitation—with a same-sex or different-sex partner— is far less of a challenge to the dominant order. We would therefore expect red states and blue states to differ in their approach to custody. They do, but not as starkly as the battles over legislative issues might suggest. Instead, the judiciary in *every* state has exercised leadership to defuse the issue, sometimes by calling attention to shared values and sometimes by narrowing the issue to procedural grounds that can command consensus support. Nonetheless, the potential for the type of fracture that has characterized federal abortion decisions remains, and Alabama, discussed at the end of the chapter, provides a telling example.

The chapter begins with a brief description of the evolution of the law in this area. Virtually all states require courts to determine which of two fit parents is to receive custody in accordance with a relatively open-ended "best interests of the child" standard. Following this initial decision, either parent may request a change in custody, typically by showing a change in circumstances. At one time, most states considered the morality of the parents' conduct in determining the result and viewed nonmarital cohabitation, with a different-sex or, particularly, a same-sex partner, to be a relevant if not automatically disqualifying factor.[5] Today, while some courts continue to presume harm from a nonmarital partner's presence in the home or the parent's bedroom while the child is present,[6] most require a more direct showing of adverse effect on the child before they restrict parental contact[7]—at least in the context of heterosexual relationships.[8]

The courts are more divided on the issue of homosexual relationships. While courts throughout the country have overwhelmingly held that sexual orientation per se should not be a basis for denying parental contact with the child,[9] many continue to condition custody or visitation on the absence of overnight visitors or explicit displays of affection.[10] To determine whether these differences correspond to the two different family systems we have described, we prepared a list of ten states based on the average age at marriage—perhaps the best marker we have identified of regional differences—and examined the decisions in each state to determine the patterns. As part of the process, we read every reported appellate case that addressed the issue that we could find through a Lexis search. The states with the highest average ages at first marriage are Massachusetts, New York, Rhode Island, Connecticut, and New Jersey (all blue and all in the Northeast).[11] The states with the lowest average ages are Utah, Oklahoma, Idaho, Arkansas, and Kentucky (all red).[12]

Unsurprisingly, these two sets of states approach the issue somewhat differently. The courts in the states with the lowest average ages at marriage—all of which are in the South, the Mountain West, or the border between the North and South—have been slower to move away from policing the morality of the litigants before them, and they remain more likely to reaffirm traditional moral values as part of their decisions. The states with the highest average ages at marriage, in contrast, have been much more eager to review lower court decisions to ensure equality and fairness for gay and lesbian parents. Nonetheless, the decisions in both groups of states have evolved in a much less polarized fashion than might be expected from voting patterns and responses to other family values issues.

## THE STATES WITH THE HIGHEST
## MEDIAN AGES AT MARRIAGE

The five states with the highest median ages at marriage (Massachusetts, New York, Rhode Island, Connecticut, and New Jersey) are also among the most liberal in the country when it comes to numerous issues, including a parent's sexual choices. Massachusetts, most obviously, has mandated the recognition of same-sex marriage as a matter of basic equality.[13] The New Jersey courts have required recognition of a status comparable to marriage, and Connecticut, which initially adopted domestic partnership legislation,[14] now allows same-sex marriage.

Nonetheless, the issue is not whether these states take different positions on nonmarital opposite-sex or same-sex cohabitation from those in red states, but *when* they did so.

Massachusetts has ruled from the early 1980s that "a parent's lifestyle, standing alone, is insufficient ground for severing the natural bond between a parent and a child."[15] In a 1980 decision, the Massachusetts Supreme Judicial Court reversed a dependency case that proposed to deny custody to a mother who wanted to reclaim her children from a third party who had taken care of them in the past because "[t]he environment in which [the mother] proposes to raise the children, namely, a Lesbian household, creates an element of instability that would adversely affect the welfare of the children."[16] "Instability," then and now, has been used a basis to object to nonmarital relationships, and it is true that nonmarital cohabitation is less likely to endure than marriage. Nonetheless, for couples who cannot legally marry, such concerns often become blanket disapproval. The Massachusetts court accordingly ruled that the mother's sexual preference could not be a basis for denying efforts to be reconciled with her children. The Massachusetts appellate court extended the ruling in 1983 to a divorce proceeding, holding that the mother's relationship with a lesbian cohabitant was not grounds to grant sole custody to the father.[17] As it did in the later cases that addressed same-sex marriage, the Massachusetts high court played a leadership role in insisting on equal treatment for gay and lesbian litigants. Heterosexual cohabitation, in contrast, seems to be sufficiently uncontroversial that we could find no appellate cases on point.

The New York cases of *Di Stefano v. Di Stefano*[18] and *In re Jane B.*,[19] decided in the '70s, have been cited by other jurisdictions as precedents for restricting the custodial rights of gay or lesbian parents.[20] Both cases granted custody to the fathers over lesbian mothers, finding that same-sex cohabitation "creates an improper environment" for children.[21]

Despite the earlier New York precedents, the appellate division in 1986 upheld a transfer of custody from the mother to a gay father living with a male partner in one of the first reported cases in the country to do so.[22] In this case, the father had stepped in and helped to turn around the life of a troubled adolescent. The boy's progress deteriorated when he moved back with the mother, but she wanted to move with him and his two siblings to Florida. The court distanced itself from the New York decisions of the '70s and adopted a nexus test that made sexual orientation irrelevant absent a showing that the children are emotionally affected.[23] It also cited with approval another New York case, striking restrictions on the presence of the father's male partner as pointless and punitive.[24]

Rhode Island has relatively few cases on point. In 1989, the state supreme court upheld conditions that prohibited a custodial mother from having overnight male visitors even without a showing of negative impact on the child.[25] By 2000, however, the supreme court had no trouble affirming a trial court's finding that a request for such an order was frivolous.[26] Rhode Island has also recognized lesbian partners as de facto parents under state law.[27]

In Connecticut in 1981, the state supreme court upheld a restriction on the father's visitation that excluded overnight visitation "where the defendant is living with another woman without the benefit of wedlock."[28] By 2000, however, Connecticut courts were rejecting a mother's request to limit the father's visitation in light of his nonmarital (heterosexual) relationship because there was no evidence that it adversely affected the children nor that the children, who were Catholic, expressed religious concerns about it.[29] In addition, the superior court had no difficulty changing a joint custody order to sole custody for a lesbian mother living with her partner in light of the father's mental health issues, commenting only that both parents had "nontraditional households."[30] The state also has long recognized the standing of same-sex partners to seek visitation, and its recent recognition of same-sex marriage makes it even more accepting of same-sex cohabitation.[31]

Finally, New Jersey has had the most complete transformation. In the early 1970s, a New Jersey court restricted the visitation rights of a father who took his three children to gay marches and rallies. The court declared that, during visitation, the father was required to "not cohabit or sleep with any individual other than a lawful spouse...not involve the children in any homosexual related activities or publicity [and] not be in the presence of his lover."[32]

The New Jersey Supreme Court, in its 2006 decision requiring the state to extend recognition to same-sex couples on the same terms as marriage, referred explicitly to this case as an example of discrimination.[33] The 2006 ruling capped the state's long transition to equal rights for same-sex parents; indeed, as early as 1979, the state appellate court reversed a trial court order that transferred custody from the mother to the father as a result of the mother's homosexuality.[34]

Today, none of these five states would transfer custody on the basis of a parent's nonmarital cohabitation alone nor would any condition custody or visitation on the absence of overnight visitors without a specific showing that the parent's conduct posed potential harm to the child. In reaching these positions, the courts have exercised leadership in recognizing changing mores within these states toward heterosexual relationships and in insisting on nondiscriminatory provisions for gays and lesbians as a matter of equal justice. Unlike later decisions in many of the same states on same-sex marriage, these decisions have carried the day below the public radar with little dissension.

## THE STATES WITH THE LOWEST MEDIAN AGES AT MARRIAGE

The states with the lowest median ages at marriage are Utah, Oklahoma, Idaho, Arkansas, and Kentucky, in that order. All voted Republican in the last several election cycles, but they are notably different from each other in several respects. Utah and Idaho are Mountain West states, with substantial Mormon populations. Oklahoma, Arkansas, and Kentucky are relatively poor border states. Moreover, while all of the blue states have *appointed* high court judges, these red states have *elected* judiciaries—except for Oklahoma. Nonetheless, before 1980, the law in the two sets of states did not differ significantly, because they both considered nonmarital sexual relationships to be relevant to custody determinations. Since then, the law has diverged, with four of the five red states continuing to adhere to a more-traditional approach to the relationship between nonmarital sexuality and the best interests of children.

In Utah, the courts have consistently chosen to affirm the role of moral principles in custody cases. The leading Utah Supreme Court case on the issue is *Kallas v. Kallas*,[35] decided in 1980. The father appealed the trial court's grant of overnight visitation to the mother on the grounds of her lesbianism and former drug use;[36] the supreme court agreed, finding that this "evidence bears clearly on the defendant's ability to deal appropriately with the three minor children."[37] The court explained its decision by emphasizing "the psychological impact on the children resulting from more extended visits with a mother who may, as a role model, at least to some extent cause serious conflict in the minds of the children concerning certain basic life-styles."[38] Citing cases from New York and New Jersey, the court suggested that overnight visits might not be appropriate or that such visits might be conditioned on a prohibition of nonmarital cohabitation in the children's presence.[39]

The Utah Supreme Court revisited the issue in 1994. In *Tucker v. Tucker*,[40] the intermediate appellate court had reversed a trial court decision to transfer custody from the mother to the father, finding that the trial court had failed to link its findings of emotional instability and moral unfitness to the mother's parenting ability and gave disproportionate weight to her lesbian relationships.[41] Although the appellate decision reflected a nationwide insistence on more-specific findings showing a nexus between the child's well-being and the parent's sexual conduct, the Utah Supreme Court reversed the court of appeals and reinstated the trial court decision. It observed:

> The issue was not whether a trial court could properly question a parent's morality where that parent merely cohabited with a member of the same sex. Rather, the issue was whether a trial court could properly question the morality of a parent who had cohabited with another person before the divorce and while still married. The trial court found that the occurrence of this conduct during the marriage and in the presence of the child demonstrated [the mother's] lack of moral example.[42]

This was, the state supreme court held, an entirely appropriate judgment. While moving away from the visitation restrictions in *Kallas*, designed to shield children from their parent's homosexuality, the Utah Supreme Court still upheld the relevance of more-nuanced moral determinations in a best-interest analysis. In doing so, the court affirmed the continuing importance of fidelity within marriage as a moral principle the courts could recognize and support.

The Idaho Supreme Court, with elected justices, addressed the issue in 2004, and like Utah, affirmed a trial court decision taking the parents' conflict over the father's homosexuality into account in modifying a joint custody decree. In *McGriff v. McGriff*,[43] the initial divorce decree provided for joint physical and legal custody, with the two daughters spending roughly equal time with each parent. After the mother discovered that the father was gay and that his male companion had moved into the home, she sought a modification in the custody decree. The magistrate agreed, granting the mother sole physical custody and providing the father with visitation on the condition that he not reside with his male partner during their visits. The magistrate found, inter alia, that "Father's decision to openly co-habit with [his partner]...is a change that will generate questions from the girls and their friends regarding their Father's lifestyle." The court further criticized the father for minimizing the potential effect of the issue given the conservative culture and mores in which the children lived and for "insensitivity to the girls' needs regarding his lifestyle."[44]

The father appealed, maintaining that the mother had difficulty accepting his sexual orientation and that her motion to change custody was entirely based on his sexual orientation without a showing of detriment to the children. The Idaho Supreme Court affirmed the trial court's order. While it emphasized that a change of custody could not be based on sexual orientation per se,[45] it found that the magistrate had made specific findings concerning the effect on the children resulting from the growing hostility between the parents, from the father's partner's actions toward the mother, and from the father's refusal to respect the mother's wishes for joint communication with the children about the father's homosexuality.[46]

The Arkansas Supreme Court, again with elected justices, emphasized that behavior, *not* appearances, mattered in *Taylor v. Taylor*;[47] decided during the same time period as the Idaho case. In *Taylor*, the mother shared her home with an "admitted lesbian," who paid rent and sometimes slept in the mother's bed.[48] The children occasionally joined them.[49] The mother testified, however, that she believed that homosexuality was wrong and that she did not have a sexual relationship with the woman.[50] The trial court granted the father's motion to modify custody, observing that the mother's decision simply to let a lesbian live in her house with the children "even without sex is inappropriate behavior. . . . It is at least poor parental judgment on the part of defendant to allow a well known lesbian to both reside with defendant and the children and sleep in the same bed with defendant."[51]

The Arkansas Supreme Court reversed. Although it acknowledged that "this court has held that a parent's unmarried cohabitation with a romantic partner, or a parent's promiscuous conduct or lifestyle, in the presence of a child cannot be abided,"[52] it emphasized "the absence of proof that a homosexual relationship was occurring" and the evidence showing that the children were well-adjusted and happy and "had not been adversely affected" by their mother's living arrangement.[53]

The distinction between homosexuality per se and nonmarital cohabitation in the child's presence remains good law in Arkansas. In a 2007 case affirming a change of custody from the mother to the father, the intermediate court of appeals claimed that its decision did not depend on the mother's sexual orientation, but the fact that she "had six different sexual partners in a four-and-a-half year period." In every instance, the mother cohabited with her partner in the presence of the child, despite an explicit court order that forbade extramarital cohabitation in front of the child.[54]

The Arkansas Supreme Court has applied the same test to heterosexual couples, upholding a transfer of custody in 2005 based on the mother's nonmarital cohabitation, remarking that it indicated instability in the child's life.[55] Arkansas courts continue to affirm the importance of sexual morality to custody decisions.

In contrast to the other states, Kentucky has almost no reported opinions on point. The last one is from 1980, when the Kentucky Court of Appeals stated:

> Without question, in my opinion, there is social stigma attached to homosexuality. Therefore [the daughter] will have additional burdens to bear in terms of teasing, possible embarrassment and internal conflicts. Also, there is excellent scientific research on the effects of parental modeling on children.... [The daughter] may have difficulties in achieving a fulfilling heterosexual identity of her own in the future. There would seem to me to be no rational reason for purposely submitting a child to these additional and potentially debilitating influences.[56]

In 1989, a Kentucky court refused to apply a similar standard to heterosexual cohabitation, finding that there must be a nexus between the "misconduct" and an adverse effect on the child to justify changing custody.[57] At the same time, Kentucky has continued to apply more-traditional standards to same-sex parenting, refusing to recognize a lesbian partner as a de facto parent.[58]

Demographically and politically, Oklahoma is one of the most conservative states in the country. Nonetheless, the Oklahoma Supreme Court, the only red state court in this sample whose justices are appointed rather than elected, has been more willing than the others to rule in favor of gay and lesbian parents. In the 1995 case of *Fox v. Fox*,[59] the court considered whether to grant a father's petition for a change of custody because the mother was a lesbian. The trial court had granted the father's motion, transferring custody to the father. The Oklahoma Supreme Court reversed, finding that the mother's sexual behavior did not constitute "a significant change of circumstance that directly and adversely affects the children."[60] This standard is consistent with the majority approach in both red and blue states to the impact of heterosexual cohabitation on custody—and it is similar to the *blue* state rulings discussed above. (It differs only in that it did not go as far as the New Jersey and New York decisions to affirm the principle of equal treatment; instead, it emphasized the nexus test necessary to justify a change of custody.) It differed from most of the other red states in its willingness not only to adopt a nexus test, but to meaningfully review trial court determinations accordingly.

Taken as a whole, the red states in this group certainly differ from the blue states. Of the five red states with the lowest median age at marriage, only one (Oklahoma) expressly reversed a trial court's consideration of a parent's same-sex cohabitation because it did not make specific findings of adverse effect. Three states (Utah, Idaho, and Arkansas) have upheld the relevance of such considerations, with Arkansas and Idaho doing so in relatively recent decisions. In contrast, in the five blue states with the highest median age at marriage in the country, the most-recent decision we could find addressing nonmarital sexuality and custody or visitation was the 1989 Rhode Island decision affirming restrictions on overnight heterosexual cohabitation. Massachusetts and New Jersey were reversing trial court decisions based on sexual orientation by 1980, and New York expressly affirmed the transfer of custody from a fit mother to a gay father in the mid-1980s. None of the five blue states has reported decisions within the last decade restricting custody or visitation on the basis of the parent's sexual activity.

Aside from the results, the tone of the cases differs as well. The state supreme courts in Utah, Idaho, and Arkansas expressly affirmed the lower courts' consideration of parents' morality, while the blue state courts were more likely to use the language of equality.[61] Moreover, even when the red states applied the same legal standards, they were less likely to reverse trial court decisions modifying custody after a parent's sexual orientation had become an issue.

Notwithstanding these differences in rhetoric and results, the reported judicial decisions show significantly less polarization than the parental notification cases or legislation on abortion and same-sex marriage. *All* of the reported decisions reject sexual orientation as a per se factor precluding custody or visitation, and *all* require factual findings that tie sexuality to an impact on the children, even though they differ with respect to how this could be shown.[62] Moreover, even the red states appear to be moving in the direction of less rather than more regulation of sexuality.[63] The most telling aspects of the custody story may not be the cases on the record, but the relative silence from states such as Kentucky, which are unlikely to rule out such considerations altogether. Overall, however, courts sensitive to cultural context seem to have the ability to manage legal evolution without exacerbating political divisions.

# ALABAMA: A CAUTIONARY TALE?

Nonetheless, the question of whether *elected* state courts can effectively police the fairness of trial courts in the face of partisan pressures remains open. A series of Alabama custody decisions demonstrates how the injection of polarized rather than consensus values into judicial decision making can undermine the role of courts in mediating public morality. Just as happened in the Supreme Court parental notification cases, once an issue becomes one of partisan positioning, the appellate courts lose the ability to provide guidance at all and may withdraw from the field.

The former chief justice of the Alabama Supreme Court, Roy Moore, was renowned for his insistence on displaying the Ten Commandments in the courthouse, and Alabama eventually removed him from office because of his defiance of the federal order requiring that he stop doing so.[64] Less well known is his invocation of religious authority in family law decision making. His efforts came to a head in *Ex parte H.H.*,[65] decided in 2002. In that case, the mother was living with a lesbian partner in California when she sought to modify an order granting the father custody. She claimed that the father was physically abusive toward the children, whipping them with a belt and slapping at least one of the children hard enough to cause a nosebleed.[66] The father disputed the characterization and severity of the events. The trial court ruled in his favor, but the court of appeals reversed, finding that the mother had proved her claim of physical abuse.[67] The Alabama Supreme Court reversed again, reinstating the trial court's judgment on procedural grounds. It held in a brief opinion that the appellate court should have deferred to the trial court judge, who had evaluated "the credibility of the testimony and who observed the demeanor of the witnesses, [and] found that, although the father's disciplinary actions may occasionally be excessive, no abuse had occurred."[68]

Justice Moore wrote a separate opinion to emphasize that "the homosexual conduct of a parent—conduct involving a sexual relationship between two persons of the same gender—creates a strong presumption of unfitness that alone is sufficient justification for denying that parent custody."[69] He insisted further:

> Homosexual conduct is, and has been, considered abhorrent, immoral, detestable, a crime against nature, and a violation of the laws of nature and of nature's God upon which this Nation and our laws are predicated. Such conduct violates both the criminal and civil laws of

this State and is destructive to a basic building block of society—the family.

He continued by denouncing the behavior as "an inherent evil against which children must be protected."[70]

The contrast between the majority opinion and the concurrence is striking. In earlier cases, the Alabama Supreme Court had held that a trial court could restrict custody and visitation to avoid children's exposure to nonmarital cohabitation even without a showing of detriment to the child.[71] The court did not mention these prior rulings, which would have provided an alternative basis for the result. Instead, the court used technical grounds for the reversal, finding that the intermediate court had not given sufficient deference to the trial court's findings of fact. Justice Moore, in one of the most intemperate opinions in the country, used the occasion not only to reaffirm the earlier rulings, but to condemn homosexuality with references to "Sodom and Gomorrah."[72]

The Alabama Supreme Court, increasingly wary of the issue, demonstrated similar deference to the trial court in a heterosexual cohabitation case decided the same year.[73] The parties had divorced as a result of the mother's adultery, and the mother had moved in with her boyfriend while the father was stationed with the army in Korea.[74] By the time of the appellate decision, she had also given birth to a child with the boyfriend.[75] The court of appeals nonetheless affirmed the trial court's refusal to grant the father's motion to modify custody, and the Supreme Court declined to grant certiorari.[76] Justice Moore filed an impassioned dissent, writing, "[f]or years there has been a steady deterioration of this Court's standard regarding the fitness of an adulterous parent in a custody case. Prior decisions of this Court establish a conclusive presumption that a parent who has committed adultery is unfit to have custody of a minor child."[77]

Justice Moore, elected to his position on the Alabama Supreme Court,[78] used his opinions to reaffirm the centrality of Christian standards of morality to family law decision making. The other justices, by contrast, shifted to more-technical and procedural grounds for their decisions—and also declined to take another nonmarital cohabitation (heterosexual or homosexual) case for at least five years after Justice Moore's opinions.[79] During that time, the Alabama appellate courts have neither actively policed the fairness of trial court decisions[80] nor claimed a role as arbiters of family morality with the same confidence as the courts in earlier eras.[81]

# CONCLUSION: IS FAMILY LAW
# FEDERALISM POSSIBLE?

Family law—the determination of the rules governing marriage, divorce, and parenthood—is state law, and it has always varied substantially across the United States. Indeed, the variation began, in a manner not so different from modern developments, with radically different laws—and cultural understandings—in the early colonies. The New England states, then as now in the forefront of legal reforms, treated divorce as a civil matter, with judicial authority to sever marital bonds beginning in the seventeenth century. The southern states, in contrast, adopted English ecclesiastical law and did not permit the courts to grant final divorces at all until largely after the Civil War.[82] The differences remained substantial even then, and legislation was introduced in almost every session of Congress between 1884 and 1940 to nationalize the regulation of marriage and divorce. The split between liberals and conservatives doomed the effort.[83]

The determination of individual rights, in contrast, is to a much greater degree national law, with the constitutional order guaranteeing every individual a place within the legal community. The question of who controls access to family status and to the mechanisms (from contraception to gametes donation to adoption) that determine family formation accordingly lies on the fault line between state and federal authority. Drawing the line involves a balance between federal guarantees and local governance. It also involves choices about what is possible and when. Before the Civil War, for example, slavery was treated as a matter of domestic relations and relegated practically and legally to the states. The Civil War and the 13th Amendment changed it irrevocably to a national issue, even if the balance between federal and state authority would be reframed again and again on the issue of civil rights.[84] Divorce reform, in contrast, has remained with the states, with no-fault provisions nonetheless sweeping the United States between 1969 and 1985, after a century of stalled federal efforts caught in the liberal versus conservative polarization of an earlier era.

Part II of this book has charted the role of law in establishing, giving symbolic expression to, and mediating the conflicts between the two paradigms. High-profile constitutional decisions broke open the pathways to blue family life, securing rights to contraception and abortion. Similarly high-profile legislative measures have given voice to the red paradigm backlash. Despite the intractability of issues such as same-sex marriage at the federal level, there has been substantial, albeit gradual, progress at the state level. This chapter has examined the role of the courts in avoiding and defusing potentially destructive conflicts in custody cases. Full appreciation of the role of law in a federal system that divides responsibilities between the national government and the states is essential to finding a way beyond the conflicts between the two paradigms.

The final part of the book charts the proposals necessary to revitalize support for all American families. The success of such policies will depend not just on the merits of the policies themselves, but also on the ability to create political support for a legal infrastructure that transcends the current debates.

# PART III

# THE MAP TO THE FUTURE

## CHAPTER 10

# Marriage Advice in Shades of Pink

M ARRIAGE IS IN crisis in the United States, but, as we have argued throughout this book, the significance of that crisis is very much in dispute. Contrary to the claims of traditionalists, marriage is an institution that is neither universal nor unchanging. Nonetheless, to a greater degree than modernists like to acknowledge, the power of marriage as an institution comes from its shared meanings, including its creation of a culture of trust.[1]

The forces that once produced consensus on the meaning of marriage—contributing to the couple's trust that their understandings would be upheld by family and community—are no more. The existence of effective and reliable contraception, a changing economy that makes possible female as well as male autonomy, and a centuries-long change in reproduction from managing as many children as a couple could handle to investing in a chosen few have all necessarily altered the meaning of marriage, and they have done so over the last half-century in ways that have torn apart our understandings.

If consensus on marriage is still possible, it is on the role of marriage in producing commitment between adults and in channeling resources from one generation to the next. To remake marriage so that it fits the needs of red and blue families, it is critical to change the subject—at least as a matter of law and policy—from the intrinsically divisive issue of controlling sexuality to marriage's role in promoting commitment. Agreement will still not exist, however, on the nature of the rebuilding.

Harvard political scientist James Q. Wilson, in his 2002 book, *The Marriage Problem: How Our Culture Has Weakened Families*,[2] called for "a powerful cultural reassertion of the value of marriage" that would promote its "authority."[3] Wilson indicted the Enlightenment, with its emphasis on reason and individual fulfillment and its promise of greater gender autonomy, as a source of the problem, and he sought to reinstill the right values through custom, religion, and law.[4] By contrast, legal scholar Nancy Polikoff sees marriage as an outdated and repressive institution. She would dismantle its authority and replace it with a variety of individually negotiated arrangements between friends and lovers, parents with children, and partners undertaking any number of different types of relationships.

The differences between such views cannot be reconciled; James Q. Wilson and Nancy Polikoff are unlikely to ever agree on very much about the institution of marriage or its role in society. Part of the difference between them is that they have lived different lives, as parts of different generations, with different family arrangements, in different (and—Massachusetts, California and the District of Columbia—not so different) parts of the country. For similar reasons, it is hardly accidental (as chapters 3 and 4 noted) that the prevalence of marriage in a community has become a powerful predictor of voting preferences. Nonetheless, we are likely to rediscover a greater degree of overlap in our understandings of marriage as an institution only if different parts of the country permit the evolution of the legal and social meanings of marriage in accordance with their own values and traditions.

## THE STATE OF MARRIAGE

At the core of the tensions between family systems is the issue of what the state should promote and what it should leave to individual choice. Historically, the idea of autonomy with respect to the creation of family form would have been considered an oxymoron to the extent that the issue arose at all. The traditional family of biological mother, father, and children was often treated as prior to the state,[5] if not foundational to society itself.[6] The Supreme Court has recognized marriage as "an institution, in the maintenance of which in its purity the public is deeply interested, for it is the foundation of the family and of society, without which there would be neither civilization nor progress."[7] Nor has the state been neutral among the possible forms of marriage. When the Supreme Court confronted the issue of polygamy as an expression of Mormon religious practice in the Utah territories during the nineteenth century, it had no trouble declaring that "society may be said to be built [upon marriage], and out of its fruits spring social relations and social obligations and duties, with which government is necessarily required to deal."[8] The challenge in today's society is how to retain marriage's role in promoting stability while accepting its reduced role in ordering adult life. We believe the effort to redefine marriage, given the regional differences we have charted, will most effectively occur one state at a time.

The alternative may be to give up on shared meanings altogether. While the state continues to regulate the status of marriage, its meaning has become so contested that some on both the right, who object to same-sex marriage, and the left, who favor extending marriage more broadly, advocate separating the state institution from its varied meanings and forms.

Such proposals would eliminate marriage's status as an institution that connects the couple to the larger community and relegate its emotional core to private traditions. Some might then celebrate the private institutions as the only true marriages; others would toast the result as the appropriate conclusion to marriage's nature as a "bankrupt institution" in an era that has moved beyond it. Consider, for example, Laura Kipnis's fascinating book *Against Love: A Polemic.*[9] Instead of lifelong commitment and monogamy, she celebrates sexual desire. She argues that contemporary marriage, with its alleged punitive consequences for adultery, is an example of unwarranted public control of intimate relationships. She advocates new structures for commitment, such as one-year renewable contracts. The contemporary pervasiveness of adultery, she suggests, shows that the expectations of lifelong commitment underlying contemporary marriage are ultimately untenable. Given her emphasis on sexual freedom, she pays minimal attention to the interdependencies between partners and between parents and child that marriage addresses. Most, however, on both the left and right, would reject such an approach, criticizing Kipnis for her failure to acknowledge that relationship stability benefits children and helps to counter the uncertainty that characterizes the lives of many adults.[10]

This is, nonetheless, an arena with considerable potential overlap between the red and blue models. At the core of both the emerging blue ethic of responsibility toward childrearing and the traditionalist red emphasis on formal structures and customs is appreciation of the value and fragility of commitment. The blue paradigm's critical insight is that emotional maturity and financial independence make commitment easier to achieve. The source of legitimate red family anguish is that the circumstances of the new information economy make stability that much harder to police or ensure. Within both traditions, marriage retains its role as the institution identified with the importance of commitment. Yet, differences between the two paradigms stand in the way of embracing the shared enterprise at the core. We accordingly recognize that, while both traditions make it possible to recognize the value of marriage and while the state could—and should—attempt to re-create support for relationship stability, the success of the venture depends on the ability to chart a path that resonates with regional variations. The failure to do so risks not just defeat at the polls, but the vitality of marriage in rebuilding communities.

## OVERLAPPING VALUES

To realize the potential for marriage support, therefore, requires a measure of political wisdom often in short supply in times of cultural warfare. Accordingly, marriage promotion should occur in decentralized ways that are sensitive to regional nuances. For the blue world, the critical issue is whether marriage will continue to be important at all as a central organizing principle for family life. Already, blue states are characterized by a higher degree of nonmarital cohabitation, greater tolerance and respect for autonomy, and greater legal recognition of nonmarital relationships. Within this world, the calls are mounting for the deinstitutionalization of marriage and systematic legal reform addressing a continuum of family relationships.

Continuing roadblocks to recognition of same-sex marriage will speed these developments, and indeed already have, with domestic partnerships, as we discussed in chapter 8, expanding to include not only same-sex couples, but a variety of other relationships. Conversely, recognition of same-sex marriage has the potential to revitalize discussion about what marriage is for—and for whom it should be seen as the right thing to do. Should parents, who are otherwise committed to each other and their children, feel obligated to marry in order to underscore the seriousness of their undertaking? Should those committed partners who do marry receive recognition that their unions are qualitatively different from those who might marry and choose not to? Does the public affirmation intrinsic to the ceremonial nature of marriage continue to play an important role, one legally cognizable as the basis for legal presumptions, differential tax treatment, or other benefits and obligations? So long as same-sex couples are barred from the institution, for reasons an increasing number of people see as unjustified or antiquated, it will be difficult to continue to insist on marriage as a preferred and important legal category.

Within the red world, the focus on same-sex marriage diverts attention from the real issues undermining family stability. The inevitable fragility of marriage at young ages and the impracticability of lengthy periods of abstinence in modern society undermine a regime centered on the unity of sex, procreation, and childrearing. The ultimate challenge to the red paradigm, of course, does not come from gays and lesbians, or even from the separation of intimate unions from procreation, a separation that has already happened for many older couples. Instead, the real issue is sex—and the question of continued societal support for a principle (limiting all sex to marriage) that no longer commands support from a majority of the population even in red states. In this context, the fight over same-sex marriage is a rearguard action that allows the debate between marriage as a divinely ordained and unchanging institution and one that adapts to meet the needs of a new era to occur on grounds that affect relatively few people.

### *Why Marry? Same-Sex Couples and the Meaning of Commitment*

The issue for the entire country is how to re-create the foundation on which family stability rests. The continued expansion of marriage, one state at a time, has the potential to reinvigorate the meaning of marriage for all.

The blue family paradigm, with its emphasis on autonomy and equality, has given less voice to the need for stability (perhaps because of a recognition that the promotion of stability has often stood in the way of modernizing the institution).[11] The exclusion of same-sex couples from marriage, as Laura Kipnis might suggest, underscores the identification of the institution with gendered—and oppressive—marital roles, the policing of sexuality, and religious traditions that many modern couples do not share.[12] In contrast, when the Supreme Judicial Court of Massachusetts affirmed the right of same-sex couples to marry, it described the importance of civil marriage in "anchor[ing] an ordered society by encouraging stable relationships over transient ones."[13] The excitement of gay and lesbian couples marrying in Boston,

San Francisco, Canada, and elsewhere has sparked renewed appreciation for the institution and discussion about its meaning. Precisely because some gay and lesbian activists question the amount of energy used in the gay marriage fight, their internal debates focus renewed attention on the relationship between equality, within and without marriage, and the limitations on autonomy that inevitably come with the idea of permanence.

Same-sex couples thus provide a new image of the meaning of marriage, one that involves practical and symbolic affirmation of the values of autonomy, equality, and fairness—and commitment.[14] The discussion we hear whenever same-sex marriage becomes newly available inevitably turns toward the nature of the choice. Once the right to marry is won, when and why should couples choose to enter the institution? Some activists continue to be ambivalent, and the sensibilities involved are classically blue: that is, commitment follows from individual election rather than imposition from above. Nonetheless, the emotions that attend the rituals on the steps of city hall underscore the continuing power and mystery that the institution commands—a power enhanced with the entry of a new class of couples previously denied admission.

The power of the dialogue, however, is that much greater as it proceeds within different state traditions; it cannot immediately overcome the opposition of those who see marriage in crisis, and who believe that same-sex marriage will irreparably damage the nature of the institution.[15] Yet, same-sex marriage is different from the division that underlies the more intractable issue of abortion in two important respects. First, the idea that human life begins with conception, at least in the sense that the union of egg and sperm creates a unique entity with the capacity to become a person, is a compelling notion worthy of respect even by those who do not share either its religious foundations or the conclusion that the status of the fetus precludes the possibility of abortion. In contrast, the opposition to homosexuality, either as intrinsically sinful or as destructive to heterosexual marriage, is offensive to many Americans who do not agree with the assumptions on which it is based. They see the issue as one of equality and human rights: two people who wish to make a loving commitment to each other ought to be able to receive state recognition whatever the nature of their sexual identity.

Second, abortion, though still critical to many women's reproductive autonomy, in recent decades has become less visible and less necessary to those with access to effective contraception, driving down abortion rates nationally and increasing middle-class reliance on measures such as the morning-after pill. Gays and lesbians, in contrast, have become more visible and more accepted throughout much of the country.[16] As a result, while views about same-sex marriage and civil unions replicate many of the same divisions that underlie abortion, same-sex marriage views have shown greater generational change than those on abortion. The regional, political, and religious divisions nonetheless continue to define the opposing positions—and those divisions remain intense.

In the national polls on acceptance of homosexuality, what has been most striking is the differences in the rate of change. In the mid-1970s, most Americans thought of same-sex conduct as morally objectionable and same-sex marriage as unthinkable. In the period from 1973 to 2006, the percentage of the country as a whole responding yes to the question "Are homosexual relations always wrong?" dropped 18 points to 56%.[17] In 2002, less than half of the respondents in the 30–44 age group thought homosexual relations were always wrong, compared to 74% in 1973. Accordingly, while positions have changed—and are likely to continue to do so as younger generations grow up with friends, colleagues, and family members who have been acknowledging their sexuality more openly and at earlier ages—the public as a whole remains deeply divided in their attitudes toward the issue.

Indeed, the embrace of same-sex marriage within the blue tradition has been a long and contentious process. For the most-tolerant states, it started with the inclusion of gays and lesbians in the larger society and the recognition that antidiscrimination protection is a matter of basic fairness. It continued with the extension of state sanctions to partnership benefits and the ability to adopt. Acceptance of same-sex marriage then follows more readily, as the history in Connecticut and Vermont illustrates, once gay and lesbian relationships have already secured official status.[18] Nonetheless, in the states that have moved most readily to extend recognition to same-sex couples, a higher percentage of the public already accepts the separation of the religious tradition of marriage from the state-sanctioned institution—and this separation of the sacred from the secular is exactly what red paradigm proponents fear. We believe that, while these world views inevitably clash, state promotion of the values associated with marriage in the secular realm need not.

## How to Stay Married: Traditional Couples
## and the Creation of Commitment

The critical role of marriage for all couples is the public declaration of commitment, a ritual whose significance can be enhanced. Chief among the recent proposals that some states have tried is covenant marriage, which, as noted in chapter 8, creates two possible forms of marriage: covenant and regular. Three states—Louisiana, Arkansas, and Arizona—actually have such laws, and other states have considered them.[19] The legislation's most innovative feature is not its restrictions on divorce—those resemble traditional divorce provisions—but its precommitment efforts: those who elect the status are saying to themselves and the world "our marriage is special."

Some states disappointed by the small numbers electing covenant marriage where it is available or wary of restrictions on divorce that have failed to deter marital instability have considered mandatory premarital education programs instead. These programs generally have three components: (1) sending the message that marriage is a serious undertaking that rests on commitment; (2) reinforcing marital ideals such as equality, fidelity, and other traditions; and (3) countering the risks associated with marriage among the young and the poorly educated.

Surveys that ask the divorced what contributed to their marital breakups have influenced the design of such programs. Respondents list the factors contributing to their divorces in the following order: "lack of commitment" (73%), "too much arguing" (56%), "infidelity" (55%), "marrying too young" (46%), "unrealistic expectations" (45%), "lack of equality in the relationship" (44%), and "domestic violence" (29%). An additional 41% add that a lack of premarital preparation contributed to their divorce.[20] Moreover, other studies find that divorce risk rises with low education and income, marrying before the age of 20, premarital cohabitation, having children before marriage, experiencing a divorce growing up (and marrying someone who experienced a divorce growing up), and poor mental health.[21] A number of states have therefore reasoned that premarital education might help to prevent divorce by providing better preparation and more realistic expectations and that mandating it might reach the higher-risk group—including the young, the unprepared, and the impetuous—unlikely to elect covenant marriage.

Six states (Florida, Maryland, Minnesota, Oklahoma, Tennessee, and Utah) have adopted such measures to date.[22] The counseling incorporates the type of relationship advice, financial planning, and wedding preparation of covenant marriage, without the legal restrictions on divorce.

Preliminary studies report some success in raising the level of marital happiness, improving communication, and reducing dissolutions.[23] Critics observe, however, that the programs may be more successful with middle-class couples than with the population as a whole, and they may be more effective at persuading high-risk couples not to tie the knot at all than at changing the behavior of those who do.[24]

What these efforts—same-sex marriage in some states, covenant marriage or premarital counseling in others—have in common is a state effort to articulate the values associated with marriage and to continue to regulate the institution in the name of those values. Smaller-scale efforts have sometimes occurred in more-local arenas. Thus, a number of communities have embraced marriage education and counseling programs, and most efforts to recognize same-sex relationships have started with municipal initiatives to create domestic partnership registries, authorize adoptions by a second parent of the same sex,[25] or adopt antidiscrimination provisions. These measures have helped to create movements to change existing norms; to the extent that they succeed, they do so by persuasion and example rather than coercion.

### Respecting Autonomy

The second principle in the effort to strengthen families is respect for autonomy and restraint in the use of the coercive power of the state. While the state can articulate the shared values it wishes to promote, it is a very different matter—constitutionally and normatively—to impose such values on residents who may not share them.

The Supreme Court decision in *Lawrence v. Texas* reached the right balance. Texas had passed legislation criminalizing same-sex sodomy but, unlike older legislation in other states, not heterosexual sodomy. The statute thus clearly targeted gay sex, making gay intimate partners subject to criminal prosecution. Justice Kennedy, in declaring the statute to be unconstitutional, observed:

> These matters, involving the most intimate and personal choices a person may make in a lifetime, choices central to personal dignity and autonomy, are central to the liberty protected by the Fourteenth Amendment. At the heart of liberty is the right to define one's own concept of existence, of meaning, of the universe, and of the mystery of human life. Beliefs about these matters could not define the attributes of personhood were they formed under compulsion of the State.[26]

Justice Scalia dissented from what he has referred to as the "homosexual agenda," which is "directed at eliminating the moral opprobrium that has traditionally attached to homosexual conduct."[27] We believe that what Scalia described as the "homosexual agenda" is appropriate national policy. While the federal nature of family law creates the ability for states to articulate family ideals in different terms, the regional variations in expression should not extend to control over the most intimate and personal private behavior. The state interest in promoting stability and commitment is thus distinct from its ability to intrude into realms of private expression and meaning.

Here, as with contraception, the pathways to continued evolution should remain open. Attitudes toward sexuality—and homosexuality—have shifted gradually with each new generation, and they vary regionally not only in the intensity of the beliefs but in the rate of change.[28] The legal recognition of same-sex relationships has occurred through a series of steps in the most-liberal states, from antidiscrimination provisions to extension of employment benefits to recognition of adoption to civil unions and finally to marriage. Moreover, these shifts often start with local innovations, such as domestic partnership registries in major cities, before adoption at the state level. Family law within a federal system should continue to balance the expression of community values with the autonomy of individuals in creating separate meanings for their lives.

The recognition of diversity in state approaches to same-sex marriage, even coupled with the argument for continued evolution, is undoubtedly unacceptable to many advocates within both the blue and the red paradigms. Indeed, as with abortion, that will be inevitable given the nature of the controversies we have charted in this book. While we are among those who prefer stronger actions in accordance with our own values, we view the issue as one of what measures to take, where, and when. The federal government, however, in the Defense of Marriage Act (DOMA), preempted the states' experiment on same-sex marriage. The DOMA states that, for purposes of benefits such as Social Security, the federal government will not recognize same-sex marriages, even if a couple is legally married under state law. This override has been challenged as a threat to our federalist system, in which power is divided between the states and the national government. We believe that the federal government should continue to defer to state regulation of family issues and should do so in a way that encourages the continuing evolution of state practices.

Moreover, on the issue of homosexuality, unlike the issue of abortion, we are optimistic about the prospects for generational change and therefore see the issue as one of allowing space for the reconciliation of the critical demand of equal respect for gays and lesbians with understandings about the nature of family creation. In the meantime, there is no excuse for persecution or, as we explored in Chapter 5, punishing children for the misperceived sins of their parents.

### Supporting Families

The states, through high-profile legal rulings on same-sex unions or legislation adopting covenant marriage, articulate family ideals and help to translate changing economic and social practices into individual norms and understandings. These legal developments, however, have little practical effect on the growth of economic inequality that has made marriage so perilous for the young and the poor, and they are therefore unlikely to have any substantial effect on either marriage or divorce rates. Both same-sex and covenant marriage discussions, though they solidify symbolic shifts in the understanding of marriage, are irrelevant to the degree of support available to more-fragile couples. At the same time, the deregulation of sexuality and respect for autonomy do little to address the disparities in marriage and the aggravation of income inequalities they produce. The battle of the paradigms—between calls for greater moral purity and those for greater financial independence—does little to rebuild the practical pathways to more-stable family life.

Yet, the disparities in marriage—and the consequent perceptions of moral decline—reflect the changing economic basis for family life as much if not more than moral or political will. For more than a decade, Princeton sociologist Sara McLanahan has been working on the Fragile Families and Child Wellbeing Study, which includes 5,000 children, with about 75% of them born to unmarried mothers. She concludes that poverty and nonmarital childbearing produce reinforcing cycles as poor women are more likely to bear children without realistic opportunities to marry, and their lack of resources reduces the life prospects for them and their children, making it less likely in turn that their grandchildren will marry. Marriage programs, targeted at new parents at the time of a child's birth, and programs that teach relationship skills might, however, affect marriage rates.[29]

Economists find that the likelihood of marriage varies not only with individual income, but in accordance with the degree of male regional inequality; the greater the disparity in male incomes, the lower the overall marriage rates in the metropolitan area.[30] These patterns suggest a complex interaction between economic well-being and traditional mores. As traditionalists would predict, marriage rates have declined most in the fastest-growing (and often blue) urban areas that may be furthest removed from the institutions that reinforce traditional values. At the same time, worsening economic inequality depletes the institutional and financial resources even in more-traditional communities that might rebuild the foundation for family life. Indeed, nonmarital childbearing, which was once thought of as a marker of race, has become more thoroughly identified with class. During the 1960s, the rate of nonmarital teen childbearing among blacks was 12 times that of whites; in 2004, it was a little more than twice as high, reflecting a decrease in the rate for blacks and an increase in the rate for whites.[31] The economic forces that remade African-American communities, particularly in the rustbelt inner cities during the '60s and '70s, now also affect working-class whites. As we discussed in chapters 2 and 3, the "rates of marriage and marital stability have remained relatively constant among women who have completed college," while both measures have declined substantially for women with less education and have accentuated the long-standing association between male achievement and marriage.[32]

These factors create a dilemma for those who would strengthen the family by any means. To begin with, different groups have different traditions and different practical needs. Thus, McLanahan's groundbreaking studies of low-income families draw two striking conclusions: the likelihood of marriage both reflects and contributes to male income growth, and infidelity and lack of trust are major factors in people's reluctance to marry. She emphasizes that both partnership instability, that is, mothers' multiple relationships, and multi-partner fertility, including men's procreation with different mates, discourage marriage and reproduce similar patterns in the next generation. McLanahan concludes that the interaction of these factors complicates effective interventions. She accordingly counsels that a delay in first births until mothers find more-reliable long-term partners would produce the greatest payoffs.[33]

As we have suggested throughout our analysis, teens from lower-income families begin sexual activity earlier and are less likely to use contraception. An inadvertent pregnancy, in communities in which they are the norm, poses little deterrent to sexual activity; yet, numerous studies find that delays in childbearing, even without marriage, increase mother and child prospects—and lower fertility, intended and not. Indeed, in predicting the likelihood of incarceration of the next generation, the mother's age and whether she finishes high school are important independent variables—and incarceration in turn makes marriage less likely.[34] Accordingly, marriage promotion by itself is likely to be ineffective, and limiting sexual activity in communities in which it is widespread is virtually impossible. Greater attention to family planning is the indispensable link, but it too is unlikely to be effective absent more systematic support for education, comprehensive health care, and job opportunities.[35] Johns Hopkins sociologist Andrew Cherlin, who has been studying family formation for more than 30 years, notes that policy makers have a dilemma: punitive policies that attempt to promote marriage by denying support for the poorest families, which are overwhelming headed by single parents, will replicate family dysfunction in the next generation, because the best marriage promotion policy is one that secures the well-being of children in their formative years.[36]

The same may not be true for more-stable communities on what they perceive as the moral brink (our communities on the cusp). Here, high school education classes that focus on relationships, premarital counseling, and church efforts have greater likelihood of success. Ironically, these programs, in their focus on relationship quality, demonstrate more overlap between red and blue values than the fights over whether they should exist in the first place. Social science evidence finds that what works is preaching blue values—delaying marriage until the couple has established a stable foundation, anticipating financial needs and planning accordingly, recognizing the warning signs for domestic violence, encouraging mutual respect, and keeping open the lines of effective communication—and a red emphasis on finding a partner with shared religious commitments and marital ideals and giving birth within a relationship built on such principles.[37] Although such programs need not and should not emphasize their conclusions in ideological terms, the most effective are designed to assist young couples in dealing with a world of more-egalitarian relationships, in which women enjoy greater opportunities and independence—and are more likely to initiate divorce if their needs are not addressed. After all, young women who have relatively traditional family ideals still expect young men to be attentive, faithful, and productive. Early efforts to assess the effects of such programs have not yet effectively controlled for different populations nor determined whether they have the greatest effect only on those who are already good marriage risks. Moreover, we would predict that the effects, if the programs are successful, are likely to be small. But such efforts could help to reinforce new understandings of marriage—ones that couple the idea of commitment with recognition of the importance of mutual respect.

Conversely, virtually every study has concluded that legal restrictions on divorce do little to promote marriage. In studies of why people stay married, those who perceived rewards, such as love, from their relationship were much happier than those who explained their cohesiveness based on barriers to leaving, including commitment to the norm of marriage.[38] The researchers concluded:

> [Barriers to divorce] such as religious beliefs, concerns about children, or worries about financial independence may act as cohesive forces to the extent that they keep unhappily married couples together for a period of time. But barriers do not appear to be as powerful as rewards in maintaining cohesion. Without a strong attraction between spouses (as reflected in love, friendship or positive communication), many people eventually find ways to overcome existing barriers and leave their marriages.[39]

Marriage promotion programs are thus most effective when they help couples to create and maintain a shared foundation for their union.


## CONCLUSION

Legal and societal norms can and should help couples remain in long-term relationships, but the challenge becomes greater when society itself disagrees on the basis necessary to promote stable unions.[40] The question of changing norms to encourage marriage is highly complex and political.[41] Moreover, perhaps the biggest point of disagreement is the notion of what works: the blue family world combines autonomy with support, which produces healthier families more likely to choose constructive paths, while the red family paradigm counsels more prescriptive (and traditional) roles for men and women with a greater insistence on consequences for those who deviate from them.

We have argued in this chapter that the areas of greatest overlap are those giving voice to shared aspirations. While those who prize autonomy may be wary of celebrating traditional marriage, most do not begrudge efforts to encourage commitment, educate young people in the qualities that effectively promote relationship stability, or establish voluntary marriage promotion programs. Moreover, marriage education programs, practically if not ideologically, change the subject from what is right (marriage) to how to make it work (relationship quality based on shared values and mutual respect). Removed from the high-volume conflicts of the culture wars, marriage promotion efforts, whether cast in red or blue, share one practical level of overlap: both emphasize the importance of marital bliss whether to combat extramarital temptation (see on-line sites proclaiming "Christian Sex is Hot," "ABC News: Christians Promote Hot Sex in Marriage," "Sexy Christian Wives") or dual career family exhaustion (How one busy couple had sex—every single night!). Perhaps they might both agree to fund innovative scholarly inquiries, such as Helen Fisher's work on the nature of intimate attraction and the role of the hormones, oxytocin, and dopamine in keeping couples together.

We suspect, however, that taking a little blue pill is no more a solution for marital woes than restrictions on divorce. The more-effective measures, as chapter 11 shows, focus on delay—and that requires a commitment to contraception.

## CHAPTER 11

# Making Ready for Baby

## *Painting the Nursery Sky Blue*

W HEN WE WERE in high school, we learned about how not to become pregnant. Fertility control meant abstaining or using condoms, a diaphragm, or birth control pills to make sure that we did not have a child when we were not yet ready. After we each married, when we decided that we wanted to have children, fertility control meant something completely different. It meant making sure that we had children because we were finally ready.

Both of us had our first child well after age 25. We live in an era where it is not just the teen and nonmarital birthrates that are increasing—so too is the rate of births to women over the age of 30, a rate that has been going up for the past several decades.[1] Fertility control for red and blue families rests on entirely different conceptions (please forgive the pun). For blue families, contraception supports the deferral of marriage and childbirth, and reproductive technology allows every couple to choose the appropriate time for family formation. By contrast, for red families, who associate moral responsibility with channeling sexuality into marriage, contraception eliminates the most important consequences of sexual transgressions and undermines their insistence that the appropriate transition from teen abstinence to adult roles is through courtship and marriage.[2] For couples who marry at younger ages, fertility-enhancing technology is less important (though, of course, children provide an important gateway to participation in the community, so infertility may be a difficult burden).

Missing from both paradigms, however, is full consideration of the populations that do not carefully plan for childbearing, do not enjoy attractive opportunities for marriage, and do not have access to assisted reproduction if they defer childbearing. The fight between red and blue is most destructive in its failure to provide a framework that acknowledges the interests of those most affected by the intersection of changing economic conditions and family needs. The high-profile stalemates over abortion and abstinence education obscure the growing inequality of access to contraception and the disproportionately high unintended pregnancy rates among low-income women. If there is any place where the connection among sexuality, childbearing, and marriage has broken down, it is in the childbearing practices of unmarried women in their early 20s. And, if there is anywhere the model of responsible family planning does not exist, it is among the same group. Yet, these young adults are both outside the reach of mandatory abstinence classes and do not have ready access to family-planning facilities.

This chapter brings together the full range of issues in fertility control, from the need to prevent conception to the need to promote conception, to show how the differences among different groups—demographic as well as ideological—must be addressed to reach shared solutions. While red and blue families may never agree on policy solutions, such as support for contraception, that bridge the values gap, they may agree on policy solutions that ameliorate undesirable racial and class consequences. This chapter proposes that the more-constructive approaches can only come from changing the subject: first, from abortion to contraception as the indispensable component in preventing improvident births; second, from high school students to young adults as the critical group that can improve the health of the nation's families; and, third, from single-minded programs to more-diverse strategies capable of addressing the needs of the country as a whole.

## CONTESTED TERRAIN

The sexual revolution began with birth control, and any revitalized national agenda should start with fertility. The connections among contraception, fertility, and sexual activity are fundamentally important, both symbolically and practically. Contraception is an issue whenever we consider sexual activity, and it is an issue that affects most women's lives for decades. It is the *moral meaning* of contraception, rather than its ubiquity, that is contested terrain in today's polarized discourse on fertility control: is a public embrace of the importance of contraception implied approval for nonmarital sexuality or part of a renewed definition of individual responsibility?

The most telling evidence of the differing approaches between red and blue—and of their limitations—came in the fight over who deserved credit for the drop in teen births in the 1990s, a development both groups applauded. The conservatives wished to attribute the decline, which included a reduction in the number of abortions during the same period, to greater abstinence, the liberals to greater use of birth control. They are both right—abstinence and contraception both played a role—in the case of younger teens, where the shared fight against teen pregnancy has shown the greatest gains. For older teens (18–19), abstinence appears to have had no effect, and the liberals have the better case. A careful study of data from the National Survey of Family Growth examined the bases for the declining teenage pregnancy rate from 1995 to 2002.[3] The researchers found the changes shown in table 11.1.

These figures show a small decline in the level of sexual activity only for younger teens, a substantial increase in the use of contraception for all teens, and a large drop in pregnancy risk.[4] Teen births declined significantly as well, with a greater decline for African-Americans than for whites. Nonetheless, the improvements that came from better contraceptive use were very much a race- and class-based affair.[5] Among teens in the '90s, contraceptive use increased more for whites than nonwhites, with 25% of African-American females unprotected at the time of their last reported sexual encounter in comparison with 10% of whites.[6] African-American teen births fell as much as they did in large part because abortion rates, which dropped substantially for white teens, remained much higher for minority teens. Unfortunately, the gains that occurred in the '90s are eroding, with teen pregnancies rising in 2006 for the first time since 1991, and black females aged 15–19 showed the largest increases.[7]

TABLE 11.1

| Age | Sexual Activity | Condom Use | Pregnancy Risk |
|---|---|---|---|
| 15–17 | –10% | +20% (58% of total) | –55% |
| 18–19 | No change | +16% (50% of total) | –27% |

The decline in teen pregnancies during the '90s did not carry over to unintended pregnancies for adult women; yet, women in their early 20s have dramatically more children (105.9 per 1,000 for women aged 20–24 compared to 41.9 per 1,000 teens aged 15–19) and therefore have disproportionately more impact in shaping the next generation.[8] While the percentage of teen births that occurs outside of marriage has always been relatively high, the dramatic rise in the overall percentage of nonmarital births has been driven by women in their 20s.[9] In 2006, 57.9% of births to women between the ages of 20 and 24 were to unmarried mothers compared to 31% of the births to women in their late 20s, and under 20% to women over 30.[10]

Neither the programs that encourage abstinence nor those that provide comprehensive sex education target women over 18. Among this group of young adults, the high percentage of unintended pregnancies has been driven by widening income and racial disparities.[11] In addition, overall rates of contraceptive use have declined since 2002, largely because fewer low-income women of color are using contraception,[12] with cost an important barrier to securing access to more-effective techniques.[13] Latina adults, for example, are three to four times more likely than white women to use no method of contraception.[14]

It follows that access to abortion is more critical to reproductive choice for poorer women and for women of color who are more likely to become unintentionally pregnant. Indeed, while half of all pregnancies in the United States are unintended (82% for teens and 70% for women in their 20s), the rate for African-American women is 69% compared to 54% for Latinas and only 40% for white women.[15] The disparities in abortion rates underscore the different racial and class patterns. Rebekah Smith emphasizes that, while overall abortion rates were declining in the '90s,[16] the women obtaining abortions were increasingly "never-married, low-income, non-white or Hispanic, and usually the parent of at least one child."[17] Poor women constituted 30% of all women of reproductive age in the United States, yet they obtained 57% of the abortions in 2000. White women had the lowest pregnancy rates and the lowest abortion rates (18%). Among blacks, 43% of conceptions ended in abortion. Latinas terminated their pregnancies 25% of the time.[18] The most-recent studies show that, while abortion rates have fallen for the entire population, they have fallen most dramatically for whites, increasing the percentage of abortion by nonwhite and Latina women to 67% of the total.[19]

Perhaps surprisingly, the reduction in abortions through the '90s was *not* primarily due to legal restrictions on abortion: "Almost two-thirds of the decline in the total number of abortions can be traced to eight [blue] jurisdictions with few or no abortion restrictions.... These jurisdictions also help women avoid unintended pregnancies by making contraception widely available."[20]

The link between contraception and abortion remains a site of political controversy, with social conservatives maintaining that an emphasis on abstinence and marriage should correlate with both less contraception (presumably because of less sex outside of marriage) and less abortion. Credible empirical studies, however, draw the opposite conclusion, showing that increases in the availability of effective contraception decrease the abortion rate more effectively.[21] Abstinence might delay sexual activity for small, self-motivated groups; as policy for the society at large, however, it cannot address the high rates of unplanned pregnancy for unmarried women in their 20s, and for the most economically vulnerable women, it is pointlessly cruel. The analysis that created the consensus for the contraceptive reform of the 1960s and '70s remains accurate: increased contraception produces dramatically greater declines in both unwanted births and abortions than do abstinence efforts alone, and public efforts are disproportionately important to poor women, who have less control over their own sexuality and less systematic access to birth control information or techniques.

The claim that abstinence alone can guide the transition to adulthood does not therefore address the real-world consequences of restrictions on the availability of birth control. The net result of such restrictions has been to reinforce the patterns that existed before the legalization of contraception; viz, secure access for the affluent and the sophisticated and declining availability for the most vulnerable, especially those dependent on government services.

## CONTRACEPTION: SECURING COMPREHENSIVE ACCESS

While the red and blue models differ in their approaches to when the use of birth control is appropriate, relatively few (outside of the Catholic Church) would favor making it entirely illegal—nor, as a practical matter, could they muster the political support necessary to do so.[22] Moreover, when the issue becomes appropriate state policy, as opposed to understandings within intimate relationships, it would be difficult to justify restrictions on the public as a whole on the basis of particular beliefs—the unacceptability of premarital sex and the insistence that the possibility of pregnancy not be averted—that cannot command more than minority support.

Part of the reason is that contraceptive use is close to universal. Among major religions, only Catholicism prohibits artificial contraception; yet, three-quarters of American Catholics favor relaxing the *church's* position on birth control.[23] Moreover, 97% of sexually active women report using contraception at some point in their lives, including 96% of Catholics. Indeed, a 2006 Wall Street Journal Online/ Harris Interactive Health-Care Poll found that 81% of all Americans (which included 81% of the Catholics and 75% of the born-again Christians who were surveyed) agree that greater access to birth control is an effective way to lower the number of abortions.[24]

We suspect that widespread public discussion of the availability of contraception would underscore the tensions within the red paradigm: many social conservatives see contraception as a linchpin in the cultural shift away from marriage.[25] On the other hand, the overwhelming majority of American women in both red and blue families use birth control at some point in their lives, the vast majority have sex before they marry (96%), and more than half of Americans (61%) approve of premarital sex, with a majority of only those over the age of 60 disagreeing.[26] Moreover, while the identification of sex with marriage is an important component of the *religious* core of the red paradigm, many social conservatives who would insist on the importance of marriage for childrearing would not necessarily favor restrictions on sexual activity.[27] Indeed, even among evangelicals, true abstinence is a minority strategy. That is, though evangelical Protestants show greater commitment to the idea of traditional sexual values, they are as likely as the rest of the population to engage in nonmarital sexuality. The substantial differences in behavior, like the major political divides, are those that separate the most devout, perhaps 25% of evangelical teens, from the less devout. While the former may in fact delay sexual activity to a greater degree than their less-pious peers, the level of nonmarital sexual activity among evangelicals as a group—and the corresponding need for contraception both within marriage and without—is at least as great as it is for everyone else.[28]

The question, then, is how to move away from the current impasse on control of fertility. At least part of the answer must be to rebuild the emphasis on contraception and move the discussion away from abortion. Fertility control is the core of reproductive autonomy, abortion the fallback that increases in importance when contraception fails. Renewed focus on the effect of minority activism in undercutting a principle that commands overwhelming support might help to reframe the issue in more compelling terms. Every woman, whether married or not, should have routine access to effective and reliable contraception, and she should be educated in ways that enable her to make an informed choice—not just while she is in high school but through the long years of potential fertility. Moreover, avoiding improvident births that shortchange the lives of the children who result, and who are likely to ultimately burden the public treasury, is a moral issue that should command public attention as an issue of its own. Finally, those committed to abortion rights should acknowledge that almost every abortion that occurs is one that could have been prevented through more readily available access to contraception.

The second part of the answer, however, involves reconsideration of the basis for protection of class interests within modern democracies. The Supreme Court has been willing to hold that the government cannot forbid access to birth control and abortion, but it has been much less willing to rule that the government must fund access that would make such "rights" meaningful.[29] Consequently, in the context of reproductive liberty, this distinction has served to reinforce the class-based nature of access to contraception. Emory historian David Garrow emphasizes that this division was true both before and after the Supreme Court's 1973 decision in *Roe*.[30] The matter of guaranteed access to basic services such as contraception must therefore be part of a broader effort to redefine the basic elements of middle-class life. Contraception, after all, is not just about wayward teens; it is an important part of adult life for all but a tiny fraction of women.

These issues will become more complex in the future as contraceptive options become more varied, often more expensive, and more dependent on access to medical care. Accordingly, comprehensive sex education, systematic access to contraception, nondiscriminatory access to birth control for unmarried women, and teen access should be seen as intertwined issues.

First, the choice between comprehensive sex education and abstinence-only education has profound consequences, particularly for lower-income women. Comprehensive sex education includes arguments for abstinence *as well as* medically accurate information about contraception. The issue is not whether the values underlying abstinence should be taught; it is whether they should be taught to the exclusion of other views.

One of the ironies of the fight over sex education in schools centers on the recent findings about virginity pledges. These studies conclude that such efforts are most effective when they are not part of a mandatory schoolwide program. Instead, it is the creation of a community of committed members, who voluntarily opt into such programs and who feel special because of the more-selective nature of the group membership, that has the biggest impact on teen behavior.[31]

At the same time, studies of contraceptive failure indicate that a lack of preparation and training is a bigger factor than lack of access per se. There is a failure "to teach, understand, admit or care that unprotected sex can lead to the creation...of a developing human being,"[32] and that individual and social responsibility requires systematic preparation for the consequences of sexuality on a lifelong basis, not just for what might occur in the backseat of the car on the night of the prom. Accordingly, strategies to deter teen births should not try to craft a one-size-fits-all approach. Targeted programs that focus on younger, more religious, or more committed teens might help to promote abstinence for longer periods among select groups. Information about effective contraception might also be packaged as part of the marriage preparation and promotion activities discussed in chapter 10. Special programs could be designed to focus on the most-at-risk teens, and more programs should be aimed at older teens and young adults, especially those at community colleges or those lacking access to health care. Finally, a critical component of the 1990s efforts focused on preventing sexually transmitted diseases, including HIV/AIDS, and these efforts have waned. A significant portion of young people fear STDs as much or more than they fear pregnancy.[33]

The second critical issue concerns guaranteeing comprehensive access to contraception. For adults, contraception access is largely a matter of funding and convenience. The most reliable methods are long-acting ones such as sterilization, intra-uterine devices, and hormonally based methods, such as Depo Provera or the birth control pill or patch. These methods, unlike lower-tech devices such as condoms, can be expensive and require access to a doctor and/or the ability to fill prescriptions. Accordingly, the reliability of contraceptive use corresponds to access to health care.[34]

Yet, the politicization of sexuality has produced systematic cutbacks in women's access to contraception because of (1) poorer women's general lack of access to medical insurance; (2) declining medical insurance coverage for women in their 20s; (3) cutbacks in the Medicaid program that restrict immigrants' eligibility generally, disproportionately affecting Latinas, and increasing documentation requirements that delay or frustrate access even for those women who are eligible;[35] (4) lack of adequate funding for Title X and other public family-planning efforts (now funded at 61% of 1980 levels); (5) restrictions on federal funding of abortion and related services, which have the effect of not only reducing access to abortion but of limiting abortion providers' ability to provide contraception as part of their follow-up care; (6) lack of coverage for reproductive services, including contraception, in many private health plans;[36] and (7) legal changes that have discouraged pharmaceutical companies from contributing discounted contraceptives to family-planning clinics.[37]

The figures on contraceptive access, however, are not entirely bleak. The number of private medical insurance programs covering contraception, for example, increased at the same time as public funding decreased;[38] the availability of emergency contraception such as the morning-after pill increased as abortion services available later in a pregnancy declined.[39] Removed from the public spotlight, moreover, the states have increased spending on some forms of contraception, if only because the financial savings from pregnancy prevention are so great. Medicaid finances 40% of American births. Reducing the number of unplanned pregnancies thus saves substantial expenditures of public funds. The states have been authorized to apply for "Medicaid waivers," allowing them to use federal funds for family-planning efforts for women who would not otherwise be eligible for Medicaid benefits. Initially, only a few states applied, but today half of the states have received permission for Medicaid waivers, covering more than two-thirds of women nationally. Studies show that the Medicaid family-planning expansions result in lower birthrates, with the broad, income-based programs having the greatest impact. Moreover, the states receiving such waivers include a broad cross-section of red and blue states, including almost all of the South except for Georgia. The irony is that the major provision the Obama administration dropped from the stimulus bill as part of the compromise to get it passed was a measure that would have reduced the administrative hassles that states face in applying for the waiver. The brouhaha over the issue underscores the discrepancies between political rhetoric and state needs.[40]

Third, policy choices that ensure equal access to contraceptives for unmarried women continue to be important. The distinction between married and unmarried women, though important to those who would like to insist on the unity of sexuality and marriage, is unlikely to reemerge as a barrier to contraception. Even if the Supreme Court should disavow the line of privacy cases that began with *Griswold* and includes *Roe v. Wade*, equal protection principles are likely to continue to protect unmarried women's access to birth control within the constitutional framework.[41] This is particularly true given that distinctions based on marriage correspond to important race- and class-based inequalities. More than 70% of African-American births, for example, are nonmarital compared to half that rate for whites and 50% of Latina births. Moreover, as discussed above, the least-educated quartile of women have a nonmarital birthrate over 40% compared with less than 10% for the most-educated quartile. Any restriction in access by marital status would thus compound class- and race-based inequalities.

Finally, adolescent access to contraception remains a much more divisive issue, particularly access without parental consent. Although the Supreme Court decision guaranteeing contraceptive access to teens remains good law, a number of states have taken measures that undercut ready access, and the current Supreme Court might well cut back on teen access to contraception just as it has on teen access to abortion.

In almost half of the states, a minor has an explicit right of access to contraceptives without parental notification or consent (that is, state law guarantees access even without federal constitutional protection), and most other states provide minors access if they are married or have ever been pregnant, are a high school graduate, or receive a physician's referral.[42] Massachusetts and New York even fund a program that provides confidential contraceptive services for minors,[43] although two states—Texas and Utah—explicitly require parental consent for state-funded programs.[44] Moreover, a number of states that have received Medicaid waivers limit their programs to women over the age of 19.[45] The federal programs, including Title X and Medicaid, require that their services be provided on a confidential basis, precluding parental notification or consent, and, as discussed in chapter 5, the courts have upheld such requirements.

The issue of adolescent access is a critical one because teen pregnancy has more negative consequences on mothers and children and because parental consent requirements overwhelmingly result in less teen contraceptive use. On the other hand, the issue of parental authority touches a responsive chord in many parts of the population, with minority parents, in particular, often favoring parental involvement laws.[46]

This is an arena where the effects of polarized political discourse are particularly pernicious. Scholars and government officials who work closely with teens recognize that parental involvement laws largely have the effect of discouraging contraceptive use without necessarily deterring teen sexuality. For the teens from the poorest and most-troubled families, it reinforces a sense that things happen without much ability to plan for or control them. Political attention focused on parental consent produces counterproductive results. As the *Ayotte* case demonstrated in the context of abortion, partisan fights over family values undermine the leadership role of the courts in defusing the issues and leave standing cynical policies that disproportionately disadvantage the most vulnerable—all in the name of "moral" values.

## EMERGENCY CONTRACEPTION: INCREASING THE OPTIONS?

Contraceptive use is likely to become more complicated and varied in the future as options expand. Already, officials recommend the use of multiple methods, including the pill, an IUD, or an implantable to provide long-term protection; condoms as barriers that prevent the transmission of disease; and the morning-after pill as a backup measure if other methods fail. Yet, controversy over new methods such as emergency contraception demonstrates the political hurdles that red-blue divisions create to more systematic prevention of unplanned births.

The Food and Drug Administration approved Plan B, or levonorgestrel (the morning-after pill), as a prescription drug in 1999.[47] For maximum effectiveness, the pills must be taken within 72 hours of unprotected intercourse because they are designed to interfere with the processes leading up to implantation. Plan B, which is also called emergency contraception, differs from RU-486 in that the latter can dislodge an existing pregnancy even after the embryo has implanted in the uterine wall, and it can be effective within 49 days after the beginning of the women's last period.

In April 2003, the company that manufactured Plan B (now Barr Pharmaceuticals) filed an application to make Plan B available without a prescription. The result, of course, would be to make it more widely available and less expensive to obtain. Later that year, two FDA advisory committees voted (23–4) to approve the application, without any limitation on the age of the recipient, and relevant FDA staff indicated their support. Nonetheless, the FDA issued a statement of non-approval, explaining, among other reasons, that it was concerned about the safety of Plan B for women under the age of 16. Barr filed a second application in July 2004, asking that the drug be approved without a prescription for girls and women aged 16 or older. Almost two years later, the Food and Drug Administration finally approved the over-the-counter availability of Plan B, but only for women 18 years or older. Minors need a prescription to obtain the drug. The FDA based this restriction on a lack of adequate data concerning the safety of Plan B for minors—even though numerous medical groups, including the American Academy of Pediatrics, supported its availability.[48]

The background story is far more interesting. During the first phase of the FDA's deliberations, when it was considering the initial application, several employees of the FDA testified in depositions that they were told that rejecting Plan B was a political necessity. The *New York Times* reported that Dr. John Jenkins, who directed the agency's Office of New Drugs, said in a deposition that his boss, Dr. Steven Galson, told him:

> [H]e felt he "didn't have a choice" but to reject the application.... "And he characterized that in a sense that he wasn't sure that he would be allowed to remain as center director if he didn't agree with the action," Dr. Jenkins said.... Dr. Florence Houn, director of the office that evaluated the Plan B application, said that she was told by Dr. Janet Woodcock, a deputy F.D.A. commissioner, that a rejection was necessary "to appease the administration's constituents, and then later this could be approved."[49]

Indeed, an internal memo of the FDA expressed the concern of Janet Woodcock, the deputy operations commissioner, that "we could not anticipate or prevent extreme promiscuous behaviors such as the medication taking on an 'Urban Legend' status that would lead adolescents to form sex-based cults centered around the use of Plan B."[50]

When the Government Accountability Office subsequently investigated the FDA's process in considering the drug, it found that the FDA deviated from its usual procedures for approval of new drugs.[51] The FDA's high-level management was much more involved in the Plan B application than in comparable applications concerning over-the-counter status. Moreover, the rationale for the non-approval—that data on older adolescents could not be applied to younger adolescents and that the over-the-counter status of Plan B might have an effect "on the propensity for younger adolescents to engage in unsafe sexual behaviors because of their lack of cognitive maturity"—simply "did not follow FDA's traditional practices."[52] Instead, the FDA had previously relied on data for older adolescents in deciding on a drug's safety for younger adolescents, and the agency had not previously considered "behavioral implications due to differences in cognitive development." Indeed, in a subsequent lawsuit about the FDA's actions, a federal court found that there was "a strong preliminary showing" of "bad faith or improper behavior" on the part of the FDA.[53]

During the second phase, while the FDA was considering the amended application, Susan Wood, who was the director of the Office of Women's Health at the FDA, resigned in frustration. She told Ted Koppel on *Nightline* that she quit because she "felt that science was being overruled at [the] FDA and women's health was being damaged."[54] A few months later, Dr. Frank Davidoff, a former editor in chief of the *Annals of Internal Medicine*, resigned as a member of an FDA advisory committee, explaining that he could "no longer associate myself with an organization that is capable of making such an important decision so flagrantly on the basis of political influence."[55]

So what was behind all of this political maneuvering? The Plan B controversy demonstrates the conflation of the anti-abortion religious stance—the mere possibility that the drug might make implantation in the uterine wall less likely is enough for some opponents to label it "abortion"—with the determination to bring back pregnancy as the penalty for improvident sex.[56] Some opponents treat Plan B as a form of abortion because they fear it may interfere with the implantation of a fertilized egg in the uterine wall. Plan B, which uses a large dose of the same hormones used in the birth control pill, is primarily designed to prevent ovulation, and animal studies indicate that it does not block implantation of a fertilized egg.[57] Nonetheless, it is impossible to rule out the possibility that it will interfere with implantation and thus act after, rather than before, conception.

Church opposition, especially by Catholics, might therefore be understandable. In fact, however, almost all opponents, including the Catholic Church, almost immediately added concern about encouraging sexuality to their anti-abortion arguments. As one witness testified at hearings held in December 2003 on the drug, "It is self-evident that over-the-counter availability of the morning after pill will lead to increased promiscuity and its attendant physical and psychological damage."[58] The Concerned Women for America alleged that it would result in an "increase in the already too high STD rates by encouraging risky sexual activity, and be given by statutory rapists to adolescents to cover up the continuing abuse."[59] In its "fact" sheet on contraceptive mandates, the U.S. Conference of Catholic Bishops alleges that improved access to contraception does not decrease the number of unwanted pregnancies.[60] It is also concerned that mandating insurance coverage of contraceptives for minors would subvert parental rights over their children.[61]

In contrast, those advocating the wider availability of Plan B argued that emergency contraception could provide significant help in reducing the number of unplanned teen pregnancies and abortions.[62] In their testimony supporting the availability of Plan B, representatives of the National Partnership for Women and Families pointed out that about one-half of the unplanned pregnancies in the United States each year result from contraceptive failure and that women could be trusted to use Plan B responsibly.[63] While studies have not yet established whether widespread use of Plan B will reduce the pregnancy rate, the initial testing suggests that it does not affect the rate of unprotected sex and that the ease of access makes women more likely to use it.[64] In other countries that permit its use, the primary result has been a decrease in the abortion rate.[65]

The FDA's regulations determine the availability of emergency contraception for the entire country. In addition, different states determine how it will be distributed. More than half of all states require that, if private insurance policies cover prescription drugs, then they must also cover all FDA-approved contraceptives, including emergency contraception, with most other states providing for general coverage except for certain insurance plans and employers; indeed, only 2 states (North Carolina and Arkansas) explicitly exclude emergency contraceptives from this mandate.[66] Nonetheless, in other states, Plan B may be excluded from Medicaid coverage. By contrast, in 15 states, emergency rooms are required to provide information about emergency contraceptives, and, in more than two-thirds of these states, emergency rooms can dispense Plan B upon the request of a sexual assault victim.[67]

The arguments that Plan B will affect sexual behavior, though not implausible, are not fundamentally different from those about contraception more generally. It is certainly true that the widespread availability of reliable forms of contraception such as the pill has had an impact on sexual practices, and particularly on the acceptability of nonmarital intercourse. Nonetheless, the change in mores was established without the availability of Plan B, and the greater availability of emergency contraception is unlikely to have much impact on overall sexual behavior. Its primary effect is likely to be in cases of contraceptive failure in preventing pregnancy.

The larger issue here, though, is about the integrity of national institutions—and the willingness to use contraception as a wedge issue to rally support for the red paradigm. At the height of the controversy over Plan B, the Bush White House refused to respond to a question from reporters about whether the president supported the right to use contraception.[68] As the FDA controversy illustrates, the moral concerns of Plan B opponents are not scientific reasons to block national approval nor to require a prescription (as opposed to over-the-counter sale), and the FDA is not charged with oversight of American sexual behavior. This type of action at the national level thus represents the imposition of the views of one side of an ideological dispute on the country as a whole.

## ABORTION: RIGHTS TALK DEEMPHASIZED

If contraception is essential to women's reproductive autonomy, then abortion is more tangential. That is, abortion is an important fallback when contraception fails, but so long as contraception is readily available, the greater or lesser availability of abortion is unlikely to have a major impact on sexual behavior or family formation. Instead, it is important to the construction of family understandings in two critical ways. First, restrictions on abortion, like restrictions on contraception, disproportionately harm the most-vulnerable women. Second, abortion, to a much greater degree than contraception, serves as a political flashpoint that galvanizes opposing forces. And divisions on abortion, unlike divisions on contraception, have become greater over time. The use of abortion as a political issue reflects the determination to exacerbate or ameliorate the differences between the two family systems. The only way to deemphasize the attention paid to abortion is to place greater emphasis on contraception, not as a compromise measure, but as the critical pathway to reproductive autonomy.

Let's start with the practicalities. Difficulties in access to contraception affect the abortion rate. Few women would "choose" abortion if they could otherwise avoid the pregnancy in the first place. Instead, abortion rates are largely a consequence of unintended pregnancies. Unintended pregnancies and subsequent abortions, of course, are more common for those who lack access to effective contraception. As public family-planning efforts have waned, the percentage of abortion by minority women has increased (two-thirds of the total), and the 30% of women who are poor had 57% of the abortions. Any greater restrictions on abortion would therefore disproportionately disadvantage poorer women and potentially lead to the return of dangerous, back-alley abortions.

Nonetheless, abortion remains intrinsically divisive: 60% of liberal Democrats believe that abortion should be generally available in comparison with only 17% of conservative Republicans, while 50% of conservative Republicans believe that abortion should be illegal with few exceptions compared to only 13% of liberal Democrats.[69] Moreover, these positions have hardened over time.[70] In May 2009, a Gallup poll found that more Americans described themselves as "pro-life" (51%) than as "pro-choice" (42%), the first time a majority had done so since Gallup started asking the question in the mid-1990s, and the largest reason for the change was the increase in the number of Republicans (from 60% to 70%) identifying as pro-life.[71]

Finally, as poor and minority women dominate the group resorting to abortion, the support for the type of abortions that poor women have may decline. The most-recent indications are that the number of abortion clinics has decreased nationally, and readily available access exists primarily in urban areas. Guttmacher Institute researchers report that 92% of nonmetropolitan women and 24% of those in metropolitan areas lack an abortion facility in their county.[72] The only increases in the number of abortion facilities have come from those using nonsurgical methods such as "the abortion pill," RU-486, which are easier to integrate into nonspecialized medical settings. Nonsurgical methods, however, can only be used in the early part of pregnancy, and women who lack access to health care or who must raise the money for the procedure often wait until later in the pregnancy, making surgical techniques the only possibility.[73] The gestational age at which abortions occur has shifted to earlier in the pregnancy, with the percentage of abortions occurring within the first six weeks of pregnancy doubling from 14% in 1992 to 28% by 2004. Sixty percent take place within the first eight weeks, and 90% in the first trimester.[74] Later abortions overwhelmingly occur because of later detection of the pregnancy, difficulties in arranging funding, reluctance to tell others (such as parents or partners), or unanticipated health risks to the mother or fetus.[75] The latter category, which includes the type of medical issues that prompt late-term abortions, are rare; the other factors correspond to the wealth and sophistication of the women involved. As a result, middle-class women increasingly rely on more-effective contraception, the morning-after pill, and chemical abortion, potentially undermining support for the later surgical abortions, which are of greater importance to the less affluent.

The best strategy is one that changes the subject. We must emphasize that the most-effective way to reduce abortions is to increase the use of contraception. The issue should not be the acceptability of abortion; all of us would prefer to reduce its incidence. Instead, government policy should turn on the most-effective methods of doing so.

## MORE FERTILITY?

Contraception allows for more control over the timing of pregnancy and facilitates a blue lifestyle with later childbearing. The corollary to this delay is support for the choices that come with emotional maturity and financial independence. Childbearing once followed automatically from sexual activity; infertility occurred mysteriously and often unpredictably in the context of marriage. Today, some men and women are childless by choice. For those who want children, but delay childbearing, a predictable consequence is greater difficulty with conception—and therefore greater demand for assisted reproduction, or medical procedures that involve handling both egg and sperm. Women's fertility declines as they age, particularly after the age of 35, and more than 1 million women each year have a medical appointment about infertility. In 2006, more than 50,000 children were born through in vitro fertilization (IVF) and similar procedures.[76] Yet, the systematic provision of services—research, testing, regulation, insurance coverage, and financing—has been caught up in the same political divisions that hamstring more systematic approaches to contraception. We believe that the two issues are related; the high level of unintended pregnancy in the United States masks falling fertility rates for significant portions of the population. We also believe that the time has come to make the use of assisted reproductive technologies (ART) a regulatory issue rather than a moral one.

Legislative and regulatory oversight of assisted reproduction, especially at the national level, has been characterized by moral posturing and regulatory gridlock. Although the issue commands less political attention than abortion, it also starts with disagreement on the moral status of the embryo. Restrictions on embryo research (many of which were lifted early in the Obama administration), for example, meant that the federal government would not fund studies designed to improve ART success rates. Moreover, the topic of assisted reproduction is often associated with lifestyles that inflame cultural tensions. Significant portions of the public have no sympathy, for example, for the professional woman who delayed motherhood to establish her career, the single woman who would like a child without marriage (perhaps because of a ticking biological clock), or the gay or lesbian couple who cannot produce a child on their own. Yet, these prospective parents are much more likely than those who become accidentally pregnant to bring careful planning, maturity, and significant emotional and financial resources to parenting—and they are likely to have children whether or not the techniques they use to do so are the subject of government oversight.

While the basic *moral* issues involve the acceptability of any form of ART—the Vatican is vehemently opposed—the most basic *regulatory* issues involve the relationship between funding and oversight. In Europe, states subsidize assisted reproduction to a considerable degree within state health systems, so government can also guide practices through selective funding. Many European countries, for example, have limited multiple births even with the potential trade-off of lower success rates. In the United States, the cost of ART, combined with a lack of public funding and, in many cases, of private insurance coverage, increases the pressure to use techniques more likely to produce a pregnancy (such as transferring multiple eggs during an IVF cycle), even if these techniques increase the risk of birth defects.[77]

The question of acceptable reproduction similarly turns on the ability of a prospective parent to find a clinic that will provide services. The result combines systematic (and sometimes arbitrary) discrimination by many clinics with the development of for-profit services that cater to those able to pay for them. A survey of fertility clinics found that approximately half of them indicated that they were likely to turn away a man without a wife or partner, 20% would not provide services to a woman without a spouse, 17% would not provide services to a lesbian couple, and 5% would not offer services to a biracial couple.[78]

Among the list of prescriptions excluded from Medicaid coverage in most states are those for fertility, alongside those for weight loss. Although these limitations on access to infertility services only concern funding issues, they express policy judgments concerning who should be able to reproduce on a variety of levels. First, by excluding funding for infertility services for those receiving public benefits, states exclude poorer infertile people from being able to reproduce. While not the same as sterilizing the "mentally unfit," this decision about how to allocate state funding deprives a group of people of the means of reproduction. Second, by not requiring insurance plans to cover a range of infertility services, states are deciding that infertile people should not be treated in the same way as those who are eligible for pregnancy and other health-related services. Finally, by limiting coverage to heterosexual married couples, some states are reinforcing the exclusion from parenthood of people who are single and of gays and lesbians.[79]

Full discussion of these issues is beyond the scope of this book. Instead, we observe that, just as the red family prescriptions may be pointlessly cruel to those who lack the means to avoid unwanted pregnancies, the blue paradigm prescriptions of mature family planning may lead any number of women into involuntary childlessness. Later childbearing inevitably means lower rates of fertility, even if later childbearing produces healthier childrearing. Poorer women experience infertility issues at younger ages than the more affluent, in part because of their lack of access to health care that might prevent diseases that interfere with reproduction. And without insurance coverage, the most-successful techniques are beyond the reach of many of those with middle-class incomes. Recognition of the shifting patterns of family formation therefore suggests a growing need for honesty in the consideration of the resulting costs. What we would like to see is greater support for the inclusion of reproductive services as part of a wholesale discussion of health care reform.

We nonetheless recognize that the trade-offs in any comprehensive approach will be difficult to negotiate in a divisive environment.

First, assisted reproduction is expensive and controversial. Since the most-educated women are the most likely to postpone childbearing, any wholesale public subsidization of assisted reproduction would be a wealth transfer to the most affluent. While we believe reproductive health care should be treated on the same basis as other health services, fair-minded reform can only take place in the context of a comprehensive overhaul of a system that currently fails to provide basic health services to those most in need.

Second, where public health care systems have included assisted reproduction, they have paired widespread support with widespread limitations. These limitations typically include not only safety-based regulation, such as restrictions on the number of embryos transferred in a cycle of assisted reproduction, but also cost-saving measures, such as limitations on the number of IVF cycles permitted, and eligibility rules that often exclude the unmarried. These restrictions are at odds with the American tradition of private medical decision making; yet, public discussion of eligibility criteria might undermine support for extending coverage at all.

Third, religious objections might make it difficult to muster the appropriate public support or skew the terms of the coverage provided. The Catholic Church has repeatedly affirmed its opposition to in vitro fertilization, for example, and California, which otherwise mandates insurance coverage for fertility treatments, excludes the portion of reproductive services associated with IVF, most likely in response to the religious objections.[80] The most telling experience, however, may well be that around the issue of reproductive cloning. With anti-abortion activists favoring wholesale restrictions on embryo manipulation or research while other legislators favored restrictions only on reproductive cloning itself, the U.S. Congress and most state legislatures have found that they can pass no legislation at all.[81]

These moral clashes, once again, have significant consequences for how men and women pursue an education, find a job, find a partner—and have children. Throughout the industrialized world, biological and social imperatives are on a collision course. The established and mature produce healthier children, but have a harder time conceiving them. Poorer women, by having children at younger ages, risk locking themselves and their offspring into cycles of poverty, but they face an even greater likelihood of childlessness than better-off women if they wait. Religious ethicist Karey Harwood, after an extensive study of infertility, recommends that women consider having children in their 20s, before the biological reality of infertility—even if that means that they are not yet established in their careers.[82] Indeed, reconfiguring the blue world to permit women to return to the workforce after they have their children may be an easier project than reconfiguring relationships to allow parents to both marry young and stay together at least through their children's minority. A technological solution—harvesting and freezing sperm and eggs in secure vaults until the propitious moment—may actually be easier than the social engineering necessary to bring our socioeconomic and biological lives back in sync.

Nonetheless, if we are to address the issue of fertility in all of its guises, we need to examine the trade-offs among family and education and career. In the final chapter, we turn to discussions of balance between family life and career, exploring marriage and then some dilemmas of work/family.

## CHAPTER 12

# Work and Family

## *Retooling the Foundation in Deep Purple*

THE REVOLUTION IN moral values we have charted in this book is most fundamentally about a long-term restructuring of the relationships between work and family, which has required, in turn, restructuring relationships between men and women. The largely agricultural world of the colonies experienced no separation between home and market. Commercial production took place on family farms and in urban shops with families nearby, ready to help out. The separation of the two arose with industrialization; the man of the household commuted to an office or factory while his wife, at least in the families wealthy enough to permit it, stayed home to preside over a reconstituted family realm that invested more in its offspring. The information economy is now transforming the separate spheres of the industrial economy.

Family formation has been profoundly affected by the greater demands of the information economy for formal education, for specialized experience, and for the nimbleness to change jobs repeatedly. While the increasing pressures to devote more energy to career preparation and job development encourage later family formation, they simultaneously undermine the economic opportunities available to those ready to start family formation at early ages. As women move out of the home and into the workforce, this makes investment in and supervision of children that much harder to ensure.

The immediate result of these economic changes has been to increase the disparities between social classes and regions: inequalities in wealth, wages, and family well-being have grown. An increasing literature maintains that the stakes have risen not just for those on the losing end of this transformation, but for the country as a whole. America's rise to prominence, according to an impressive body of research, rested on the superior education of its citizens, and yet, over the last half-century, the country as a whole has lost ground to the rest of the industrialized world.[1] Remarkably little of that literature addresses the family changes we have documented in this book. We believe that at the core of the challenge posed by the reorganization of the relationship between work and family is the need to rethink human capital formation—human capital that depends both on the effective instruction of children and on rebuilding the pathways from adolescence into adulthood.

This interaction between work and family differs for our prototypical blue and red families. The blue family strategy, which invests heavily in human capital acquisition for both its sons and its daughters, puts biology and economics on a collision course: women's biological clocks stop ticking just as they are ready to start a family. The irony is that women's ability to provide additional resources for their children increases as their overall fertility is decreasing—reducing the number of children born to well-educated parents optimally prepared to care for them.

This irony creates a new set of dilemmas: because well-educated women have more human capital, they have an easier time finding more-flexible workplaces. But as every student of the "mommy track" knows, departure from the model of full-time worker brings disproportionate decreases in benefits and pay—and these decreases may be even more disproportionate for the fathers who would like to spend more time with their children.[2] These situations often peak at the point in the late 30s and early 40s when older couples experience the greatest reproductive and work tensions. We consider in this chapter whether these issues are, at least in part, ones of transition that might benefit from greater public discussion and oversight.

Red communities are more likely to be built around marriage and childrearing, and the early to mid-20s is the time to start families in these communities. Yet, the current economy fails to provide the jobs that facilitate men's and women's assumption of family responsibilities, family-friendly workplaces that allow parents to combine work and children without shortchanging either, or the integration of educational opportunities into the workplace so that parents can continue to acquire human capital while they financially support their families. As a result, early marriage and childbearing may interfere with the educational attainment necessary to provide a secure future, and the lack of security threatens family stability, which in turn worsens the prospects for the next generation. The challenge is to more effectively integrate the overlapping worlds of work and family to permit those who begin family lives earlier to continue to acquire the education and skills needed for their families to flourish, while ensuring that those who have families only after their careers are established do not face disproportionate penalties for contributing to their children's lives.

For both red and blue families, work/family balance is thus a critical part of the response to the second demographic transformation. Everyone benefits from family-friendly pathways into the workforce and family-friendly workplaces. Notwithstanding the universality of the problem, however, proposing solutions falls into the red-blue ideological and political chasm about the relationship between government and markets:[3] questions about whether private actors should band together to push for workforce reform or whether government mandates should prompt more universal measures show the political complexity of developing solutions.

Remaking the workforce to facilitate childbearing and two-parent childrearing is the uncompleted component of the blue family revolution and, as the Europeans have already realized, a necessary support for preserving fertility.[4] For red family rebuilding, reestablishing the links between employment and family stands as the missing element: young men who lack the means to be effective providers are unlikely to establish strong families, and young women who must work in unsatisfying jobs to compensate for the lack of family income are likely to be less tolerant of their husband's shortcomings. Work/family issues are just as important for red, working-class families as they are for blue, upper middle-class professionals. Accordingly, this chapter proposes changes in the structures that support the transition to adulthood and that support the integration of work and family. These reforms include laws that apply, first, to the workplace itself; second, to support for women's continued human capital acquisition; and third, to the structure of employment for men; in short, they address the pathways *into* the workplace as well as the pathways to balance *within* the workplace.

# PATHWAYS INTO THE WORKPLACE: TOEING THE LINE?

In the era that followed World War II, education, work, and family occurred in lockstep. That is, Americans completed their educations—typically, high school—and women married soon after they finished school. Men entered the workforce, and shortly thereafter, they undertook family responsibilities, often staying with a single employer through retirement. If an inopportune pregnancy prompted earlier marriage, it derailed educational plans, and family responsibilities made it more difficult to return to school or to change careers.

Today, the security of long-term employment is harder to come by. At the same time, employers provide less training and place more emphasis on hiring workers who have acquired their skills elsewhere. Updating education and skills, whether through experience, individual efforts, or a return to school has also become more important. The lockstep world is gone.

These changes in the economic world have had the most disproportionately negative effects on young men, who have become less likely than young women to complete college and who may find the stepping-stones to secure employment more treacherous. As we have argued throughout the book, this has resulted in greater underemployment as well as employment instability for men in their 20s.

For young women, these economic changes have increased the price of inopportune pregnancies. These pregnancies continue to derail education at the same time that working-class families have become more dependent on dual incomes. These young women lose out in multiple ways as early pregnancies (often unplanned) depress their own earnings on a lifetime basis, make divorce and single-parenthood more likely, and reduce the resources they have to invest in their children.

## Educational Flexibility for Women

The negative cycles at the core of a traditional family strategy that promotes abstinence, early marriage, and childbearing stem from the educational disruption involved. In today's economy, these changes affect both men and women.

While men continue to earn somewhat more than women, the differences among women have become a much more significant factor in family well-being. In 2004, for example, women with college degrees earned an average monthly income of $2,851, while women with high school educations earned less than half—$1,357—and those with graduate degrees earned even more, $4,837.[5]

The impact of early childbearing aggravates these disparities. New parents in less-privileged families may feel great pressure to drop out of high school and/or to enter the labor market as soon as they can get a job. It takes considerable discipline for any teen to manage a baby and stay in school. Almost 60% of teens with a school-age pregnancy drop out of high school compared to the 25% dropout rate of teens who do not have a child before they turn 18.[6] Only 2% of teen mothers will graduate from college, while four times that number of women who don't have children until 20 or 21 will graduate.

Educational attainment also affects the likelihood that a mother will stay in the workforce. Economist Heather Boushey found that the "child penalty," the effect of having a child on labor force participation rates, is negligible for highly educated women, while it is considerable for women with less education; the employment rate for women with less education who had children at home was 21.7% less than for those women with the same education who did not have children at home, while for women with a graduate degree, the penalty rate was 1.3%.[7] The disparity most likely reflects a number of factors: less-educated women are more likely to find that the cost of child care exceeds the amount of money they would make by working; with less-reliable child care, they may find it more difficult to stay employed; they are more likely to hold traditional values about women's roles; they are less likely to be able to secure satisfying jobs; and the jobs they are able to find are less likely to be flexible about children's illnesses or babysitting emergencies. Whatever the source, lesser income in turn reduces the resources that the parents can bring to childrearing.

This lack of resources affects the marital and employment prospects of the next generation as well. Eighty-two percent of children whose parents do not have a high school diploma live in poverty. Seventy-five percent of unmarried teen mothers begin to receive welfare within five years of their first child. Children of teen mothers don't perform as well in school as children of older mothers; for example, they are 50% more likely to repeat a grade.[8] Moreover, as we discussed above, divorce rates—and single-parenthood from all sources—are likely to be greater for those women who either marry at younger ages or fail to complete school.

Clearly, early childbearing has a negative impact on human capital attainment and the lifetime opportunities for success for these mothers and their children. Ameliorating this negative impact involves focusing on the ability of young mothers to continue their schooling in conjunction with meeting familial responsibilities and while also working part-time or full-time. This means developing policies that focus on

- the cost of higher education, especially for those who have families to support. Calculation of university expenses for financial aid purposes should include, for example, the cost of child care and medical insurance.[9]
- more-flexible programs, including community college classes that can be scheduled either to correspond to elementary and high school schedules, or with on-site day care to allow older women to return to school. Some of the most promising developments may be the expansion of online courses and degree programs that make it easier to tailor individual schedules around child care needs.[10]
- community college and apprenticeship programs designed to allow less-skilled workers to return to school to retool their skills or to obtain the education they need to switch jobs or receive promotions.
- enforcement of age discrimination and "maternal wall"[11] regulations that specifically target the ability of women to return to work as their children become more independent.

The tools to implement these programs already exist. Consider, for example, community colleges, which enroll almost one-half of all undergraduate students.[12] Community colleges are a much more affordable alternative to four-year institutions, they have open admission programs, and they are usually geographically accessible. For low-income students, blacks, and Latinos, community colleges are their primary method for beginning higher education.[13] Many community colleges are developing programs that help all students to stay in school as well as programs focused on young mothers. Child care centers provide an important service for parents, and some community colleges offer classes to help students think through their reproductive health. On the other hand, almost two-thirds of entering community college students are not academically prepared for college-level courses,[14] creating an enormous challenge to ensuring students' success. States are also experimenting with "career pathways" that connect "educational programs with integrated work experience, on-the-job training, and support services."[15]

Once people obtain desirable jobs, then they need assurances that taking care of a child will not jeopardize their employment opportunities; they need some workplace flexibility as well as family-related benefits. Law professor Joan Williams has defined a "maternal wall" that many women confront: "the strong negative competence and commitment assumptions triggered by motherhood."[16] Both men and women may also, she argues, experience "family responsibility discrimination," in which employees experience discrimination because of their caretaking obligations.[17] The number of lawsuits with such claims has been steadily increasing, and both the states and the federal government are developing new policies in this area. In 2007, the federal Equal Employment Opportunity Commission set out guidelines on the types of actions that might qualify as caretaker discrimination, including stereotyped assumptions about women's potential familial responsibilities and denying opportunities to men that are available for women based on gendered assumptions about caretaking obligations.[18]

### Pathway Support for Men

Young men remain less likely than young women to have full-time child care responsibilities, and unskilled men have more leisure time today than they did a generation ago. The challenge for young men, therefore, is the need for more-stable employment and employment that still allows them to share child care responsibilities with the mothers of their children. Again, we note the class divide that underlies our blue and red paradigms more generally. For middle-class men, the demands of the workplace are similar to, if not greater than, those that women face; the need to create workplaces that encourage middle-class men to take family leave is a priority. For working-class men, who tend to form families at younger ages and who enjoy diminishing workforce prospects, the larger struggle is to obtain employment at all. Yet, stable employment is essential not only to men's income opportunities, but to their prospects for successful families.

Accordingly, it is critical to support young men in entering and staying in the workforce. The same programs we discussed for women, including improved community college programs and protection from caretaking discrimination, are critical for men as well. More focused efforts might also include:

- attention to the affordability and flexibility of higher education, in ways that affect both men's and women's distinctive needs and life patterns;

- apprenticeship programs likely to lead to permanent positions;
- community college programs directly tied to job placement; and
- keeping community college programs affordable.

Universal service opportunities or requirements, which could include a variety of military and volunteer obligations of various kinds, might provide reinforcement for the transition from school to adult responsibilities. These opportunities might involve mentoring, pay commensurate with the positions, service in a variety of needed occupations, and some job training or skills acquisition.

## TOWARD A FAMILY-FRIENDLY WORKPLACE

Keeping parents, particularly women, in the workplace means paying attention to people's lives outside of the workplace. Our work and home lives are separate, and therein lies the problem. When a child is sick, or when there's a parent-teacher conference, a parent may risk losing pay—or even her job—in order to leave work to care for the child or to talk to the teacher. As Joan Williams has eloquently maintained, the existing American workplace is the product of the nineteenth-century family that emerged from the first demographic transformation.[19] This family, which generated the male investment that created the middle class of the industrial era, produced "ideal workers" with spouses who oversaw the domestic realm. The newly enhanced domestic realm, shorn of the family's earlier productive activities, included not only childrearing, but the housekeeping activities—cooking, laundering, errand running, and entertaining—necessary to support the employee spouse. Modern studies of family time, in contrast, indicate that, with dual-earner families, women spend as much time as they did in the earlier era with their children, men spend more, and the time spent on housekeeping has plummeted.[20] What has not kept pace is the redesign of workplaces to complement the reorganization of family responsibilities.

The term for this workplace reform is "work/family balance," and its goal is to achieve the balance that makes it possible for women to remain in the workplace without shortchanging their children and for men to contribute more at home without risking their jobs. Tension between the two may be inevitable, but it is not inevitable that employees must choose between losing their jobs or staying home to care for a sick child, nor is it inevitable that enrolling a child in Little

League requires leaving work at 2 P.M. to drive the child to practice at 3 P.M. Family support policies, such as family leave, state-supported preschools, longer school days and years, and flex-time can help in balancing the needs of society and families.

## THE IDEOLOGICAL DIVIDE

All families experience work/family tensions, and both Obama and McCain included the issue in their presidential platforms. The two parties agree, fundamentally, on the need to provide support to ensure that family members can work and that workers can be family members, recognizing the significance of this issue for most Americans. On the other hand, they disagree on the optimal mix of incentives versus government mandates to ensure support. This disagreement obscures both the source of the problem and the potential for broad-based policies.

First, the discussion cloaks the fact that the issue of work/family balance takes on different meanings for different groups within American society. A larger number of Americans work longer hours per week than do employees in most of the industrialized world; a larger number of women do so in the United States than anywhere else on the globe.[21] Americans do so for a variety of reasons that include cultural differences between the United States and other countries,[22] lesser regulation of hours and working conditions in the United States than in Europe, a shift toward "lean production" techniques that include a reduction in the number of permanent workers but increased hours worked to maintain a constant flow of goods and services, and an increase in the cost of benefits, such as health care, that make benefit-paying positions more expensive.[23] The increase in hours worked, however, is very much a class-based affair. In 1965, the correlation between hours worked and leisure time did not vary by class.[24] Today, it varies inversely with socioeconomic status. Certain high-paying and high-status positions command the greatest number of hours of employment. At the same time, less-skilled men work fewer hours today than in the recent past, in large part because of underemployment. Less-skilled women work more than they once did (also in part because of male underemployment) and more than they would prefer to work, but not necessarily more than other workers in the economy.[25] Looking at the last several decades, the biggest shift has been in the number of weekly hours worked by *families* rather than individuals, exacerbating time binds[26]—

and the largest of these increases has been among the most-educated, where both high-status men's and women's workforce involvement have shown the greatest growth.

This greater inequality in the distribution of both income and hours increases pressures in different ways. For highly skilled, high-income workers, the issue is the threat of the "mommy track" for men and women alike. With often-extraordinary rewards for those fully committing to careers, the falloff can be substantial for those who cut back to "part-time work" of 35 hours (or even more). For less-skilled workers, the lack of flexibility and family-related benefits makes family-related obligations even more difficult to fulfill. With the economic downturn, these pressures are exacerbated for workers who may perceive the choice in terms of retaining a much-needed job or risking unemployment if they become more expendable because of attention to family. The starkness of the differences ratchets up the pressure to work longer hours or opt out of a career ladder altogether.

Changing these patterns is a complex process. Much of it involves remaking the social contract between employers and workers, a process that is already ongoing. Under what circumstances should employees have a right to attend to a sick child, make temporary changes in starting or quitting times, work fewer hours, or expect workplace support for family responsibilities? These issues can be the subject of gradually changing private norms (employers sometimes use family-friendly proposals to recruit the most-valued employees) or publicly mandated shifts in acceptable practices. Legislation contributes to this process, especially when it systematizes practices that have already begun to spread voluntarily, or when it makes it easier for employers to act by streamlining administrative requirements or by coordinating tax incentives. Thus, the federal Family and Medical Leave Act has established minimum national requirements for some employees while state laws have expanded the scope of such efforts, making more employees eligible to take leave, requiring some form of paid leave, or providing tax benefits to employers for family-friendly workplaces.[27]

Second, the ideological divisions about the role of government skew the proposals for reform. Economic conservatives, who oppose large-scale government solutions, reflexively oppose comprehensive health care solutions, for example, despite the distorting effects of employer-supplied health care on jobs. These differences also shape the possibilities for workplace reform. Republicans call for more-flexible workplaces, including the opportunity to work from home, flexible schedules (so long as this has no negative impact on productivity), and the portability of health care and retirement benefits.[28] Democrats call for work/family balance, including the expansion of the FMLA, financial incentives to encourage more states to offer paid leave, expanding afterschool care options for children, protecting against discrimination based on family responsibilities, and greater flexibility in the workplace.[29] Republicans focus almost exclusively on encouraging greater flexibility for *employers* in redesigning jobs rather than allowing additional governmental regulation, while Democrats include greater use of legal and governmental efforts to compel changes and greater public spending to underwrite the costs.

A primary difference between the two types of proposals is their class effects. A focus on private incentives provides the largest benefits for the most-valued employees and for employers who might wish to redesign their workforces for reasons of their own. By contrast, a focus on publicly funded mandates can provide more general benefits, but imposes greater burdens on employers or the public treasury. Nonetheless, in terms of achieving change, the most striking aspect of the two types of proposals may be their level of agreement: work/family stresses concern a large part of the electorate.

## WORKPLACE PROPOSALS

We see three different sets of work/family proposals. The most far-reaching are those that would remake the nature of work to redress growing economic inequality and would provide a firmer foundation for family life. These proposals include increasing the minimum wage or the earned income tax credit;[30] reducing the time that individual employees work, such as by reducing the work week or restructuring incentives to change the way overtime is regulated;[31] and adopting a government-run health care system that does not tie benefits to individual employers. Almost two-thirds of the states have established a minimum wage that is higher than the federal standard, and many states have expanded Medicaid to include some low-income working families.[32] Fully implementing each of these proposals, however, while undoubtedly benefiting both red and blue families, would be controversial and would involve a long-term transformation of the workplace; indeed, each proposal could be the subject of a book-length treatment in its own right.

A second set of proposals, which may be easier to implement, involves rethinking the relationship between employment and elementary and secondary education, focusing on supports outside of the workplace that benefit workers. This might involve extending school hours and lowering the age at which school starts in order to provide publicly financed full-day preschool. Tracee Sioux, a blogger, points out that the school day and the work day are on entirely different schedules: "It's insane that our school day and our work day aren't aligned. It's like we're pretending that our nation's workers and our nation's parents are two separate people. They're not."[33] True. School days typically end by 3 P.M., while the standard work day ends at 5 P.M., not including commuting time. The school calendar, with its extended summer break, was developed based on the demands of farm families and originated in the days before air conditioning.[34]

Restructuring the school day and year and providing additional afterschool possibilities would immediately ease child care concerns and facilitate work/family balance. And working parents need additional options for summer, such as year-round schools or public support for camps.[35]

These changes face numerous obstacles. First, many would oppose lengthening the school day on the basis that it might be too difficult for many children. One way of addressing this concern would be by starting the initiative incrementally with, for example, optional programs or separately financed day care, before or after school, on school grounds.[36] A second obstacle to current efforts has been the failure to coordinate day care regulations and school construction; renovation efforts could be required to build in a provision for day care or other afterschool activities.

The most significant obstacle is money. Extending the school day and lowering the age at which public education becomes available would strain our already underfunded educational system. These costs would have to be balanced against the efficiencies of scale, and they might be financed through a combination of sliding scale fees for additional programs and the consolidation of programs that already serve children. The costs, moreover, might be justified by the benefits to children, especially if extended school days offered significant evidence of advancing educational achievement or child health and well-being.[37]

The third type of proposal focuses on encouraging accommodation with the existing employment structure by making the workplace more flexible and more supportive. Many of these proposals command substantial public support, as the McCain and Obama platforms indicated. Proposals include (1) changing the work week by restructuring part-time work or adding flex- and comp-time; and (2) revising and expanding family and medical leave policies and encouraging both men and women to use the available leave.[38]

### Restructuring the Work Week

The inflexibility of workplace structures disadvantages virtually every employee who has tried to combine work and family obligations. Implementing policies that allow flex-time and "flex-place" (such as telecommuting) can help employees and may also benefit employers with increased employee retention.

Part-time work is another example of flexible workplace design. Part-time work is, however, marginalized in terms of benefits available and promotion opportunities. The difference between full-time and part-time work is not necessarily hours, but the structure of the positions. Men who work less than 40 hours a week are more likely to be termed "underemployed." They may be self-employed, work sporadically in full-time positions, or engage in various forms of multiple jobs or contract labor. In contrast, workers officially classified as part-time are primarily women. In fact, women are more than twice as likely to be in part-time jobs as are men: 25% of all employed women work part-time, while only about 10% of men do so.[39] Women are much more likely to prefer to work part-time than are men, and both women who work part-time and those who do not work outside of the home believe that they are better parents than do women who work full-time.[40]

Part-time workers are typically paid less per hour than their full-time counterparts and receive fewer benefits;[41] the primary advantage, of course, is that this schedule gives workers more flexibility in managing their time. While some companies have created good part-time jobs, particularly in seasonal or retail occupations that lend themselves to part-time work, the examples remain isolated, and part-time work constitutes a small proportion of jobs, with employees who receive disproportionately lower wages and fewer benefits.

The distinctions between part-time and full-time positions have multiple roots. First, hiring more part-time workers is often less efficient in part because of returns on scale: it costs more to process, train, and supervise one employee than two. Second, even if a job can be easily divided between multiple workers, benefits pose less-tractable issues. Is half a health care plan better than none? Should part-time workers pay double the premium of full-time workers for full coverage? Moreover, the meaning of part-time work varies with class, gender, and type of employment.[42]

This marginalization disadvantages families in two complementary ways. For the well-educated, it sets up often-painful choices between staying on a fast track to professional success versus accepting more-flexible employment at dramatically reduced salary and benefits. Women (and it is primarily women) who make these marginalizing choices are overwhelmingly able to do so because of marriages that allow them to trade material benefits for more family-friendly environments.

Less well-off couples increasingly need not only two incomes, but more-consistent benefit packages. With less-educated men working fewer hours and enjoying less-reliable opportunities for stable employment, lower-income mothers and fathers may both need to be employed to ensure consistent access to health care and steady combined levels of income.

In this context, more-flexible policies could address both sets of needs. Restructuring employment to remove the disadvantages of part-time work is difficult, but possible. The single easiest way to spur creation of more part-time positions is the adoption of a single-payer, government-run health care system that would remove the cost of health care from private employers. Part-time work would allow women (and, we hope, more men) flexibility not only to cut back on their work hours, but also to move into more-demanding positions as their children require less supervision, which would ease the dilemmas that attend the timing of childbearing.

### *Changing Family and Medical Leave*

On the federal level, the principal legislative initiative in the work/family area has been the Family and Medical Leave Act (FMLA).[43] The FMLA provides up to 12 weeks of unpaid leave for qualified employees for the birth or adoption of a child and to care for the serious illness of themselves or specific family members.[44] The FMLA has been a Democratic effort: President George H. W. Bush repeatedly refused to sign it, and it was the first piece of legislation that President Bill Clinton signed when he took office in 1993. The partisan divide continues: Obama advocated extending it in his 2008 presidential platform, while McCain embraced the Republican opposition.

The care picture is complicated by limits in FMLA coverage, the inability to take unpaid leave, and limited access to paid leave.

First, almost 40% of employees are not at worksites subject to the FMLA,[45] and, because not all of the other employees have satisfied the prerequisites, only 54% of the workforce is eligible to take FMLA leave.[46] Second, even among those workers who are covered, many (according to one study, more than three-quarters) cannot make use of the opportunity because they cannot afford to take unpaid leave.[47] Third, access to paid leave, which FMLA does not address, is overwhelmingly a function of income. For those working parents who have incomes less than 200% of the federal poverty level, 40% have no access to paid leave at all (no paid sick days, vacation, or personal days).[48] Among low-wage workers, 76% do not have access to paid sick leave.[49] Indeed, as a general matter, low-wage workers are less likely than higher-income workers to be covered by family leave policies, to be eligible to take even unpaid family leave, or, much less, to receive paid family leave.[50] They are also less likely to have access to flexible scheduling.[51]

While highly educated, higher-income women are more likely to have access to paid leave than are women with less education and lower incomes, 35% still lack access to any form of paid maternity leave. The number without paid maternity leave rises to 47% of women who have less than a high school education.[52] Women with a college degree were three times more likely to take paid leave following the birth of their first child (58.7%) than women with less than a high school education (17.8%); while 56.4% of women with less than a high school education took unpaid leave, only 38.6% of women with a college degree used unpaid leave.[53]

The National Partnership for Women and Families examined a series of different laws in developing a state-by-state scorecard of parental leave programs. California, New Jersey, and Washington (all blue) have enacted paid family leave legislation, and there are campaigns in a number of others—all blue.[54] While, politically, this is a red-blue issue because it involves more governmental regulation of the workplace, the vision it embodies, of promoting family formation, involves shared values. Unpaid leave has proved to be minimally helpful as a form of extended leave, particularly for low-wage women who typically have the least financial means to avail themselves of unpaid leave.

As one step forward, the FMLA has been a success. It provides some help, it begins the national conversation on family leave, and it may have some effect in reframing the discussion of workplace norms.[55] On the other hand, the FMLA's limits have prevented more workers from using its protections. To help the FMLA realize its potential, there must be meaningful access to leave opportunities for both men and women, which means requiring smaller workplaces to be covered, shortening the waiting period for employee eligibility—and ensuring that working-class men buy into these roles.

## CONCLUSION

Red and blue families both must develop improved responses to the changing relationship between work and family that is associated with the information economy. The missing piece for both paradigms, as the commercial market intrudes ever further into the family, is to rebuild support for family life within the world of work.

As we have stressed throughout the rest of this volume, the process is complicated not only by the ideological divisions between red and blue, but also by the class divisions they represent. These divisions have undermined the creation of a coalition for more thoroughgoing workplace reform. Indeed, it is easy to lampoon proposals for affordable child care and many versions of flex-time as subsidies for the wealthy, who have become dramatically more likely to work longer hours but who have more easily repackaged jobs. Nonetheless, rebuilding the routes into the workplace and maintaining balance while there affects every family—and necessarily affects the resources available for children.

# Conclusion

As we completed this book, we reviewed and updated the statistics on American families, including those showing a resurgence in teen births since 2006. Just as we were finishing the chapter on fertility control, we received a link to a post from someone involved in the marriage movement whom we deeply respect, commenting on the most-recent statistics:

> [T]he unmarried birthrate appeared for a few years around 2000 to have halted its breathtakingly rapid rise.... But in the last five years, unmarried childrearing has resumed its inexorable rise. 38% of all babies are born out of wedlock, which implies probably more than half of women who become mothers for the first time do so while not married.
>
> Is it mere coincidence that this resurgence in illegitimacy happened during the five years in which gay marriage has become (not thanks to me or my choice) the most prominent marriage issue in America—and the one marriage idea endorsed by the tastemakers to the young in particular?[1]

We were stunned. We had seen the same statistics, and we had also ranted to each other about them—with much the same tone of anger and anguish. Our rant, to be sure, had focused more on the increase in teen births (up for the first time in 14 years) than on nonmarital births. Nonetheless, we were certain—with no more social science evidence in front of us than that in the blog—that the causes of both increases were apparent and were due to the promotion of abstinence-only education, the failure to ensure the availability and use of effective contraception, the cutbacks in the accessibility of abortion, and the deterioration of the economy. An increase in births to teens, the poor, and those ill prepared to care for the resulting children was the predictable result.

Such is the nature of the culture wars. Even those of us enmeshed in the literature on the changing American family do not agree on the meaning of what we see before our eyes. We regularly consult and trust those in whom we have confidence, which largely means those who agree with our views. The Internet makes it possible to instantly check our initial impressions, with the National Review Online, the National Association for the Repeal of Abortion Laws (NARAL Pro-Choice America), and countless blogs with an endless variety of facts and opinions, each tailored to reinforce the views of its readers.

The discovery that election returns follow family forms is perhaps not surprising. Family formation may indicate much about a society and certainly the more traditionalist versus modernist inclinations of its voters. We think, however, that we have discovered something else. The forces that have created the blue family paradigm—technology, a return to education, globalization, and the erosion of the society built on manufacturing—affect the entire industrialized world. These forces, however, do not compel a uniform response. Some parts of society have embraced them, remade the bases for their family lives, and prospered because of it. Other parts of society have seen their lot worsened, with fewer ways to secure the future for their children and downward cycles of poverty resulting. A third group, however, is mad as hell. They recognize, quite accurately, that their way of life is being threatened. They perceive the more successful (the ultra-blue "liberal elite") as condescending and indifferent, if not downright hostile, to their plight. They feel that the only solution is a return to age-old pieties—and opposition to their beliefs only strengthens their determination.

The challenge is to recognize and respect the sentiments that underlie these differences and to figure out a way to prevent them from derailing our ability to realize shared objectives. After all, all sides of this debate want a bright future for our children, one that we recognize has to come from parental commitments to children and the ability to marshal societal resources for the well-being of the next generation. We have argued in this book that we will transcend the disagreements that divide us only by recognizing our differences and tailoring the responses to the needs of diverse communities. To do so at a time of increasing inequality and regional differences requires rediscovering the advantages of family law federalism and changing both the subjects of discussion and the principal forums for resolution. We can transcend the increased partisanship of the era only by reconnecting decision makers with those affected by their decisions. The decentralization at the core of a federalist approach will do so more effectively than high-profile ideological fights, and the ability to change the subjects of discussion accordingly depends on the ability to tailor the approach in each of the areas central to the re-creation of family life. While we may not be able to convert either side to the other's view, we might be able to focus on the pressure points that change family dynamics.

First, marriage promotion should be handled in decentralized ways through the federalist system, allowing each part of the country to redefine family aspirations in regional terms based on shared values. Let Massachusetts permit same-sex unions, Louisiana experiment with covenant marriage, Utah provide for high school courses in marriage preparation, and 1,000 counties prescribe premarital education. Free from the glaring publicity of congressional posturing or Supreme Court decisions, municipalities and regions can determine what works and what fits within local culture and traditions. We predict that the most-effective programs will be those that emphasize planning and delay and that encourage prospective spouses to make sure the relationship is one based on shared interests and a capacity for mutual respect. Such efforts will succeed, however, only if we rebuild support for the transition to adulthood that takes place between the end of high school and full integration into the adult worlds of work and family.

Second, let's change the focus of fights over family planning from abortion to contraception and from single-minded objectives to programs that can succeed with diverse groups—and let's make sure to include not just teens but those in their early 20s. Reducing the high number of unwanted pregnancies in the United States would do more than any effort at marriage promotion to reduce the number of abortions, improve family stability, and enhance the well-being of the next generation. As the experience with Medicaid funding has proved, coupling funding for pregnancy with funding for pregnancy prevention appears to be an effective way to encourage state efforts: states that have to pay for the births appear to be much more eager to prevent the next one. The harder issue politically—and the issue worth fighting for—is more-effective strategies to prevent pregnancies in the teens and early 20s. Early childbearing, whether it increases the nonmarital birthrate or initiates a cycle of marriage and divorce, benefits no one.

Third, comprehensive reform of the health care system must take family needs into account. Fertility concerns, whether they involve contraception or assisted reproduction, should be a central part of heath care reform. Women need access to medical care to delay fertility, to avoid the premature infertility that comes from untreated illness, and to enhance later fertility. At the same time, the current system of employer-provided care magnifies the inflexibility of the workplace in addressing the balance with family responsibilities while the wholesale disappearance of insurance coverage for young adults has almost invisibly worsened family-planning efforts. Changing the subject to medical care might do more to advance family interests than continuing the values debate.

Fourth, promoting healthy families can only come with reconsideration of the relationship among work, family, and education. Postponing family formation into the late 20s makes sense in the information economy; creating a society in which women cannot begin family life until the point when fertility diminishes makes no sense at all. Restructuring the interaction between work and family thus has three vital components. First, undertaking family obligations, whether at the beginning of adult life or later, should not derail career expectations. This can only occur with greater flexibility in the workplace itself, encouraging flex-time, family leaves, and both male and female assumption of family responsibilities. Second, the continued acquisition of the education, training, and experience that increase human capital should be a lifetime enterprise. We should rethink the ways in which we support parents' ability to return to school *after* the birth of their children, to reenter the workforce as family responsibilities change, and to switch to positions of lesser and greater responsibility in tandem with the waxing and waning of children's needs. Third, we need to rethink the transition to adulthood for those unlikely to complete college. Apprenticeships, family-friendly community colleges, vocational training, and more direct links between education and employment might do more to promote family stability than marriage promotion efforts.

All of these, however, require leadership committed to defusing values conflicts rather than manipulating them for political advantage. We have a long-established model for doing precisely that: the federalist system of family law.

# Notes

## *Introduction*

1. DREW WESTEN, THE POLITICAL BRAIN 178 (2007).
2. *See, e.g.*, Delia Baldassarri & Andrew Gelman, *Partisans without Constraint: Political Polarization and Trends in American Public Opinion* (June 13, 2007), *available at* http://www.stat.columbia.edu/~gelman/research/unpublished/ BGpolarization4.pdf; *see also* Edward L. Glaeser & Bryce A. Ward, *Myths and Realities of American Political Geography* (Harvard Inst. on Econ. Res., Discussion Paper No. 2100, 2006) (concluding that American political divisions have reverted to their pre–New Deal form and have become increasingly religious and cultural). For legal analysis, see Robert Post & Reva Siegel, *Roe Rage: Democratic Constitutionalism and Backlash*, 42 HARV. C.R.-C.L. L. REV. 373 (2007). On the debate itself, see John W. Evans, *Have Americans' Attitudes Become More Polarized? An Update*, 84 SOC. SCI. Q. 71 (2004); MORRIS P. FIORINA, SAMUEL J. ABRAMS, & JEREMY C. POPE, CULTURE WAR? THE MYTH OF A POLARIZED AMERICA (2004). Instead, we focus on the increasingly intense values divide that has emerged since the mid-'80s, which is focused on issues such as abortion and sexuality.
3. BILL BISHOP, THE BIG SORT 26 (2008).
4. Stephen Ansolabehere, Jonathan Rodden, & James M. Snyder Jr., *Purple America*, 20 J. ECON. PERSP. 97, 107 (Spring 2006), *available at* http://web.mit. edu/jrodden/www/materials/purplefinal.pdf.
5. *See* ROSE M. KREIDER, CURRENT POPULATION REPORTS: LIVING ARRANGEMENTS OF CHILDREN: 2004 (2008), *available at* http://www.census. gov/prod/2008pubs/p70–114.pdf. The number of children living with two parents varied by race, with 87% of Asian children living in these families compared to 38% of black children. *Id.* at 3. Note that single-mother families are much more closely associated with poverty than single-father families: 37% of children living with their unmarried mother, as opposed to 17% of children living their unmarried father, lived in poverty, compared to 31% of

children living with two unmarried parents and 10% of children living with married parents. *Id.* at 7.

6. National Campaign to Prevent Teen and Unplanned Pregnancy, *Why It Matters: Teen Pregnancy and Overall Child Well-Being, available at* http://www.thenationalcampaign.org/why-it-matters/pdf/child_well-being.pdf.

7. John C. Green & Mark Silk, *Why Moral Values Did Count*, Religion in the News (Spring 2005), *available at* http://www.trincoll.edu/depts/csrpl/RINVol8No1/WhyMoral%20ValuesDidCount.htm.

## Chapter 1

1. *See, e.g.,* Ron Lesthaeghe & Lisa Neidert, *The "Second Demographic Transition" in the U.S.: Spatial Patterns and Correlates* (Mar. 2006), *available at* http://www.psc.isr.umich.edu/pubs/pdf/rr06–592.pdf; Ron Lesthaeghe & Lisa Neidert, *Voting and Families: America's Second Demographic Transition*, New Geography (Dec. 11, 2008), *available at* http://www.newgeography.com/content/00461-voting-and-families-america%E2%80%99s-second-demographic-transition.

2. Child Trends Databank, *Teen Birth Rates Ranked Lowest to Highest* (2003), *available at* http://www.childtrendsdatabank.org/pdf/13_PDF.pdf.

3. *Id.*

4. The pattern for African-Americans is a little harder to gauge than that of whites. The states with the lowest African-American teen birthrates are New Hampshire, Utah, New York, and Rhode Island, with California, Massachusetts, and New Mexico tied for fifth. New Hampshire (under 1%), New Mexico (under 2%), and Utah (2%) have such small African-American populations as to make analysis difficult. The states with the highest rates of African-American births are not concentrated by region and include Wisconsin, Arkansas, Illinois, Mississippi, and Ohio. Accordingly, the low overall teen birthrates for the states in the upper part of New England may reflect a lack of diversity, and the high rates in the Southwest may reflect the percentage of Latinos. The teen births for whites alone diverge most between the core northeastern states and the southern states.

5. Latinos constitute 42% of the population of New Mexico, 32.4% of California, 32% of Texas, and 25% of Arizona. Moreover, since the Latino population in these states is substantially younger than the white population, and fertility rates are higher, the effect on the teen birthrate is substantial. *Id.* Over half of all births in these states are to Latinos; *see* Guttmacher Institute, *U.S. Teen Pregnancy Statistics: National and State Trends by Race and Ethnicity* 11 (Sept. 2006), *available* at http://www.guttmacher.org/pubs/2006/09/12/USTPstats.pdf [hereinafter Guttmacher, *U.S. Teen Pregnancy Statistics*]. Hispanic voters are relatively conservative on values issues, but they are more likely to vote Democratic than whites with similar concerns.

6. Shan Carter et al., *Electoral Shifts*, NYTimes.com, Nov. 5, 2008, http://www.nytimes.com/interactive/2008/11/05/us/politics/20081104_ELECTION_RECAP.html?scp=1&sq=counties%20voted%20more%20Republican%20in%202008%20than%202004&st=cse.

7. *Id.*

8. Indeed, in 2004, Massachusetts and Rhode Island are the two "bluest" states, Maryland is fifth, and Connecticut is tied for sixth.

9. ChildTrends, *Facts at a Glance* 3, Table 1 (2006), *available at* http://www .childtrends.org/Files/FAAG2006.pdf.

10. *Election Results*, NYTimes.com, *Dec. 9, 2008*, http://elections.nytimes. com/2008/results/president/map.html.

11. Guttmacher, *U.S. Teen Pregnancy Statistics*, *supra* note 5, at 4, Table 1.0, *available at* http://www.guttmacher.org/pubs/journals/3227200.pdf.

12. These states, except for Massachusetts, have fewer restrictions on teen abortions than do virtually all of the red states.

13. Guttmacher, *U.S. Teen Pregnancy Statistics*, *supra* note 5, at 11. If we were to measure abortion rates as opposed to ratios, New Jersey, New York, and Maryland would remain in the top five, but Massachusetts and Connecticut would be replaced by Nevada and California. *Id.* The lowest abortion rates also would change, with the five lowest states being Utah, South Dakota, North Dakota, Kentucky, and West Virginia.

14. Vermont, New Hampshire, and Maine, among the states with the lowest teen birthrate, also had high percentages of nonmarital teen births: in Vermont, it was 87%, New Hampshire 89%, and Maine 88%. *Id.* The percentage of births to teen mothers with respect to all births in the state was highest in New Mexico (17%), followed by Mississippi (16%), Arkansas and Louisiana (15%), and Alabama and Oklahoma (14%). *Id.* The lowest percentages were in Massachusetts, New Hampshire, New Jersey, and Vermont (6%), and Connecticut, Minnesota, New York, and Utah (7%). *Id.*

15. Teen pregnancy, as opposed to birthrates, suggests a somewhat different regional distribution. The lowest teen pregnancy rates were in North Dakota, Vermont, New Hampshire, Minnesota, and Maine. *Id.* at 11. The states with the highest teen pregnancy rates were Nevada, Arizona, Mississippi, and Texas. *Id.*

16. Racial distribution affects some of the overall state averages, as we noted above, because African-Americans nationally have more than double the pregnancy rates (178.9 versus 82.6 per 1,000 women) and almost triple the abortion rates (62.9 versus 22.6) of whites. New York, New Jersey, and Maryland all report more pregnancies and births among African-American than among white teens. The New England states, however, with even lower teen birthrates, have significantly smaller percentages of African-Americans and lower abortion rates than the Mid-Atlantic states. *Id.* at 11.

17. Tallese Johnson & Jane Dye, Indicators of Marriage and Fertility in the United States from the American Community Survey: 2000 to 2003, Table 1 (2005), *available at* http://www.census.gov/population/www/ socdemo/fertility/mar-fert-slides.html.

18. Infoplease, Median Age at First Marriage, http://www.infoplease.com/ipa/ A0005061.html (last visited Feb. 27, 2009). In 1890, the median age at first marriage was 26.1 for men and 22.0 for women.

19. *See* U.S. Census Bureau, American Fact Finder, American Community Survey 2007, http://factfinder.census.gov/servlet/ GRTTable?_bm=y&-geo_id=01000US&-_box_head_nbr=R1204&-ds_

name=ACS_2007_1YR_G00_&-redoLog=false&-mt_name=ACS_2005_
EST_G00_R1204_US30&-format=US-30 (last visited Aug. 19, 2009).
Kansas is fifth in terms of overall totals, but Wyoming is fifth for women
(24.1), while Alabama is for men (26.2).

20. *See* Table 1.1. For earlier data, see T. J. Mathews & Brady E. Hamilton, *Mean
Age of Mother, 1970–2000*, 51 NAT'L VITAL STAT. REP. 1, 10, Table 3 (Dec.
11, 2002), *available at* http://www.cdc.gov/nchs/data/nvsr/nvsr51/nvsr51_01.
pdf. The average age of first birth has increased less than the average age of
marriage because fewer women have been marrying.

21. Looking at just the 1990s, however, the areas with the biggest jump in age
at first birth were the District of Columbia, Massachusetts, Michigan, New
Hampshire, New Jersey, North Carolina, and Virginia. The states with the
least change were Wyoming and Alaska, which showed declines in age; New
Mexico, which stayed the same; and South Dakota and North Dakota. *Id.*

22. Jane Lawler Dye, *Fertility of American Women: June 2004*, 20–555 CURRENT
POPULATION REP. 1, 4, Table 2 (2005), *available at* http://www.census.gov/
prod/2005pubs/p20-555.pdf. It was 48% in the Northeast, which includes
Maine, New Hampshire, Vermont, Massachusetts, Rhode Island, Connecticut,
New York, New Jersey, and Pennsylvania; and 42.5% in the Mid-Atlantic and
South, which included Delaware, Maryland, the District of Columbia, Virginia,
West Virginia, North Carolina, South Carolina, Georgia, Florida, Kentucky,
Tennessee, Alabama, Mississippi, Arkansas, Louisiana, Oklahoma, and Texas.
The statistics did not include a further breakdown by state.

23. Steve Sailer, *Birth Gap: How Birthrates Color the Electoral Map*, AM.
CONSERVATIVE (Dec. 2004), *available at* http://www.amconmag.
com/2004_12_06/cover.html. In the United States, there are 1,182 children
born for every 1,000 women. U.S. CENSUS BUREAU, TABLE S1. FERTILITY
INDICATORS FOR WOMEN 15 TO 44 YEARS OLD BY STATE OF RESIDENCE:
JUNE 2004 (2004), *available at* http://www.census.gov/population/socdemo/
fertility/tabS1.xls. Washington, D.C., is, once again, an outlier, with a fertility
rate of 776. States with the lowest fertility rates for never-married women
were mixed, with Utah, a red state, with the lowest rate of 208, followed
by Delaware (213), Minnesota (234), North Dakota (241), Idaho (247), and
New Hampshire (254). *Id.* Alaska has the highest fertility rate, with 1,435
children born per 1,000 women, followed by Arkansas (1,418), Utah and
Mississippi (1,393), and South Dakota (1,368). The states with the lowest
fertility rates are Maryland (991), Vermont (1,000), Massachusetts (1,020),
Maine (1,022), and Delaware (1,023). *Id.* Unsurprisingly, the states with the
highest percentages of childless women track the fertility rates: Vermont .
(53.5%), Massachusetts (51.2), Delaware (49.1), New York (48.5), and Maine
(48.2)—all blue. The states with the lowest percentages of childless women
are Arkansas (35.3%), Mississippi (35.4), Alaska (38.0), Alabama (38.7), and
Georgia (39.3)—all red. *Id.*

24. Laurie D. Elam-Evans et al., *Abortion Surveillance—United States, 2000*,
MORBIDITY & MORALITY WKLY. REP.: CDC SURVEILLANCE SUMMARIES 1, 29,
Table 3 (Nov. 28, 2003), *available at* http://www.cdc.gov/mmwr/preview/
mmwrhtml/ss5212a1.htm.

25. *Id.* Florida and Louisiana had low rates as well, but did not report the number of abortions with respect to in-state residents. *Id.*

26. *Id.* States with incomplete measures were again excluded, as was the District of Columbia.

27. Washington, while more diverse than the upper New England states, was still 78.9% white, with only 3% African-Americans. Cynthia A. Brewer & Trudy A. Suchan, Mapping Census 2000: The Geography of U.S. Diversity (2001).

28. These data were also less complete than others, with a number of southern states missing from the tables.

29. Tallese Johnson & Jane Dye, Indicators of Marriage and Fertility in the United States from the American Community Survey: 2000 to 2003, Table 2 (2005), *available at* http://www.census.gov/population/www/ socdemo/fertility/slideshow/table02.csv.

30. Nevada's divorce rate, like its marriage rate, however, most likely reflects its tradition of relatively lax residency requirements.

31. The CDC figures on divorce rates, which include rates for each of the five years from 1999 to 2004, provide a better sense of patterns over time than the census figures. These tables also show the states with the highest divorce rates as Nevada, Arkansas, Wyoming, and Idaho, with West Virginia and Alabama ahead of Kentucky over the five-year period. The CDC tallies include Massachusetts, Illinois, and Pennsylvania in the bottom five, but show New Jersey and Wisconsin with more consistently low rates than North Dakota or Connecticut. Division of Vital Statistics, National Center for Health Statistics, Centers for Disease Control, *Divorce Rates by State: 1990, 1995, and 1999–2004* (Oct. 19, 2005), *available at* http://www.cdc.gov/nchs/ data/nvss/divorce90_04.pdf.

32. *See* Paul R. Amato & Stacy J. Rogers, *A Longitudinal Study of Marital Problems and Subsequent Divorce*, 59 J. Marriage & Fam. 612, 621 (1997); A. Booth & J. Edwards, *Age at Marriage and Marital Instability*, 47 J. Marriage & Fam. 67, 67–75 (1985); Barbara Dafoe Whitehead & David Popenoe, *State of Our Unions: The Social Health of Marriage in America*, Box 2 (2004), *available at* http:// marriage.rutgers.edu/Publications/SOOU/TEXTSOOU2004.htm#Divorce.

33. Paul R. Amato et al., Alone Together 79 (2007).

34. Dye, *supra* note 22. If we were to consider only the birthrates to unmarried women from 2000 to 2003, however, we would pick up in the top ten Colorado and New Jersey, states with considerably more-diverse populations. Johnson & Dye, *supra* note 29. The states with the highest birthrates to never-married mothers are Mississippi (690), Georgia (678), Michigan (600), Alabama (570), and Alaska (556). *Id.* If we were to look instead at recent births, the top five would be Mississippi, Louisiana, South Carolina, New Mexico, and Alabama. *Id.*

35. *Births: Final Data for 2004*, 55 Nat'l Vital Stat. Rep. (Sept. 29, 2006), *available at* http://www.cdc.gov/nchs/data/nvsr/nvsr55/nvsr55_01.pdf.

36. For an in-depth look at differences among religious groups, see, in particular, Mark D. Regnerus, Forbidden Fruit: Sex & Religion in the Lives of American Teenagers (2007).

37. Steve Sailer, *Value Voters*, AM. CONSERVATIVE, Feb. 11, 2008, *available at* http://www.amconmag.com/article/2008/feb/11/00016; *see* ANDREW GELMAN, RED STATE, BLUE STATE, RICH STATE, POOR STATE: WHY AMERICANS VOTE THE WAY THEY DO 170 (2008) ("Republicans do better among married voters, who are more likely to end up in more affordable states that also happen to be more culturally conservative").

38. Lesthaeghe & Neidert, *Second Demographic Transition, supra* note 1; Lesthaeghe & Neidert, *Voting and Families, supra* note 1.

## Chapter 2

1. E. A. WRIGLEY & R. S. SCHOFIELD, THE POPULATION HISTORY OF ENGLAND, 1541–1871, at 162 (1989); LAWRENCE STONE, THE FAMILY, SEX AND MARRIAGE IN ENGLAND, 1500–1800, at 39–41 (1979).

2. *See, e.g.*, Sara McLanahan, *Diverging Destinies: How Children Are Faring after the Second Demographic Transformation*, 41 DEMOGRAPHY 607 (2004).

3. *See, e.g.*, MARY P. RYAN, CRADLE OF THE MIDDLE CLASS: THE FAMILY IN ONEIDA COUNTY, NEW YORK, 1790–1865, at 184–85 (1981).

4. *See, e.g.*, Ronald Lee, *The Demographic Transition: Three Centuries, of Fundamental Change*, 17 J. ECON. PERSP. 167 (Autumn 2003).

5. *See generally* ANDREW J. CHERLIN, THE MARRIAGE-GO-ROUND: THE STATE OF MARRIAGE AND THE FAMILY IN AMERICA TODAY (2009); Ron J. Lesthaeghe & Lisa Neidert, *The "Second Demographic Transition" in the U.S.: Spatial Patterns and Correlates* (Mar. 2006), *available at* http://www.psc.isr.umich.edu/pubs/pdf/rr06–592.pdf.

6. JUNE CARBONE, FROM PARTNERS TO PARENTS: THE SECOND REVOLUTION IN FAMILY LAW, chapters 1–3 (2000). Becker argued that the woes that come from greater family instability come from less specialization between men and women and thus smaller returns from marriage as men and women move away from traditional gender roles. However, what Becker describes as specialization in the home (cooking, cleaning, looking after the children) is the work of a generalist, and market substitutes are available for these activities at relatively low prices. Moreover, as husbands and wives both enter the labor force, they often do so in different industries, creating a form of portfolio diversification (the wife employed in the medical field can support the laid-off accountant husband, providing a cushion in hard times). A better description of the two transformations focuses on specialization for the paid labor market. What Becker describes as lower returns from marriage, in turn, can be more accurately described as a redistribution of the power relationships within family life, with women enjoying greater independence and thus an ability to demand better terms for their participation.

7. For example, Naomi Cahn, *The Moral Complexities of Family Law*, 50 STAN. L. REV. 225 (1997).

8. PIPPA NORRIS & RONALD INGELHART, SACRED AND SECULAR: RELIGION AND POLITICS WORLDWIDE 162 (2004).

9. RYAN, *supra* note 3, at 184–85.

10. *Id.* at 107–10.

11. The economic changes have been accompanied by what Joan Williams has termed the ideology of domesticity, which focused on the "separate spheres" of home and market and produced the "cult of true womanhood." JOAN WILLIAMS, UNBENDING GENDER: WHY FAMILY AND WORK CONFLICT AND WHAT TO DO ABOUT IT (2000).

12. *See* Jane E. Larson, *Women Understand So Little, They Call My Good Nature "Deceit": A Feminist Rethinking of Seduction*, 93 COLUM. L. REV. 374, 388–90 (1993) ("Victorian culture exalted sexual restraint and designated women as caretakers of society's sexual virtue"); *see also* CARL N. DEGLER, AT ODDS: WOMEN AND THE FAMILY IN AMERICA FROM THE REVOLUTION TO THE PRESENT 180–83 (1981) (describing declining birthrates that followed women's greater ability to decline sexual intercourse).

13. LINDA HIRSHMAN & JANE LARSON, HARD BARGAINS: THE POLITICS OF SEX 92 (1998). Larson, *supra* note 12, at 392.

14. Larson, *supra* note 12, at 392.

15. HIRSHMAN & LARSON, *supra* note 13, at 92; Larson, *supra* note 12, at 392.

16. For a thoughtful and comprehensive discussion of the changes, see generally Joan Williams, *Toward a Reconstructive Feminism: Reconstructing the Relationship of Market Work and Family Work*, 19 N. ILL. U. L. REV. 89 (1998); Janet Galligani Casey, *Farm Women, Letters to the Editor, and the Limits of Autobiography Theory*, 28 J. MOD. LIT. 89 (2004) (drawing on letters to the editor in women's magazines to show the influence of and resistance to middle-class models of femininity).

17. RYAN, *supra* note 3, at 184–85. The Catholic working classes, in contrast, often depended on their children's labor for their families' survival, creating incentives for larger families that transcended religious differences. Moreover, factory employment, which for working-class families could start even before the teen years, made parental supervision that much more difficult and further encouraged younger marriages. *See* Elizabeth Pleck, *A Mother's Wages: Income Earning among Married Italian and Black Women, 1896–1911, in* THE AMERICAN FAMILY IN SOCIO-HISTORICAL PERSPECTIVE 490–515 (Michael Cordon ed., 3d ed. 1983).

18. *See, e.g.,* ELIZABETH FOX-GENOVESE, WITHIN THE PLANTATION HOUSEHOLD: BLACK AND WHITE WOMEN OF THE OLD SOUTH 192–241 (1988) (describing the gulf between slaveholding and enslaved women in the antebellum American South); JACQUELINE JONES, LABOR OF LOVE, LABOR OF SORROW: BLACK WOMEN, WORK, AND THE FAMILY FROM SLAVERY TO THE PRESENT 1–151 (1985) (comparing the experiences of free and enslaved black women in the southern United States); *see also* Linda K. Kerber, *Separate Spheres, Female Worlds, Woman's Place: The Rhetoric of Women's History*, 75 J. AM. HIST. 9, 10 (1988).

19. *See, e.g.,* Richard G. Harris, *The Knowledge-Based Economy: Intellectual Origins and New Economic Perspectives*, 3 INT'L J. MGMT. REVS. 21 (2001).

20. *See* Betsey Stevenson & Justin Wolfers, *Marriage and Divorce: Changes and Their Driving Forces*, 21 J. ECON. PERSP. 27 (2007), *available at* http://bpp.wharton.upenn.edu/jwolfers/Papers/MarriageandDivorce(JEP).pdf.

21. Carol Sanger brilliantly describes the role of cars and suburbanization in allowing teens to escape parental restraints. Carol Sanger, *Girls and the Getaway: Cars, Culture, and the Predicament of Gendered Space*, 144 U. PA.

L. Rev. 705, 730–33 (1995); *see generally* Beth L. Bailey, From Front Porch to Back Seat: Courtship in Twentieth-Century America (1988) (explaining how the invention of the automobile contributed to the rise of dating by giving young people both privacy and mobility).

22. Stephanie Coontz, The Way We Never Were: American Families and the Nostalgia Trap 25–26 (1992).

23. Hirshman & Larson, *supra* note 13, at 92.

24. Andrew J. Cherlin, *American Marriage in the Early Twenty-First Century*, 15 Future of Child. 33, 35 (Fall 2005).

25. *See* Linda C. McClain, The Place of Families: Fostering Capacity, Equality, and Responsibility (2006).

26. *See* George A. Akerlof, Janet L. Yellen, & Michael L. Katz, *An Analysis of Out-of Wedlock Childbearing in the United States*, 111 Q. J. Econ. 277, 277–303 (1996) (arguing that the availability of contraception and abortion ironically contributed to the increase in nonmarital births as women assumed responsibility for avoiding pregnancy and men no longer felt obligated to marry unintentionally pregnant partners).

27. Barbara Whitehead notes that 90% of women born between 1933 and 1942 were either virgins when they married or had engaged in their first intercourse with the man they subsequently married. Today, in contrast, the average age at first intercourse for women is 17 while the average age at first marriage is 25. Barbara Dafoe Whitehead, *The Changing Pathway to Marriage: Trends in Dating, First Unions, and Marriage among Young Adults, in* Family Transformed: Religion, Values, and Society in American Life 168, 170 (Steven M. Tipton & John Witte Jr. eds., 2005).

28. Frank Newport, *The Poll Editors: Sexual Norms: Where Does America Stand Today?* Gallup Poll (Dec. 1997), *available at* http://www.hi-ho.ne.jp/taku77/refer/sexnorm.htm.

29. Based on these data, Lawrence Finer concludes that "[a]lmost all Americans have sex before marrying." Lawrence B. Finer, *Trends in Premarital Sex in the United States, 1954–2003*, 122 Pub. Health Reps. 73 (Jan.–Feb. 2007).

30. Akerlof, Yellen, & Katz, *supra* note 26.

31. *Id.* at 308 (noting also that agency adoptions fell by one-half in the five years following the legalization of abortion).

32. Coontz, *supra* note 22, at 167.

33. *See* chapter 7, *infra*.

34. *See* Finer, *supra* note 29, at 76.

35. U.S. Census Bureau, Estimated Median Age at First Marriage, by Sex: 1890 to the Present (Sept. 21, 2006), *available at* http://www.censusbureau.biz/population/socdemo/hh-fam/ms2.pdf.

36. *See* Coontz, *supra* note 22, at 166.

37. Sara S. McLanahan & Gary Sandafur, Growing Up with a Single Parent: What Helps, What Hurts 109–10 (2006).

38. For example, Sara McLanahan observes, "Children who were born to mothers from the most advantaged backgrounds are making substantial gains in resources. Relative to their counterparts 40 years ago, their mothers are more mature and more likely to be working at well-paying jobs. These

children were born into stable unions and are spending more time with their fathers." McLanahan, *supra* note 2, at 608.

39. *Id.* at 611.

40. *Id.*

41. *Id.* at 609.

42. It should be noted, however, that fertility rates have also dropped, especially for teens. Between 1960 and 2000, for example, births to 15- to 19-year-old women fell by more than half. The composition of the remaining births varies by race and class. White women, for example, have higher birthrates in every age group above 25, while African-Americans have higher birthrates in every cohort under 25, even though both races report substantial declines in teen childbearing. *See* Child Trends Data Bank, Percentage of Births to Unmarried Women, http://www.childtrendsdatabank.org/indicators/75UnmarriedBirths.cfm (last visited Mar. 1, 2009).

43. For a summary of the benefits of later marriage and childbearing, *see* ELIZABETH GREGORY, READY: WHY WOMEN ARE EMBRACING THE NEW LATER MOTHERHOOD 8–10 (2007) (women who give birth at 34 live longer with fewer health issues than women who give birth at any other age, and older women generally have more resources and are happier, more stable, and more egalitarian marriages).

44. *Levi Johnston Speaks on Bristol Palin, Obama and Baby*, PROPELLER. COM, comment posted by PsychoHosebeat, http://www.propeller.com/story/2008/10/13/levi-johnston-speaks-on-bristol-palin-obama-and-baby (last visited Mar. 1, 2009).

45. *See, e.g.*, Reynolds v. United States, 98 U.S. 145, 164–67 (1879) (upholding ban on polygamy, describing the United States as a nation of European immigrants, and finding that polygamy "has always been odious among the northern and western nations of Europe").

46. *See, e.g.*, MARTHA ALBERTSON FINEMAN, THE NEUTERED MOTHER, THE SEXUAL FAMILY AND OTHER TWENTIETH CENTURY TRAGEDIES (1995) (describing the role of marriage in limiting the rights and development of women).

47. *See* Carol Sanger, *Infant Safe Haven Laws: Legislating in the Culture of Life*, 106 COLUM. L. REV. 753, 781–88 (May 2006) (discussing the role of moral panic in generating support for little-needed or punitive policies); *see also* Amy L. Wax, *Engine of Inequality: Race, Class, and Family Structure*, 41 FAM. L. Q. 567 (2007).

48. MARK D. REGNERUS, FORBIDDEN FRUIT: SEX AND RELIGION IN THE LIVES OF AMERICAN TEENAGERS 127, 154 (2007). Regnerus distinguishes between "dynamic religiosity" and "affiliation," finding: "Affiliation with an evangelical congregation doesn't make someone devout.... [M]ost research conclusions about evangelicals are from studies of affiliation or self-identity alone, not combined with religiosity." *Id.* at 154. In other words, evangelicals as a group begin sexual activity earlier than those who report membership in other religions, such as mainline Protestants, Jews, or Mormons. In all of these religions, however, the behavior of the devout, generally those who attend church or synagogue once a week or more, differs from that of the less devout. So, among evangelicals, Regnerus finds that the roughly 25% who constitute the devout

delay the beginning of sexual activity to a significantly greater degree than the non-devout. Nonetheless, evangelicals as a group, including the devout and the less devout, begin sexual activity earlier on average (by a few months) than mainstream Protestants, a group where even the devout have somewhat more flexible attitudes toward sexual activity.

49. *Id.* at 206.

50. *Id.* at 121.

51. *Id.* at 154.

52. *See, e.g.,* David Loughran & Julie M. Zissimopoulos, *Why Wait: The Effect of Early Marriage and Childbearing on the Wage Growth of Men and Women* (RAND Corp., Working Paper Series No. WR-482-1, Mar. 2007), *available at* http://papers.ssrn.com/sol3/papers.cfm?abstract_id=999824 (finding that, while childbearing depresses only women's wages, early marriage depresses both male and female earnings growth).

53. Barbara Dafoe Whitehead, *Close the Parent Gap*, BLUEPRINT (May 31, 2005), *available at* http://www.dlc.org/ndol_ci.cfm?kaid=114&subid=144&contenti d=253357.

54. REGNERUS, *supra* note 48, at 203.

55. *Id.* at 99. The most robust effects show, for example, differences between abstinence pledgers and non-pledgers that result in 99% of the non-pledgers, but only 88% of the pledgers, engaging in premarital intercourse within the period measured by the study.

56. Institute for American Values, Ctr. for Marriage & Family, *Marriage and the Law: A Statement of Principles, Executive Summary* (2006), *available at* http://www .americanvalues.org/pdfs/mlawstmnt_exsumm.pdf.

57. JAMES Q. WILSON, THE MARRIAGE PROBLEM 216–17 (2002).

58. Amy L. Wax, *The Two-Parent Family in the Liberal State: The Case for Selective Subsidies*, 1 MICH. J. RACE & L. 491, 494 (1996).

59. Personal Responsibility and Work Opportunity Reconciliation Act of 1996, 104 Pub. L. No. 193, 110 Stat. 2105, § 101 (codified at 42 U.S.C. § 601 (2007)); *see also* GWENDOLYN MINK, WELFARE'S END 43 (1998) (emphasizing the legislative history of marriage, marital parenting, and paternal involvement); Tonya L. Brito, *From Madonna to Proletariat: Constructing a New Ideology of Motherhood in Welfare Discourse*, 44 VILL. L. REV. 415 (1999).

## Chapter 3

1. Colleen Shaddox, *Juvenile Justice and the Theatre of the Absurd*, MILLER-MCCUNE (Nov. 4, 2008), *available at* http://www.miller-mccune.com/ article/765 (quoting interview with Baird).

2. W. BRADFORD WILCOX ET AL., INSTITUTE FOR AMERICAN VALUES, WHY MARRIAGE MATTERS: SECOND EDITION: TWENTY-SIX CONCLUSIONS FROM THE SOCIAL SCIENCES 6 (2005).

3. Jeffrey Jensen Arnett & Nancy L. Galambos, *Culture and Conceptions of Adulthood*, 100 NEW DIRECTIONS FOR CHILD & ADOLESC. DEV. 91, 91–92 (2003).

4. *See, e.g.,* LAWRENCE STONE, THE FAMILY, SEX AND MARRIAGE IN ENGLAND, 1500–1800, at 401–2, 408 (1979) (commenting on the relationship between class and female chastity and the extraordinary levels of sexual repression

necessary to limit births and contain them within marriage); David J. Hacker, *Rethinking the "Early" Decline of Marital Fertility in the United States*, 40 DEMOGRAPHY 605 (2003) (also noting fertility levels in England and comparing them to circumstances in the United States).

5. *See* SUSAN MOLLER OKIN, GENDER, JUSTICE AND THE FAMILY 157–59 (1991).

6. Steven L. Nock & W. Bradford Wilcox, *What's Love Got to Do with It? Equality, Equity, Commitment and Women's Marital Quality*, 84 SOC. FORCES 1321 (2006).

7. Elizabeth Fussell & Frank F. Furstenberg Jr., *The Transition to Adulthood during the 20th Century: Race, Nativity and Gender, in* ON THE FRONTIER OF ADULTHOOD: THEORY, RESEARCH, & PUBLIC POLICY 29 (Richard A. Settersten Jr. et al., eds., 2005) (noting that, for men of Western European origin, stable employment was a precursor to the ability to form a family, and in the first half of the twentieth century, such employment was generally attainable by age 20, but no longer is today).

8. George A. Akerlof, Janet L. Yellen, & Michael L. Katz, *An Analysis of Out-of-Wedlock Childbearing in the United States*, 111 Q. J. ECON. 277, 279 (1996).

9. *See, e.g.,* MILTON C. REGAN JR., FAMILY LAW AND THE PURSUIT OF INTIMACY 28 (1993).

10. *See, e.g.,* Frank F. Furstenberg Jr., Ruben G. Rumbaut, & Richard A. Settersten Jr., *On the Frontier of Adulthood: Emerging Themes and New Directions, in* ON THE FRONTIER OF ADULTHOOD, *supra* note 7, at 3.

11. CLAUDIA GOLDIN & LAWRENCE F. KATZ, THE RACE BETWEEN EDUCATION AND TECHNOLOGY (2008); CLAUDIA GOLDIN & LAWRENCE F. KATZ, LONG-RUN CHANGES IN THE U.S. WAGE STRUCTURE: NARROWING, WIDENING, POLARIZING (2007).

12. Men exceed women among high school dropouts by 22.4% to 17.1%. Network on Transitions to Adulthood, Fast Facts: Work and Education (2006), http://www.transad.pop.upenn.edu/trends/facts_wa.htm (last visited Oct. 27, 2009).

13. *Id.*

14. *Id.*

15. *Id.*

16. For a comprehensive examination of this issue, see ORLANDO PATTERSON, RITUALS OF BLOOD, CONSEQUENCES OF SLAVERY IN TWO AMERICAN CENTURIES (1998). He reports that, by the 1990s, not only were African-American women substantially more likely to graduate from college than African-American men, but they had also become more likely to acquire a professional degree. *Id.* at 18.

17. The figures are stunning. Stephen Raphael reports:

> Young men in their early twenties are especially likely to have served time. Their risk of imprisonment has tripled between 1979 and 2001. For all racial and ethnic groups, less-educated men are considerably more likely to be incarcerated than more educated men. However, less-educated black men have the highest incarceration rates. The author calculates, using California prison data, that 90% of black male high school dropouts now aged 45 to 54 have been or are in jail.

> STEPHEN RAPHAEL, NETWORK ON TRANSITIONS TO ADULTHOOD, POLICY BRIEF: EARLY INCARCERATION SPELLS AND THE TRANSITION TO ADULTHOOD 1 (2006). *See also* Stephen Raphael, *Early Incarceration Spells and the*

*Transition to Adulthood, in* The Price of Independence: The Economics of Early Adulthood (Sheldon Danziger & Cecilia Rouse eds., 2007) (demonstrating that incarceration delays or derails more conventional aspects of that transition, such as employment, education, marriage, and living independently).

18. Henry S. Farber, *Is the Company Man an Anachronism? Trends in Long Term Employment, 1973–2005, in* The Price of Independence, *supra* note 17, at 57.

19. *Id.*

20. Furstenberg et al., *supra* note 10, at 3.

21. *Id.*

22. *Id.* at 10.

23. *Id.* at 1.

24. Elizabeth S. Scott & Laurence Steinberg, *Blaming Youth*, 81 Tex. L. Rev. 799, 811–13 (2003).

25. Craig M. Bennett Abigail A. Baird, *Anatomical Changes in the Emerging Adult Brain: A Voxel-Based Morphometry Study*, 27 Human Brain Mapping 766 (2005), *available at* www3.interscience.wiley.com/cgi-bin/fulltext/112162278/main.html,ftx_abs. at 9.

26. *Id.*

27. *Id.*

28. Abigail A. Baird, *Adolescent Moral Reasoning: The Integration of Emotion and Cognition*, Moral Psycholy. (forthcoming), *available at* http://faculty.vassar.edu/abbaird/about/publications/pdfs/2006-Baird-Morality.pdf.

29. Paul Arshagouni, *"But I'm an Adult Now...Sort of": Adolescent Consent in Health Care Decision-Making and the Adolescent Brain*, 9 J. Health Care L. & Pol'y 315, 351 (2006), at quoting Am. Bar Ass'n Juvenile Justice Ctr., *Adolescence, Brain Development, and Legal Culpability, in* Cruel and Unusual Punishment: The Juvenile Death Penalty 3 (2004).

30. Scott & Steinberg, *supra* note 24, at 812–13.

31. *Id.* at 816.

32. *Id.* at 812 ("the key advances during this period are gains in deductive reasoning, the ability to think about hypothetical situations, the ability to think simultaneously in multiple dimensions, the ability to think abstractly, and the ability to think about the process of thinking ('metacognition')"); *see also* John H. Flavell, Patricia H. Miller, & Scott A. Miller, Cognitive Development (1963; reprint, 1993) (outlining Piaget's theory and updating it based on new data); Barbel Inhelder & Jean Piaget, The Growth of Logical Thinking from Childhood to Adolescence (Ann Parsons & Stanley Milgram trans., 1958); Jean Piaget, Genetic Epistemology (Eleanor Duckworth trans., 1970); Robert S. Siegler, Children's Thinking (1986; reprint, 1991).

33. Cass R. Sunstein, *Adolescent Risk Taking and Social Meaning: A Commentary* 8, *available at* http://www.law.uchicago.edu/files/files/386.pdf. (explaining the role of experience in making judgments both faster and more accurately). Experience, of course, can make individuals overly cautious. Someone who has experienced an accident may have a strong association between entering an intersection and a visceral sense of fear that may interfere with efficient decision making. Moreover, the social meaning of a given act may also

influence its emotional valence. Sunstein gives the example of the different social images associated with smoking in African-American versus white communities that produce significantly lower smoking rates among African-American than white teens. *Id.* at 10–11.

34. For a particularly good summary of the relationship between brain development and moral decision making, see Baird, *supra* note 28, at 7, who argues that it is the synthesis of visceral and cognitive information that permits the development of mature judgment. She explains that a critical change in moral judgment is the ability not just to perceive the difference between right and wrong, but to experience visceral feelings associated with the thought of performing wrongful acts. Baird further observes that a brain region with a demonstrated significant relationship between age and volume (which in turn is associated with the increase in white matter) is the anterior cingulate cortex, an area known for its prominent role in the mediation and control of emotional, attentional, motivational, social, and cognitive behaviors. She suggests that this area may be particularly critical to the integration of somatic and cognitive factors essential to development of the moral habits she describes. *Id.* at 6–7.

35. Scott & Steinberg, *supra* note 24, at 813.

36. Note that these figures include women with children who range from birth to five, not just the age at which the mothers give birth. Sara McLanahan, *Diverging Destinies: How Children Are Faring after the Second Demographic Transformation*, 41 Demography 607, 609 (2004). Of course, the superiority of older parents has its limits. McLanahan notes that most of the studies finding poor-quality parenting from younger families focus on teens. *Id.*

37. *Id.* Of course, older parents may also be less energetic, less flexible, and less likely to assist adult children and grandchildren.

38. *See* Janet B. Hardy et al., *Adolescent Childbearing Revisited: The Age of Inner-City Mothers at Delivery Is a Determinant of Their Children's Self-Sufficiency at Age 27 to 33*, 100 Pediatrics 802–9 (1997).

39. *See* John Mirowsky & Catherine E. Ross, *Depression, Parenthood, and Age at First Birth*, 54 Soc. Sci. & Med. 1281 (2002) (finding maternal depression greater with younger age at first birth and the least depression in first-time mothers who are around age 30).

40. *Id.*

41. *Id.*

42. *See, e.g.*, Allan Booth & John N. Edwards, *Age at Marriage and Marital Instability*, 47 J. Marriage & Fam. 67, 68, 71 (1985) (summarizing literature and observing that age at marriage is the single best predictor of divorce); Barbara Dafoe Whitehead & David Popenoe, *The Marrying Kind: Which Men Marry and Why*, in The State of Our Unions: The Social Health of Marriage in America 6 (2004), *available at* http://marriage. rutgers.edu/publications/SOOU/ SOOU2004.pdf. Efforts to determine why this is so suggest that greater infidelity at younger ages is a significant factor. Booth & Edwards, *supra* note 42, at 71; Paul R. Amato & Stacy J. Rogers, *A Longitudinal Study of Marital Problems and Subsequent Divorce*, 59 J. Marriage & Fam. 612, 621 (1997). The first comprehensive study,

by Larry L. Bumpass & James A. Sweet, *Differentials in Marital Instability: 1970*, 37 Am. Soc. Rev. 754 (1972), found that the biggest drops in marital instability occurred as the woman's age at marriage increased from the mid-teens to the late teens (a ten-point drop), and marital stability continued to improve as women's age at marriage increased from the late teens to the early 20s (five-point drop) and from the early to mid-20s (three-point drop). *Id.* at 755.

43. Centers for Disease Control and Prevention, *Cohabitation, Divorce, Marriage and Remarriage in the United States*, 22 Vital & Health Stats. 55, Table 21 (July 2002), *available at* http://www.cdc.gov/nchs/data/series/sr_23/sr23_022.pdf. In a parallel study of cohabitation rates, however, the CDC found that the greatest improvements in stability occurred when the woman's age at the start of cohabitation was over 25, rather than in the 20–24 age group. *Id.* at 49, Table 15. In contrast with the marriage figures, the CDC found no statistically significant differences between the stability of cohabitation begun in the late teens versus the early 20s. The CDC offered no explanation for these results. It is possible that the institutional role of marriage is more critical to relationship success in the early 20s, but the results may also be explained by differences in the populations who cohabit earlier rather than later in life.

44. Paul R. Amato et al., Alone Together 79 (2007).

45. *Id.*

46. Edward O. Laumann et al., The Social Organization of Sexuality: Sexual Practices in the United States 192 (1994) (indicating that the number of partners declines dramatically with age). Anthropologist Helen Fisher speculates that relationships may become more stable with age because testosterone levels peak during the mid-20s, and the temptation to seek new partners may decline with falling testosterone levels. Helen Fisher, Why We Love: The Nature and Chemistry of Romantic Love 201 (2004).

47. Tom W. Smith, *American Sexual Behavior: Trends, Socio-Demographic Differences, and Risk Behavior* 54, Table 7 (Univ. of Chicago Nat'l Opinion Res. Ctr., General Soc. Survey Topical Rep. No. 25, 2006), *available at* http://www.norc.org/nr/rdonlyres/2663f09f-2e74-436e-ac81-6ffbf288e183/0/AmericanSexualBehavior2006.pdf.

48. U.S. Dep't of Justice, Federal Bureau of Investigation, Criminal Justice Information Services Division, *2006 Crime in the United States*, Table 38, *available at* http://www.fbi.gov/ucr/cius2006/data/table_38.html (last visited Mar. 21, 2008). The impact of imprisonment in aggravating inequality is potentially staggering.

49. Milton C. Regan Jr., Family Law and the Pursuit of Intimacy 28 (1993) (on the greater importance of gender roles in constituting identity in earlier eras).

50. For a comprehensive examination of these changes, see Network on Transitions to Adulthood, *supra* note 12.

51. *Id.*

52. *See, e.g.*, Linda C. McClain, The Place of Families: Fostering Capacity, Equality, and Responsibility 63 (2006) (on the prevalence of domestic violence in eras with higher rates of marriage).

# Chapter 4

1. For a notable example, see the litigation over Barry Bonds' premarital agreement, which produced three different outcomes, with three different rationales, at the trial, appellate, and state supreme court level, and which persuaded the legislature to amend the statute—all without becoming an issue in election campaigns. *See* Bonds v. Bonds (In re Marriage of Bonds), 83 Cal. Rptr. 2d 783 (Ct. App. 1999), rev'd, 5 P.3d 815 (Cal. 2000); S. 78, 2001–2002, Reg. Sess., Complete Bill History, at 1 (Cal. 2001); John G. Gherini, Comment: *The California Supreme Court Swings and Misses in Defining the Scope and Enforceability of Premarital Agreements*, 36 U.S.F. L. Rev. 151 (2001).

2. John T. Jost, *The End of the End of Ideology*, 61 Am. Psychol. 651, 654 (2006), proposes a similar definition. He suggests: "Conservatives consider people to be inherently *unequal and due unequal rewards;* liberals are *equalitarian.* Conservatives venerate *tradition* and—most of all—*order* and *authority;* liberals believe planned *change* brings the possibility of improvement."

3. John R. Alford, Carolyn L. Funk, & John R. Hibbing, *Are Political Orientations Genetically Transmitted?* 99 Am. Pol. Sci. Rev. 153, 157, 160 (2005) (group identification, e.g., the children of Methodists tending to be Methodists, reflects parental socialization in contrast with views on particular issues).

4. *Id.* at 164. For a mild critique, see Barry Burden, *The Genetic Bases of Political Attitudes* (Institute of Quantitative Social Science at Harvard University), *available at* http://www.iq.harvard.edu/blog/pb/2005/10/the_genetic_bases_of_political_1.html ("The process by which specific attitudes are shaped by genetics, therefore, remains largely a black box"); see also John Hibbing & John Alford, *Accepting Authoritative Decisions: Humans as War Cooperators*, 48 Am. J. Pol. Sci. 62 (2004); John Orbell et al., *"Machiavellian" Intelligences as a Basis for the Evolution of Cooperative Dispositions*, 98 Am. Pol. Sci. Rev. 1 (Feb. 2004). For an argument against these conclusions, see Elizabeth Suhay & Nathan Kalmoe, *Why Twin Studies Are Problematic for the Study of Political Ideology: Rethinking Are Political Orientations Genetically Transmitted?* (July 1, 2007) (prepared for International Society of Political Psychology annual meeting in Portland, Oregon, July 3–7, 2007), *available at* http://sitemaker. umich.edu/suhay/files/suhay__kalmoe__mcdermott_070107.pdf.

5. Alford, Funk, & Hibbing, *supra* note 3, at 158 (explaining methodology), 164–65 (describing cross-cultural packages of issues considered liberal or conservative).

6. *Id.* at 164–65.

7. *Id.* at 165.

8. *Id.* at 158–60; *see also* John R. Alford & John R. Hibbing, *The Origin of Politics: An Evolutionary Theory of Behavior*, 2 Persp. on Pol. 707 (2004).

9. Alford, Funk, & Hibbing, *supra* note 3, at 164.

10. *See, e.g.,* Shalom H. Schwartz & Lilach Sagiv, *Identifying Culture-Specifics in the Content and Structure of Values*, 26 J. Cross-Cultural Psychol. 92 (1995) (using ten values arranged in opposed pairs, e.g., openness to change (stimulation, self-direction) versus conservation (security, conformity, tradition), self-transcendence (universalism, benevolence)

versus self-actualization (power, achievement). Hedonism falls into openness to change and self-actualization). In contrast, many researchers refer to the "big five" of personality profiles: openness, conscientiousness, neuroticism, extraversion, and agreeableness. Openness tends to be the factor that best predicts liberal political views. *See also* Jost, *supra* note 2, at 662, who concludes: "There is now the possibility of explaining ideological differences between right and left in terms of underlying psychological needs for stability versus change, order versus complexity, familiarity versus novelty, conformity versus creativity, and loyalty versus rebellion."

11. Dan M. Kahan, Donald Braman, Paul Slovic, John Gastil, & Geoffrey L. Cohen, *The Second National Risk and Culture Study: Making Sense of—and Making Progress in—the American Culture War of Fact* (Yale Law School, Public Law Working Paper No. 154, 2007), *available at* http://papers.ssrn.com/sol3/papers.cfm?abstract_id=1017189.

12. George Lakoff, Moral Politics: How Liberals and Conservatives Think (2d ed., 2002).

13. *Id.*

14. *Id.*; George Lakoff, Don't Think of an Elephant! Know Your Values and Frame the Debate (2004).

15. Rockridge Institute, *The Conservative Window, available at* http://www.rockridgeinstitute.org/projects/strategic/nationasfamily/sfworldview.

16. Bonnie Azab Powell, *Framing the Issues: UC Berkeley Professor George Lakoff Tells How Conservatives Use Language to Dominate Politics*, UC-Berkeley News (2003), *available at* http://www.berkeley.edu/news/media/releases/2003/10/27_lakoff.shtml.

17. Rockridge Institute, *The Progressive Window, available at* http://www.rockridgeinstitute.org/projects/strategic/nationasfamily/npworldview.

18. *See, e.g.,* Donald Braman, Dan M. Kahan, & James Grimmelmann, *Modeling Facts, Culture, and Cognition in the Gun Debate*, 18 Soc. Just. Res. 283 (2005); Dan M. Kahan & Donald Braman, *Cultural Cognition and Public Policy*, 24 Yale L. & Pol'y Rev. 149, 163 (2006). *See generally,* Cultural Cognition Project at Yale Law School, *available at* http://research.yale.edu/culturalcognition.

19. Kahan & Braman, *supra* note 18, at 165.

20. Pew Forum on Religion & Public Life, *Religious Beliefs Underpin Opposition to Homosexuality* (2003), *available at* http://pewforum.org/docs/index.php?DocID=37.

21. *Id.* This does not necessarily mean, however, that causality is unidimensional. As Kristin Luker observed, parishioners may seek out churches whose "sexual teachings support…their own values, especially when they feel that their values [are] increasingly under assault in the larger culture." Kristin Luker, When Sex Goes to School: Warring Views on Sex—and Sex Education—since the Sixties 95–96 (2006).

22. The science on this point remains speculative, however, with intriguing suggestions about the biological basis of homosexuality that do not, at this point, provide conclusive evidence about its etiology. *See* Anthony

F. Bogaert, *Biological versus Nonbiological Older Brothers and Men's Sexual Orientation*, 103 PROC. NAT'L ACAD. SCI. 10771 (2006) (summarizing literature and concluding that having older brothers increases the incidence of male homosexuality).

23. *See, e.g.*, FRANCIS FUKUYAMA, THE END OF HISTORY AND THE LAST MAN (1992); Jost, *supra* note 2, at 651, 656.

24. ANDREW GELMAN, RED STATE, BLUE STATE, RICH STATE, POOR STATE: WHY AMERICANS VOTE THE WAY THEY DO 116 (2008).

25. *Id.* at 115. The split, of course, may reflect a variety of factors, including the change in the South from a largely Democratic to a heavily Republican area, and the reaction of the party leadership to the two wars, with the most intense divisions on Vietnam coming from within the Democratic Party.

26. *Id.* at 127.

27. *See id.* at 128–29, 168.

28. BILL BISHOP, THE BIG SORT 133 (2008).

29. *Id.* at 131.

30. *Id.*; Thomas J. Miles & Cass R. Sunstein, *The New Legal Realism*, 75 U. CHI. L. REV. 831, 839 (2008).

31. Kahan & Braman, *supra* note 18, at 155–56.

32. *Id.* at 169.

33. BISHOP, *supra* note 28, at 82.

34. *Id.* at 167–68. Social scientists identify fundamentalists, whatever their creed, as those who believe "that one religion uniquely represents the fundamental truth, that this truth is opposed by evil, and that only followers of this religion have the desired relationship with God." Lynne M. Jackson & Bruce Hunsberger, *An Intergroup Perspective on Religion and Prejudice*, 38 J. SCI. STUDY REL. 509, 512 (1999); *see also* Bob Altemeyer & Bruce Hunsberger, *A Revised Religious Fundamentalism Scale: The Short and Sweet of It*, 14 INT'L J. PSYCHOL. REL. 47 (2004) (proposing a scale to measure fundamentalism).

35. BISHOP, *supra* note 28, at 173.

36. *Id.* at 38.

37. *Id.* at 178.

38. *Id.*

39. JOHN C. GREEN ET AL., THE AMERICAN RELIGIOUS LANDSCAPE AND THE 2004 PRESIDENTIAL VOTE: INCREASED POLARIZATION 13 (2005), *available at* http://pewforum.org/publications/surveys/postelection.pdf.

40. Pew Forum on Religion & Public Life, *Religion and the 2006 Elections*, *available at* http://pewforum.org/docs/index.php?DocID=174.

41. *Id.*

42. *Id.*

43. *See* Pew Forum on Religion & Public Life, *Voting Religiously* (Nov. 5, 2008), *available at* http://pewresearch.org/pubs/1022/exit-poll-analysis-religion.

44. *NES 2004 Post Election Questionnaire* 87–88 (2004), *available at* ftp://ftp.nes.isr.umich.edu/ftp/cses/studies/module2/survey/USA_2004_English_PostElection.pdf.

45. David E. Campbell, *A House Divided? What Social Science Has to Say about the Culture War*, 15 Wm. & Mary Bill Rts. J. 59, 64–65 (2006).

46. Peter L. Francia, Jonathan S. Morris, Carmine Scavo, & Judy Baumgardner, *America Divided? Examining the Myth of the Polarized American Electorate* (2005), *available at* http://www.allacademic.com//meta/p_mla_apa_research_citation/0/4/1/5/0/pages41504/p41504-1.php.

47. Robin Marantz Henig, *Darwin's God*, N.Y. Times Mag., Mar. 4, 2007, at 37; *see also* Scott Atran & Ara Norenzayan, *Religion's Evolutionary Landscape: Counterintuition, Commitment, Compassion, Communion*, 27 Behav. & Brain Sci. 713 (2004).

48. For an empirical test of this proposition, see Bradley Ruffle & Richard Sosis, *Does It Pay to Pray? Costly Ritual and Cooperation*, 7 B.E. J. Econ. Anal. & Pol'y 1 (2007) (finding that religious males in Israel are more likely to cooperate than are secular males).

49. Henig, *supra* note 47 (quoting interview with Sosis).

50. David Barnhizer suggests that the law and courts are at the center of the "seismic" cultural conflict and that there has been little reasoned discourse from intellectuals on these issues. David Barnhizer, *Ideology, Propaganda and Legal Discourse in the Argument Culture* (Cleveland-Marshall Legal Studies Paper No. 07–141, 2007), *available at* http://papers.ssrn.com/sol3/papers.cfm?abstract_id=975256. While law is central—control of national appropriations for teen education, for example, helps to determine what teens actually learn—we see law as the result, rather than as the catalyst, of the conflict. The laws that exist reflect certain values; while they may promote the development of, or revolution against, those values, they exemplify the values of the winning position. Moreover, we see more reasoned analysis from within and outside of the academy than does Professor Barnhizer.

51. *Id.* at 929, citing David E. Campbell, *Religious "Threat" in Contemporary Presidential Elections*, 68 J. Pol. 104, 109 (2006).

52. Michael Hout & Claude S. Fischer, *Why More Americans Have No Religious Preference: Politics and Generations*, 67 Am. Soc. Rev. 165, 166, 188–89 (2002).

53. Ross Douthat, *Crises of Faith*, Atlantic (July–Aug. 2007), *available at* http://www.theatlantic.com/doc/200707/religion.

54. *See* Victor J. Stenger & Christopher Hitchens, God: The Failed Hypothesis/How Science Shows That God Does Not Exist (2007); Richard Dawkins, The God Delusion (2008); Christopher Hitchens, God Is Not Great (2008); Sam Harris, The End of Faith: Religion, Terror, and the Future of Reason (2005).

55. Christian Smith, American Evangelicalism: Embattled and Thriving 150–51 (1998).

56. Clem Brooks, *Religious Influence and the Politics of Family Decline Concerns*, 67 Am. Soc. Rev. 191, 207–8 (2002).

57. Luker, *supra* note 21, at 143.

58. *Id.* at 146.

## Chapter 5

1. Planned Parenthood, *available at* http://www.yelp.com/biz/planned-parenthood-costa-mesa (last visited Mar. 18, 2009). Yelp.com is an online forum where users can review everything from doctors to restaurants on a five-star basis in addition to writing comments about the person or place they are reviewing that anyone logging onto the Web site can read. The comment from Trish G. was posted on a review of the Planned Parenthood in Costa Mesa, California.

2. Act of March 3, 1873, chap. 258, 17 Stat. 598; *see also* J. E. Leonarz, Annotation, *Validity of Regulations as to Contraceptives or the Dissemination of Birth Control Information*, 96 A.L.R.2d 955, § 6 (2001).

3. For an example of such laws, *see* An Act Concerning Offences against Chastity, Morality and Decency, 1879 Mass. Acts 512 (codified at Mass. Gen. Laws Ann. chap. 272, § 21 (West 1992)). The act stated:

   Except as provided in section twenty-one A, whoever sells, lends, gives away, exhibits, or offers to sell, lend or give away an instrument or other article intended to be used for self-abuse, or any drug, medicine, instrument or article whatever for the prevention of conception or for causing unlawful abortion, or advertises the same, or writes, prints, or causes to be written or printed a card, circular, book, pamphlet, advertisement or notice of any kind stating when, where, how, of whom or by what means such article can be purchased or obtained, or manufactures or makes any such article shall be punished by imprisonment in the state prison for not more than five years or in jail or the house of correction for not more than two and one half years or by a fine of not less than one hundred nor more than one thousand dollars.

4. Conn. Gen. Stat. § 6399 (1878).

5. *See* Donna Dennis, Review Essay, *Obscenity Law and the Conditions of Freedom in the Nineteenth-Century United States: Nicola Beisel, Imperiled Innocents: Anthony Comstock and Family Reproduction in Victorian America*, 27 L. & Soc. Inquiry 369, 370–75 (2002).

6. Deborah Spar, *Selling Stem Cell Science: How Markets Drive Law along the Technological Frontier*, 33 Am. J.L. & Med. 541, 548 (2007). For a more complete history of these laws, see Mary Ware Dennett, Birth Control Laws 7 (1926; reprint, 1970); Note, *Some Legislative Aspects of the Birth-Control Problem*, 45 Harv. L. Rev. 723, 724–26 (1932).

7. National Center for Health Statistics, *Births to Teenagers in the United States, 1940–2000*, 49 Nat'l Vital Stat. Rep. 10 (2001), at p. 10, *available at* http://www.cdc.gov/nchs/data/nvsr49/nvsr49_10.pdf; *see also* Kristin Luker, Dubious Conceptions: The Politics of Teenage Pregnancy 196, Table 1 (1997).

8. Stephanie Coontz, The Way We Never Were: American Families and the Nostalgia Trap 39–40 (1992).

9. Claudia Goldin & Lawrence F. Katz, *The Power of the Pill: Oral Contraceptives and Women's Career and Marriage Decisions*, 110 J. Pol. Econ. 730, 731 (Aug. 2002).

10. *Id.* at 749.

11. Russell W. Rumberger, *The Market for College Graduates, 1960–1990*, 55 J. HIGHER EDUC. 433, 436 (1984), *available at* http://www.jstor.org/stable/pdfplus/1981442.pdf.

12. Nicole Stoops, *Educational Attainment in the United States: 2003*, CURRENT POPULATION REP. 4 (June 2004), *available at* http://www.census.gov/prod/2004pubs/p20-550.pdf.

13. Goldin & Katz, *supra* note 9, at 751.

14. *Id.* at 753.

15. LUKER, *supra* note 7, at 87–95.

16. COONTZ, *supra* note 8, at 202–3; *see also* LUKER, *supra* note 7, at 196, Table 1 (showing that birthrates to women aged 15–19 were 79.5 births per 1,000 in 1950, 91.0 births per 1,000 in 1960, 73.3 per 1,000 in 1965, 69.7 in 1970, and 59.9 in 1990).

17. P. MAZA, ADOPTION TRENDS: 1944–1975 (1934).

18. Goldin & Katz, *supra* note 9, at 752.

19. LORETTA MCLAUGHLIN, THE PILL, JOHN ROCK, AND THE CHURCH 106, 115–16 (1982)

20. *Id.* at 135.

21. Spar, *supra* note 6, at 551.

22. 381 U.S. 479 (1965).

23. Poe v. Ullman, 367 U.S. 497 (1961).

24. Posting of Mary L. Dudziak to Legal History Blog, *Catherine Roraback, Attorney in Griswold v. Connecticut, Has Died*, http://legalhistoryblog.blogspot.com/2007/10/catherine-roraback-attorney-in-griswold.html (Oct. 20, 2007), at 16:27.

25. Bill Baird, *The Politics of God, Government, and Sex: A Thirty-One-Year Crusade*, 13 ST. LOUIS U. PUB. L. REV. 139, 144 (1993).

26. *Vice Squad Nabs BU Birth Control Speaker*, REC. AM., Apr. 7, 1967, at 2.

27. Eisenstadt v. Baird, 405 U.S. 438, 453 (1972).

28. Carey v. Pop. Servs. Int'l, 431 U.S. 678, 687 (1977).

29. Goldin & Katz, *supra* note 9, at 754–55.

30. *Id.* In this study, the authors first introduced the factor of the average abortion rate in an individual's state of birth when the individual was 18–21. Inclusion of this variable shows a large negative and statistically significant impact of the state abortion variable on the likelihood that a female college graduate will marry by 23. The authors then added state-of-birth linear time trends, which reduce the size and significance of the abortion rate variable and increase that of access to birth control.

31. *Id.* at 758.

32. Jennifer Warner, *Premarital Sex the Norm in America*, WEBMD (Dec. 20, 2006), http://www.webmd.com/sex-relationships/news/20061220/premarital-sex-the-norm-in-america.

33. Gary Langer et al., *Poll: American Sex Survey*, ABCNEWS, Oct. 21, 2004, http://abcnews.go.com/primetime/pollvault/Story?id=156921&page=2.

34. THOMAS C. DIENES, LAW, POLITICS, AND BIRTH CONTROL 266 (1972).

35. LUKER, *supra* note 7, at 56–57.

36. King v. Smith, 392 U.S. 309, 326 (1968).
37. Sanford F. Schram & J. Patrick Turbett, *Civil Disorder and the Welfare Explosion: A Two-Step Process*, 48 Am. Soc. Rev. 408, 410 (1983).
38. Office of Policy Planning and Research, U.S. Dep't of Labor, The Negro Family: The Case for National Action (1965) (typically called the Moynihan Report after its primary author, Daniel Patrick Moynihan).
39. Martin Gilens, Why Americans Hate Welfare: Race, Media and the Politics of Antipoverty Policy 106 (2000); *see also* Guttmacher Institute, *Typical AFDC Family Smaller than 10 Years Ago: Average Number of Children Fell from 3 to 2*, 15 Fam. Plan. Persp. 31–32 (Jan.–Feb. 1983).
40. Donna L. Franklin, Ensuring Inequality: The Structural Transformation of the African American Family 164 (1997).
41. Luker, *supra* note 7, at 57.
42. *Id.* at 59.
43. *See id.*; J. Shoshanna Ehrlich, *From Age of Consent Laws to the "Silver Ring Thing": The Regulation of Adolescent Female Sexuality*, 16 Health Matrix 151, 160–62 (2006).
44. Luker, *supra* note 7, at 60.
45. 405 U.S. 438, 453 (1972).
46. 431 U.S. 678, 694 (1977).
47. *Id.* at 695.
48. G. Crum, *Health Care Policy and the Reagan Administration: The Case of Family Planning*, 12 J. Health & Hum. Resources Admin. 524–35 (1990).
49. Planned Parenthood Fed'n of Am. v. Heckler, 712 F.2d 650, 665 (D.C. Cir. 1983).
50. *See* Rachel Benson Gold, *Stronger Together: Medicaid, Title X Bring Different Strengths to Family Planning Effort*, 10 Guttmacher Pol'y Rev. 13, 18 (Spring 2007) (discussing how Title X clinics are struggling to meet the health needs of the rising numbers of immigrants ineligible for Medicaid), *available at* http://www.guttmacher.org/pubs/gpr/10/2/gpr100213.pdf; Cynthia Dailard, *Challenges Facing Family Planning Clinics and Title X*, 4 Guttmacher Rep. on Pub. Pol'y 8, 8–11 (Apr. 2001), *available at* http://www.guttmacher.org/pubs/tgr/04/2/gr040208.pdf; Adam Sonfield et al., Guttmacher Institute, Cost Pressures on Title X Family Planning Grantees, FY 2001–2004, at 4 (2006) (explaining that Title X–funded clinics reported an average cost increase of 58% from 2001 to 2004 for language assistance services for non–English speakers), *available at* http://www.guttmacher.org/pubs/2006/08/01/CPTX.pdf. Overall, Medicaid funding for family planning has increased, and much of the increase directed toward contraception has been concentrated in 14 states.
51. Rachel Benson Gold, *Rekindling Efforts to Prevent Unplanned Pregnancy: A Matter of "Equity and Common Sense,"* 9 Guttmacher Pol'y Rev. (Summer 2006), *available at* http://www.guttmacher.org/pubs/gpr/09/3/gpr090302.html.
52. Gardiner Harris, *Agency Agrees to Ease Access to Emergency Contraceptive for 17-Year-Olds*, N.Y. Times, Apr. 23, 2009, at A14.

1. WILLIAM MARTIN, WITH GOD ON OUR SIDE: THE RISE OF THE RELIGIOUS RIGHT IN AMERICA 193 (1996) (quoting Brown), quoted in Robert Post & Reva Siegel, *Roe Rage: Democratic Constitutionalism and Backlash*, 42 HARV. C.R.-C.L. L. REV. 373, 415 (2007).

2. Post & Siegel, *supra* note 1, at 420.

3. *A Special Report*, CHRISTIAN HARVEST TIMES, June 1980, at 1, *quoted in* MARTIN, *supra* note 1, at 196.

4. *See Republican Party Platform of 1980*, American Presidency Project, *available at* http://www.presidency.ucsb.edu/showplatforms.php?platindex=R1980 (last visited Mar. 21, 2009). In 1984, the Republican Party reaffirmed its "support for the appointment of judges at all levels of the judiciary who respect traditional family values and the sanctity of innocent human life." *See Republican Party Platform of 1984*, American Presidency Project, *available at* http://www.presidency.ucsb.edu/showplatforms.php?platindex=R1984 (last visited Mar. 21, 2009).

5. DREW WESTEN, THE POLITICAL BRAIN 178 (2007).

6. John R. Alford, Carolyn L. Funk, & John R. Hibbing, *Are Political Orientations Genetically Transmitted?* 99 AM. POL. SCI. REV. 153, 164–65 (2005).

7. John T. Jost, *The End of the End of Ideology*, 61 AM. PSYCHOL. 651, 666 (Oct. 2006).

8. GEORGE LAKOFF, MORAL POLITICS: HOW LIBERALS AND CONSERVATIVES THINK 267 (2d. ed. 2002).

9. Gregory Smith & Allison Pond, *A Slight but Steady Majority Favors Keeping Abortion Legal*, Pew Forum on Religion in Public Life (Sept. 16, 2008), *available at* http://pewforum.org/docs/?DocID=350.

10. *Pragmatic Americans: Liberal and Conservative on Social Issues*, Pew Center for the People & the Press (Aug. 3, 2006), *available at* http://people-press.org/report/283/pragmatic-americans-liberal-and-conservative-on-social-issues.

11. BILL BISHOP, THE BIG SORT: WHY THE CLUSTERING OF LIKE-MINDED AMERICANS IS TEARING US APART 26 (2008).

12. *See also* ANDREW GELMAN, RED STATE, BLUE STATE, RICH STATE, POOR STATE 118 (2008).

13. Stephanie Simon, *Abortion Foes' Dilemma: Confront or Cooperate?* WALL ST. J. (Nov. 11, 2008), at A6, *see also* Lydia Saad, *More Americans "Pro-Life" than "Pro-Choice" for First Time*, Gallup (May 15, 2009), *available at* http://www.gallup.com/poll/118399/More-Americans-Pro-Life-Than-Pro-Choice-First-Time.aspx?CSTS=tagrss.

14. Lydia Saad, *Abortion Issue Laying Low in 2008 Campaign* (May 2008), *available at* http://www.gallup.com/poll/107458/Abortion-Issue-Laying-Low-2008-Campaign.aspx (in October 2004, 20% of pro-life voters compared to 10% of pro-choice voters said that a candidate must share their views on abortion for the voters to be able to vote for that candidate; in May 2008, it was 15% and 11%).

15. *Pragmatic Americans*, *supra* note 10.

16. 410 U.S. 113 (1973).

17. *Id.* at 152.

18. Planned Parenthood of S.E. Pa. v. Casey, 505 U.S. 833, 852 (1992).

19. *Id.*

20. E.g., *id.* at 895; Hodgson v. Minnesota, 497 U.S. 417, 428–29, 444–45 (1990).

21. Brief of Petitioners at 10–12, Ayotte v. Planned Parenthood, 546 U.S. 320 (2006). Professor Teresa Collett notes that parental notification laws can benefit minors through improving medical care and providing protection from sexual assault. Teresa Stanton Collett, *Protecting Our Daughters: The Need for Parental Notification Laws*, 26 Vt. L. Rev. 101, 102 (2001).

22. Editorial, *Parental Notification*, N.Y. Times (July 27, 2006), *available at* http:// www.nytimes.com/2006/07/27/opinion/27thu4.html?pagewanted=print.

23. For a comprehensive statement of the benefits of parental notification laws, including claims that such laws help to reduce teen pregnancy, see Teresa Stanton Collett, *Transporting Minors for Immoral Purposes: The Case for the Child Custody Protection Act & the Child Interstate Abortion Notification Act*, 16 Health Matrix 107 (2006). For a discussion of the methodological issues underlying such claims, see Theodore Joyce, Silvie Colman, & Robert Kaestner, *Methodological Issues in the Evaluation of Parental Involvement Laws: Evidence from Texas* (Nat'l Bureau of Econ. Res., Working Paper No. 12608, 2006), *available at* http://papers.ssrn.com/sol3/papers.cfm?abstract_id=929171.

24. *See* George Lakoff, Don't Think of an Elephant! Know Your Values and Frame the Debate 104–5 (2004). Professors Robert Post and Reva Siegel note more generally that "[t]he antiabortion backlash that has so traumatized liberals reflects a constitutional vision that would preserve traditional family roles and resist secularization of the American state." Post & Siegel, *supra* note 1, at 423.

25. Chad Livengood, *House Bill Would Criminalize Coercion of Abortion*, News-Leader.com, Mar. 4, 2009, *available at* http://www.news-leader.com/article/20090304/NEWS06/903040462.

26. *See, e.g.*, Caroline A. Placey, Comment, *Of Judicial Bypass Procedures, Moral Recusal, and Protected Political Speech: Throwing Pregnant Minors under the Campaign Bus*, 56 Emory L.J. 693, 703–4 (2006); Posting of Professor Kimberly Mutcherson to Legal Affairs Debate Club, http://www.legalaffairs .org/webexclusive/debateclub_parental-notification0306.msp (Mar. 13, 2006), at 12:45.

27. Stanley K. Henshaw & Kathryn Kost, *Parental Involvement in Minors' Abortion Decisions*, 24 Fam. Plan. Persp. 196, 207 (1992).

28. Auriana Ojeda, *Should Abortion Rights Be Restricted? Introduction*, enotes .com, 2002, http://www.enotes.com/should-abortion-article/39731; *see also* Rachel N. Pine, *Speculation and Reality: The Role of Facts in Judicial Protection of Fundamental Rights*, 136 U. Pa. L. Rev. 655, 687–93 (1987) (summarizing research that shows ineffective parent-teen communications about matters of sexuality and that assumptions underlying parental notification laws are unrealistic); J. Shoshanna Ehrlich, *From Age of Consent Laws to the "Silver Ring Thing": The Regulation of Adolescent Female Sexuality*, 16 Health Matrix 151, 169–72 (2006).

29. *See* Carol Sanger, *Regulating Teenage Abortion in the United States: Politics and Policy*, 18 Int'l J.L. Pol'y & Fam. 305 (2004) (statutes serve, inter alia, to make access to abortion more difficult for minors).

30. For further discussion of the *Roe* backlash, see Post & Siegel, *supra* note 1.

31. Theresa N. Walker, Note, *California's Parental Consent Statute: A Constitutional Challenge*, 40 HASTINGS L.J. 169, 169 n.4 (1988) (23 states had enacted either parental notification or consent laws; 9 were subject to injunction, and 3 had been declared unconstitutional).

32. MASS. GEN. LAWS ANN. chap. 112, § 12P (West 2003). The Massachusetts statute required the consent, not just the notification, of both parents.

33. *See* Planned Parenthood, *Laws Requiring Mandatory Parental Involvement for Minors' Abortion*, http://www.plannedparenthood.org/issues-action/abortion/ mandatory-parental-involvement/reports/laws-requiring-mandatory-parental-involvement-minors-abortion-6132.htm (last visited Mar. 21, 2009).

34. *See* H. W. Perry Jr. & L. A. Powe Jr., *The Political Battle for the Constitution*, 21 CONST. COMMENT. 641 (2004) (summarizing the political shifts and timing the start of the political polarization on the issue to the Reagan years); *see also* Post & Siegel, *supra* note 1, at 409–25.

35. Planned Parenthood v. Danforth, 428 U.S. 52 (1976).

36. Bellotti v. Baird, 443 U.S. 622, 643–44 (1979); Planned Parenthood of S.E. Pa. v. Casey, 505 U.S. 833, 899–900 (1992).

37. 443 U.S. 622.

38. He noted:

    [W]e are concerned here with a constitutional right to seek an abortion. The abortion decision differs in important ways from other decisions that may be made during minority. The need to preserve the constitutional right and the unique nature of the abortion decision, especially when made by a minor, require a State to act with particular sensitivity when it legislates to foster parental involvement in this matter.... Indeed, considering her probable education, employment skills, financial resources, and emotional maturity, unwanted motherhood may be exceptionally burdensome for a minor.... In sum, there are few situations in which denying a minor the right to make an important decision will have consequences so grave and indelible. (*Id.* at 642)

39. *Id.* at 642–43 (opinion of Powell, J.).

40. *Id.* at 644.

41. Hodgson v. Minnesota, 497 U.S. 417 (1990).

42. *Id.* at 425 n.5 (discussing the varying requirements from state to state for a woman who seeks an abortion).

43. *Id.* at 421.

44. *See, e.g.*, Planned Parenthood v. Camblos, 155 F.3d 352, 364 (4th Cir. 1998) ("The Court in *Hodgson* was so fractured as to render its opinions collectively all but impenetrable, with five different Justices filing opinions variously concurring and dissenting in other opinions and parts of other opinions.")

45. *Hodgson*, 497 U.S. at 480 (Scalia, J., concurring in part and dissenting in part).

46. 546 U.S. 320 (2006).

47. *Id.* at 329 (citations omitted).

48. *See, e.g.*, Perry & Powe, *supra* note 34, who observed that legislatures in the era immediately after *Roe* sometimes passed legislation with the expectation that the Court would invalidate it, taking the political heat away from the legislature for the decision.

49. Planned Parenthood, *Laws Requiring Mandatory Parental Involvement, supra* note 33. Connecticut provides for counseling the teen about the possibility of parental notification, but does not mandate it. CONN. GEN. STAT. ANN. §§ 19a-600 to -601 (West 2007).

50. Pam Belluck, *New Hampshire to Repeal Parental Notification Law*, N.Y. TIMES (June 8, 2007), at A22, *available at* http://www.nytimes.com/2007/06/08/us/08parental.html.

51. *Id.* The *Ayotte* Court observed that the failure to provide an exception to the parental notification provision to protect the life or health of the mother raised potential constitutional issues, and it remanded for a determination of whether an injunction would cure the problem. Ayotte v. Planned Parenthood of New England, 546 U.S. 320 (2006).

52. The California legislature had enacted a parental involvement statute in 1987, which was declared unconstitutional in 1997 pursuant to the state's constitutional right to privacy. *See* Am. Acad. of Pediatrics v. Lungren, 940 P.2d 797, 800 (Cal. 1997) (striking down California's law because it offended the minor's right of privacy guaranteed by the California constitution). The proposition failed in 2006 by a vote of 46% to 54%. *America Votes 2006, State Races: California*, CNN.COM, http://www.cnn.com/ELECTION/2006/pages/results/states/CA.

53. *America Votes 2006, State Races: Oregon*, CNN.COM, http://www.cnn.com/ELECTION/2006/pages/results/states/OR.

54. ME. REV. STAT. ANN. tit. 22, § 1597-A(2)(A) (West 2007).

55. DEL. CODE ANN. tit. 24, § 1783(a) (2009); MD. CODE ANN., HEALTH-GEN. § 20–103(c) (West 2007) (allowing a physician to determine that parental notice is not in the minor's best interest); W. VA. CODE § 16–2F-1 (2009) (stating that a physician not affiliated with an abortion provider may waive the notice requirement). Kansas also permits physician waiver but only in the event of a medical emergency. KAN. STAT. ANN. § 65–6705(j) (2007) (allowing a physician to bypass parental notice in cases where the physician determines that an emergency exists that threatens the "well-being" of the minor).

56. *See, e.g.*, WIS. STAT. ANN. § 48.375(2)(b) (West 2005) (in lieu of parental consent, a grandparent, aunt, uncle, or sibling who is at least 25 years old may provide consent; Wisconsin is also interesting because it allows a clergy member to consult with a minor and appear on her behalf before a judge); OHIO REV. CODE ANN. § 2919.12 (Anderson 2007) (stating that notice may be given to a brother, sister, step-parent, or grandparent if certain qualifications are met). Some states broaden the class of adults to include other family members, such as grandparents, with whom the teen is living, but we view the purpose of these laws as less about parental authority. *See* Planned Parenthood, *Laws Requiring Mandatory Parental Involvement, supra* note 33.

57. Planned Parenthood lists nine states where courts have issued injunctions against enforcement of parental notification laws. Of these states, four (California, Illinois, New Hampshire, and New Jersey) are blue, though New Hampshire is a battleground state, and the remaining five are red (Alaska, Idaho, Montana, New Mexico, and Nevada), with Nevada and New Mexico battleground states. In the four blue states, none of the state laws has been reinstated through

legislative action, despite the fact that the injunctions were issued some time ago. Indeed, California voters rejected a parental notification proposition, and New Hampshire repealed its parental notification law after the Supreme Court decision in *Ayotte. See* Belluck, *supra* note 50. In the five red states, three (the battleground states of Nevada and New Mexico, which went blue in 2008, and Mountain West Montana) have taken no further action; Alaska moved promptly to reinstate the law, and Idaho is appealing the injunction. The Alaska Supreme Court found the statute to be unconstitutional in 2007. State v. Planned Parenthood, 171 P.3d 577 (Alaska 2007). In March 2007, Idaho enacted a new parental consent law to replace previous versions of the statute which the courts had held were unconstitutional and unenforceable. Planned Parenthood of Idaho, Inc. v. Wasden, 376 F.3d 908, 926 (9th Cir. 2004) (unconstitutional and unenforceable because the statute contained an inadequate medical emergency exception to protect a young woman's health), *cert. denied,* 544 U.S. 948 (2005). In Florida, by contrast, following a decision that an earlier parental notification statute was unconstitutional in N. Fla. Women's Health & Counseling Services v. State, 866 So.2d 612 (Fla. 2003), the state amended its constitution to reinstate such a requirement. FLA. STAT. ANN. § 390.01114 (West 2006) (enacted following a constitutional amendment by referendum that would permit parental notification without violating the minor's state constitutional right of privacy, as long as the parental notification requirement contained certain exceptions and a judicial bypass).

58. These states are Connecticut, Hawaii, New York, Oregon, Vermont, and Washington.

59. California rejected such a proposition at the polls, Illinois has yet to adopt a judicial bypass process a decade after the original ruling, and New Jersey has taken no action after seven years.

60. The four states are Maine, Delaware, Maryland, and Wisconsin. Delaware, however, only requires parental involvement for teens under 16. Planned Parenthood, *Laws Requiring Mandatory Parental Involvement, supra* note 33. Carol Sanger emphasizes that the contrast between nuanced consent laws for medical care, including receiving contraceptives, and the blanket consent or notification requirements for abortion underscores the politicized nature of these enactments. Sanger, *supra* note 29, at 307 ("The sweep of coverage suggests from the start that parental involvement statutes focus not on adolescence as a stage of development but rather on minority as a site of control").

61. The Massachusetts law, which originally required the consent of both parents, was limited to one parent and upheld in *Planned Parenthood League of Massachusetts, Inc. v. Attorney General*, 677 N.E.2d 101 (Mass. 1997).

62. Minnesota's restrictive law was partially upheld in *Hodgson v. Minnesota*, 497 U.S. 417 (1990).

63. R.I. GEN. LAWS § 23-4.7-6 (2004).

64. The state's parental consent law was upheld in Planned Parenthood of *Southeastern Pennsylvania v. Casey*, 505 U.S. 833 (1992).

65. Michigan's parental consent law was upheld in *Planned Parenthood of Mid-Michigan, Inc. v. Attorney General*, No. D 91-c571 AZ (Mich. Cir. Ct. Apr. 29, 1994).

66. In three states that voted red in 2004—Montana, New Mexico, and Nevada—the laws have been enjoined and no further action has been taken. Two more, West Virginia and Ohio, permit waivers or the expansion of the adults who can act in lieu of parents. South Carolina lowers the age of mandatory parental involvement to teens younger than 17 and permits grandparents acting in loco parentis to take the place of the parents. S.C. Code Ann. §§ 44–41–10(m), (n) (original statute enacted 1990), -30 (enacted 1990), -31 to -37 (enacted 1990).

67. See Barnes v. Mississippi, 992 F.2d 1335 (5th Cir.), cert. denied, 510 U.S. 976 (1993); Pro-Choice Miss. v. Fordice, 716 So.2d 645 (Miss. 1998).

68. N.D. Cent. Code §§ 14–02.1–03.1 (enacted 1981), 14–02.1–03 (enacted 1975), 14–02.1–02 (enacted 1975; last amended 1995), 14–02.1–02.1 (enacted 1991).

69. Guttmacher Institute, *State Policies in Brief: Parental Involvement in Minors' Abortions* (Mar. 1, 2009), *available at* http://www.guttmacher.org/statecenter/spibs/spib_PIMA.pdf.

70. Planned Parenthood, *Laws Requiring Mandatory Parental Involvement, supra* note 33.

71. Sanger, *supra* note 29, at 306.

72. See Naomi Cahn & June Carbone, *Empirical Research on Parental Involvement Laws* (2007) (unpublished manuscript on file with authors); Amanda Dennis et al., The Impact of Laws Requiring Parental Involvement for Abortion: A Literature Review 27 (2009).

73. Pine, *supra* note 28, at 685–87. In many jurisdictions and especially in rural or conservative areas, judges simply refuse to hear the cases, either acknowledging their personal biases or fearing that hearing the case would pose political problems with reelection. *See, e.g.,* Adam Liptak, *On Moral Grounds, Some Judges Are Opting Out of Abortion Cases,* N.Y. Times, Sept. 4. 2005, *available at* http://www.nytimes.com/2005/09/04/national/04recuse.html?ex=1146110400&en=ee4519b0fd36675e&ei=5070.

74. See Patricia Donovan, *Judging Teenagers: How Minors Fare when They Seek Court-Authorized Abortions,* 15 Fam. Plan. Persp. 259, 264 (1983) (observing that judges in rural areas are most likely to refuse to hear the cases); Lisa Pruitt, *Toward a Feminist Theory of the Rural,* 2007 Utah L. Rev. 421, 478 (noting spatial and confidentiality issues for minors in rural areas).

75. Heather D. Boonstra et al., *Abortion in Women's Lives* 26 (2006), *available at* http://www.guttmacher.org/pubs/2006/05/04/AiWL.pdf (last visited 08/19/09).

76. Rachel K. Jones, Jacqueline E. Darroch, & Stanley K. Henshaw, *Patterns in the Socioeconomic Characteristics of Women Obtaining Abortions in 2000–2001,* 34 Persp. Sexual & Reprod. Health 226, 228–32 (2002).

77. Heather D. Boonstra, *The Heart of the Matter: Public Funding of Abortion for Poor Women in the United States,* 10 Guttmacher Pol'y Rev. 12, 14–16 (2007), *available at* http://www.guttmacher.org/pubs/gpr/10/1/gpr100112.html.

78. Melanie Zurek, Letter to the Editor, N.Y. Times, Jan. 12, 2009, *available at* http://www.nytimes.com/2009/01/12/opinion/l12abort.html.

79. Maher v. Roe, 432 U.S. 464 (1977); Harris v. McRae, 448 U.S. 297 (1980). Before the Hyde Amendment, federal funds were available to women whose pregnancies caused them "severe and long-lasting physical health damage." Dep't of Labor and Health, Education, and Welfare Appropriations Act of 1979, Pub. L. No. 95–480 (1978).

80. *See* Boonstra, *The Heart of the Matter, supra* note 77, at 16 (estimating that the number is between 18% and 35%).

81. Guttmacher Institute State Center, http://www.guttmacher.org/statecenter/abortion.html (last visited Mar. 21, 2009).

82. Tim Carpenter, *Sebelius Vetoes Abortion Bill,* TOPEKA CAPITAL JOURNAL, Apr. 24, 2009, *available at* http://www.cjonline.com/at_home/2009-04-23/sebelius_vetoes_abortion_bill. *See also* THOMAS FRANK, WHAT'S THE MATTER WITH KANSAS? HOW CONSERVATIVES WON THE HEART OF AMERICA 94–96 (2004) (discussing the critical role of abortion in mobilizing the Christian right).

83. Mike Whitney, *The G.O.P. Is Finished; Let's Stick a Fork in It* (May 6, 2009), *available at* http://onlinejournal.com/artman/publish/article_4669.shtml.

## Chapter 7

1. 17 AGAIN (2009).

2. "Abstinence-plus" is the common term for comprehensive sex education (a Google search on September 6, 2007, for the term found 23,000 items). *See, e.g.,* CARMEN SOLOMON-FEARS, REDUCING TEEN PREGNANCY: ADOLESCENT FAMILY LIFE AND ABSTINENCE EDUCATION PROGRAMS 6 (2004), *available at* http://www.law.umaryland.edu/marshall/crsreports/crsdocuments/RS20873 10042004.pdf (CRS Report for Congress).

3. KRISTIN LUKER, WHEN SEX GOES TO SCHOOL: WARRING VIEWS ON SEX—AND SEX EDUCATION—SINCE THE SIXTIES 91 (2006).

4. *Id.*

5. *Id.* at 184.

6. *Id.* at 99.

7. Gary J. Simson & Erika A. Sussman, *Keeping the Sex in Sex Education: The First Amendment's Religion Clauses and the Sex Education Debate,* 9 S. CAL. REV. L. & WOMEN'S STUD. 265, 284–91 (2000). *But see* Helen M. Alvare, *Saying "Yes" before Saying "I Do": Premarital Sex and Cohabitation as a Piece of the Divorce Puzzle,* 18 NOTRE DAME J.L. ETHICS & PUB. POL'Y 7, 77–82 (2004). The Sexuality Information and Education Council of the United States has charged that "abstinence-only-until-marriage" curriculums are "based on religious beliefs…[and] rely on fear and shame." Sexuality Information and Education Council of the United States, *SIECUS Reviews Fear-Based, Abstinence-Only-until-Marriage Curricula* (2005), *available at* http://www.siecus.org/reviews.html (cited in Naomi Cahn & June Carbone, *Deep Purple: Shades of American Family Law,* 110 W. VA. L. REV. 459, 477 n.99 (2007).

8. NPR, *Sex Education in America, available at* http://www.npr.org/templates/story/story.php?storyId=1622610 (Feb. 24, 2004).

9. MARK D. REGNERUS, FORBIDDEN FRUIT: SEX & RELIGION IN THE LIVES OF AMERICAN TEENAGERS 11 (2007).

10. LUKER, WHEN SEX GOES TO SCHOOL *supra* note 3, at 104.

11. NPR, *supra* note 8.

12. Adolescent Family Life Act of 1981, Pub. L. No. 97–35, 42 U.S.C. § 300z (2006).

13. *See* U.S. Dep't of Health & Human Services, Office of Public Health and Science, Office of Population Affairs, Adolescent Family Life, http://www.hhs.gov/opa/familylife/index.html (last visited Oct. 28, 2009).

14. Bowen v. Kendrick, 487 U.S. 589, 606 (1988).

15. SOLOMON-FEARS, *supra* note 2, at 3.

16. Personal Responsibility and Work Opportunity Reconciliation Act of 1996, Pub. L. No. 104–193, 42 U.S.C. § 710(b)(2) (1996). This definition has remained virtually unchanged since 1996.

17. Laura Duberstein Lindberg, John S. Santelli, & Susheela Singh, *Changes in Formal Sex Education: 1995–2002*, 38 PERS. SEXUAL & REPROD. HEALTH 182 (2006), *available at* http://www.guttmacher.org/pubs/journals/3818206.html.

18. CARMEN SOLOMON-FEARS, SCIENTIFIC EVALUATION OF APPROACHES TO PREVENT TEEN PREGNANCY 4 (2007), *available at* http://www.opencrs.com/rpts/RS22656_20070501.pdf;

19. Omnibus Appropriations Act, Pub. L. No. 111–8, div. F (2009) (allocating $94.659 million).

20. Lindberg et al., *supra* note 17, at 184. The authors report that the percentage of males receiving only abstinence education increased from 9% to 24% and of females, from 8% to 21%.

21. REGNERUS, *supra* note 9, at 58.

22. M. J. Stephey, *A Brief History of Abstinence*, TIME, Mar. 2, 2009, at 16.

23. Interview on *Larry King Live*, CNN (Apr. 22, 2009).

24. CHRISTOPHER TRENHOLM ET AL., IMPACTS OF FOUR TITLE V, SECTION 510 ABSTINENCE EDUCATION PROGRAMS, FINAL REPORT xvii (2007), *available at* http://www.mathematica-mpr.com/publications/PDFs/impactabstinence.pdf; John S. Santelli et al., *Explaining Recent Declines in Adolescent Pregnancy in the United States: The Contribution of Abstinence and Increased Contraceptive Use*, 97 AM. J. PUB. HEALTH 150, 152–54 (2007) (comprehensive sex education programs are more effective at reducing pregnancies and sexually transmitted diseases), *available at* http://opr.princeton.edu/seminars/papers%5CRecent_declines_in_adol_pregnancy_NSFG.pdf; *see* Hazel Beh & Milton Diamond, *Children and Education: The Failure of Abstinence-Only Education: Minors Have a Right to Honest Talk about Sex*, 15 COLUM. J. GENDER & L. 12, 38–42 (2006) (summarizing reviews of the programs' effectiveness); Hannah Bruckner & Peter Bearman, *After the Promise: The STD Consequences of Adolescent Virginity Pledges*, 36 J. ADOLESCENT. HEALTH 271, 273–77 (2005). Heritage Foundation scholars, however, have criticized the findings of some of these studies. *See* Robert Rector & Kirk A. Johnson, *Adolescent Virginity Pledges and Risky Sexual Behaviors* (June 14, 2005), *available at* http://www.heritage.org/Research/Welfare/whitepaper06142005-2.cfm.

25. Douglas Kirby et al., *The Impact of Postponing Sexual Involvement Curriculum among Youths in California*, 29 FAM. PLAN. PERSP. 100, 100–108 (1997), *available at* http://www.guttmacher.org/pubs/journals/2910097.html

(concluding that California programs did not prevent sexual activity and increased the pregnancy rates of participants); Bruckner & Bearman, *supra* note 24, at 273–77; *see also* Santelli et al., *supra* note 24, at 152–54 (comprehensive sex education programs are more effective at reducing pregnancies and sexually transmitted diseases).

26. American Psychological Association, *Resolution in Favor of Empirically Supported Sex Education and HIV Prevention Programs for Adolescents* (Feb. 18–20, 2005), *available at* http://www.apa.org/releases/sexed_resolution.pdf.

27. Centers for Disease Control, Adolescent & School Healthy Programs that Work, *available at* http://web.archive.org/web/20010606142729/www.cdc.gov/nccdphp/dash/rtc/index.htm.

28. U.S. House of Representatives, Committee on Government Reform, Minority Staff, Special Investigations Division, *Content of Federally Funded Abstinence-Only Education Programs* (2004), *available at* http://www.democrats.reform.house.gov/Documents/20041201102153-50247.pdf.

29. Trenholm et al., *supra* note 24, at xvii.

30. *Id.* at xvii–xviii.

31. *Id.* at 61.

32. Lindberg et al., *supra* note 17, at 182–88.

33. James Regions, *Controversy over Abstinence Part of Larger Purity Question*, Springfield News-Leader, May 8, 2007, at 2B.

34. Cheryl Wetzstein, *Abstinence-Only on Shaky Ground: Program Funding Threatened Despite Parental Support in Polls*, Wash. Times, May 29, 2007, at A5.

35. NARAL: Pro-Choice America, http://www.prochoiceamerica.org/issues/sex-education (last visited Sept. 5, 2007).

36. U.S. Dep't of Health & Human Services, Association for Children and Families, *State Abstinence Education Program*, *available at* http://www.acf.hhs.gov/programs/fbci/progs/fbci_saep.html.

37. Kaiser Family Foundation, *Daily Women's Health Policy* (Mar. 6, 2007), *available at* http://www.kaisernetwork.org/Daily_reports/rep_index.cfm?DR_ID=43365.

38. *Funding by State, Fiscal Year 2008*, SIECUS, *available at* http://www.siecus.org/index.cfm?fuseaction=Page.ViewPage&PageID=1159.

39. Heather D. Boonstra, *Advocates Call for a New Approach after the Era of "Abstinence-Only" Sex Education*, 12 Guttmacher Pol'y Rev. (Winter 2009), *available at* http://www.guttmacher.org/pubs/gpr/12/1/gpr120106.pdf.

40. Bowen v. Kendrick, 487 U.S. 589 (1988). As two commentators note, "[i]n a significant departure from prior practice, the Court ruled that such a program, which treated religious and secular organizations neutrally, could not be challenged on its face for its overall tendency to advance religion. The Court suggested that if challengers proved that the implementation of specific grants involved distinctively religious activities, such as worship or proselytizing, or that grants were being distributed to 'pervasively sectarian organizations,' courts

would enjoin those particular grants." Ira C. Lupu & Robert W. Tuttle, *Government Partnerships with Faith-Based Service Providers: 2002 Annual Report, available at* http://www.religionandsocialpolicy.org/docs/legal/reports/12-4-2002_state_of_the_law.pdf.

41. *Bowen,* 487 U.S. at 625, 639 (Blackmun, J. dissenting). For the purposes of this book, the outcome of the constitutional challenge—that particular grants pursuant to the AFLA would be invalid if they advanced religion, but that the mere appropriation of grants to religious organizations did not invalidate the statute—is less important than the evidence supporting the religious basis for abstinence education. *See, e.g., id.* at 640 n.9.

42. *Id.* at 642.

43. *Id.* at 640.

44. Compl., ACLU of Louisiana v. Foster (June 17, 2002), *available at* Roundtable on Religion & Social Welfare Policy, http://www.religionandsocialpolicy.org/legal/legal_update_display.cfm?id=5.

45. Roundtable on Religion & Social Welfare Policy, *Government Relationships with Faith-Based Providers: The State of the Law Transcript, available at* http://www.socialpolicyandreligion.org/docs/transcripts/12-16-2002_state_of_the_law_transcript.pdf (comments of Professor Bob Tuttle).

46. Roundtable on Religion & Social Welfare Policy, *UPDATED: ACLU of Louisiana v. Foster, United States District Court for the Eastern District of Louisiana* (May 12, 2006), *available at* http://www.religionandsocialpolicy.org/legal/legal_update_display.cfm?id=7.

47. Settlement Agreement, ACLU of Louisiana v. Foster (Nov. 2002), *available at* http://www.aclu.org/FilesPDFs/foster_settlement.pdf.

48. As Professors Lupu and Tuttle explain, "In American Civil Liberties Union of Louisiana v. Foster, a court held unconstitutional a grant to faith-based organizations that provided sexual abstinence education, because the education had been conducted through intensely religious messages." Ira C. Lupu & Robert Tuttle, *The Faith-Based Initiative and the Constitution,* 55 DePaul L. Rev. 1, 86 (2005).

49. Press Release, American Civil Liberties Union, *ACLU Asks Court to Hold Louisiana's Abstinence-Only Program in Contempt, Citing Numerous Violations of 2002 Order* (Jan. 20, 2005), *available at* http://www.aclu.org/reproductiverights/gen/12754prs20050120.html.

50. Cheryl Wetzstein, *Court OKs Religious Abstinence Content,* Wash. Times, June 26, 2005, *available at* http://washingtontimes.com/national/20050625-104915-8744r.htm.

51. As it explains on its Web site:

> The Silver Ring Thing is the fastest growing teen abstinence program in the United States and is rapidly gaining international recognition for its concert-style show incorporating music, laser lights, fast-paced video, drama & comedy performances. Through this program teens are able to understand that abstinence until marriage is not only God's plan for their lives, but also the best and only way to avoid the harmful physical and emotional effects of premarital sex. By offering a message of forgiveness and new begin-

nings the program reaches out to those teens that have become
sexually active & offers an opportunity to embrace a "second
virginity."

Silver Ring Thing, http://www.silverringthing.com/history.asp (last visited
Mar. 31, 2009).

52. *Id.*, http://www.silverringthing.com/whatissrt.asp (last visited Mar. 31,
2009).

53. *Id.*, http://www.silverringthing.com/shopcategory.asp?catID=14 (last visited
Mar. 31, 2009).

54. Compl., ACLU of Massachusetts v. Leavitt, para. 1 (May 16, 2005), *available
at* http://www.aclu.org/FilesPDFs/teeneducomplaint.pdf.

55. *Id.* at para. 51.

56. *Id.* at para. 62a; *see* J. Shoshanna Ehrlich, *From Age of Consent Laws to the
"Silver Ring Thing": The Regulation of Adolescent Female Sexuality*, 16 Health
Matrix 151, 179–80 (2006).

57. Anne Faris, *Lawsuit Settlement Pulls HHS Funding for Silver Ring Thing
Abstinence Program*, Roundtable on Religion & Social Welfare Policy (Feb.
28, 2006), *available at* http://www.religionandsocialpolicy.org/news/article.
cfm?id=3918.

58. Settlement Agreement, ACLU of Massachusetts v. Leavitt, sec. 2b. (Feb. 22,
2006), *available at* http://www.religionandsocialpolicy.org/docs/legal/cases/
SRT-HHS-ACLU_Settlement%202-24-06.pdf.

59. *Id.*

60. Ira C. Lupu & Robert W. Tuttle, *Legal Update* (Mar. 7, 2006), *available
at* http://www.religionandsocialpolicy.org/legal/legal_update_display.
cfm?id=44.

61. NPR, *supra* note 8; Amy Bleakley et al., *Public Opinion on Sex Education in US
Schools*, 160 Archives Pediatric. & Adolescent Med. 1151 (2006).

62. Bleakley, *supra* note 61, at 1154–55.

63. *See* James McGrath, *Abstinence-Only Adolescent Education: Ineffective,
Unpopular, and Unconstitutional*, 38 U.S.F. L. Rev. 665, 687–89 (2004).

64. Regnerus, *supra* note 9, at 123, 156–58.

65. *Id.* at 126 (noting the effects of strategic orientation, parents' education,
risk orientation, family satisfaction, and intact families) and 204 (noting the
effects of status).

66. Testimony of Dr. John Santelli, *Committee on Oversight and Government
Reform Hearing on Abstinence-Only Programs* (Apr. 23, 2008), *available at*
http://oversight.house.gov/documents/20080423113314.pdf.

67. Regnerus, *supra* note 9, at 156.

## *Chapter 8*

1. James Kent, 2 Commentaries on American Law 76 (Oliver Wendell
Holmes Jr. ed., 12th ed., 1896).

2. Paul R. Amato et al., Alone Together 200–202 (2007).

3. Betsey Stevenson & Justin Wolfers, *Marriage and Divorce: Changes and Their
Driving Forces* (2007) (unpublished manuscript), *quoted in* David Popenoe,
*The Future of Marriage in America*, *in* The State of Our Unions 2007:

THE SOCIAL HEALTH OF MARRIAGE IN AMERICA 7 (2007), *available at* http://marriage.rutgers.edu/Publications/SOOU/SOOU2007.pdf.

4. Eduardo Porter & Michelle O'Donnell, *The New Gender Divide: Facing Middle Age with No Degree, and No Wife*, N.Y. TIMES, Aug. 6, 2006, *available at* http://www.nytimes.com/2006/08/06/us/06marry.html?scp=3&sq=men%20marriage%20rates&st=cse; *see also* Donald R. Deere & Jelena Vesovic, *Educational Wage Premiums and U.S. Income Distribution, in* 1 HANDBOOK OF THE ECONOMICS OF EDUCATION 285 (Eric Alan Hanushek & Finis Welch eds., 2006).

5. Steven P. Martin, *Women, Education, and Family Timing: Outcomes and Trends Associated with Age of Marriage and First Birth, in* KATHRYN M. NECKERMAN, SOCIAL INEQUALITY, *available at* http://books.google.com/books?id=5h2pEfBVyRwC&pg=PA98&lpg=PA98&dq=marriage+rates+of+college+graduates&source=bl&ots=LvUCi7i5eD&sig=BXj16sKDHPT_AyluXGIXzUueJlo&hl=en&ei=nBTyScaKF4GdlQeMqojLDA&sa=X&oi=book_result&ct=result&resnum=2#PPA104,M1.

6. ANDREW J. CHERLIN, THE MARRIAGE-GO-ROUND: THE STATE OF MARRIAGE AND THE FAMILY IN AMERICA TODAY 168 (2009).

7. *See, in particular,* ORLANDO PATTERSON, RITUALS OF BLOOD: THE CONSEQUENCES OF SLAVERY IN TWO AMERICAN CENTURIES (1999); DONNA FRANKLIN, ENSURING INEQUALITY: THE STRUCTURAL TRANSFORMATION OF THE AFRICAN-AMERICAN FAMILY (1997).

8. Stephanie J. Ventura, *Changing Patterns of Nonmarital Childbearing in the United States* (May 2009), *available at* http://www.cdc.gov/nchs/data/databriefs/db18.pdf.

9. The National Marriage Project, The State of Our Unions 2007: The Social Health of Marriage in America, at 14, *available at* http://marriage.rutgers.edu/Publications/SOOU/SOOU2007.pdf. (Calculations by the National Marriage Project using data downloaded from the American Community Survey, 2005.)

10. In 1960, 94% of women had been married at least once by age 45 in what may be a historical high point. *See* ANDREW J. CHERLIN, MARRIAGE, DIVORCE, AND REMARRIAGE 10 (1992); Michael R. Haines, *Long-Term Marriage Patterns in the United States from Colonial Times to the Present,* 1 THE HISTORY OF THE FAMILY 15–39 (1996).

11. JUNE CARBONE, FROM PARTNERS TO PARENTS: THE SECOND REVOLUTION IN FAMILY LAW 78 (2000); KATHRYN M. NECKERMAN, SOCIAL INEQUALITY 104 (2004).

12. *See, e.g.,* JAMES Q. WILSON, THE MARRIAGE PROBLEM (2002).

13. Steven L. Nock & W. Bradford Wilcox, *What's Love Got to Do with It? Equality, Equity, Commitment and Women's Marital Quality,* 84 SOC. FORCES 1321 (Mar. 2006). Wilcox and Nock's study reported that married women are happier if they hold traditional rather than egalitarian expectations about marriage and if they share with their husbands high levels of church attendance and commitment to the institution of marriage. The study suggested that traditional wives may be happier because they expect less, and thus, when they get less, they are not disappointed. At the same time, by expecting less, they might actually persuade their husbands to be

more emotionally responsive and to invest more, because the husbands experience less conflict with their wives over the household division of labor. In short, according to this research, socialization for commitment and for acceptance of traditional gender roles may be necessary to promote marital success. For one response to Nock and Wilcox, see Joanna Grossman & Linda McClain, *"Desperate Feminist Wives": Does the Quest for Marital Equality Doom Marital Happiness?* FindLaw's Writ: Legal Commentary (Apr. 4, 2006), *available at* http://writ.news.findlaw.com/commentary/20060404_mcclain.html.

14. Lynn D. Wardle, *The "Withering Away" of Marriage: Some Lessons from the Bolshevik Family Law Reforms in Russia, 1917–1926,* 2 Geo. J.L. & Pub. Pol'y 469 (2004).

15. Katherine Shaw Spaht, *The Last One Hundred Years: The Incredible Retreat of Law from the Regulation of Marriage,* 63 La. L. Rev. 243, 244, 306 (2003).

16. Robert Schoen & Yen-Hsin Alice Cheng, *Partner Choice and the Differential Retreat from Marriage,* 68 J. Marriage & Fam. 1–10 (2006); Arland Thornton & Linda Young-DeMarco, *Four Decades of Trends in Attitudes toward Family Issues in the United States: The 1960s through the 1990s,* 63 J. Marriage & Fam. 1009–37 (2001); *see also* Popenoe, *supra* note 3, at 16.

17. *See, e.g.,* Daniel T. Lichter et al., *Race and the Retreat from Marriage: A Shortage of Marriageable Men?* 57 Am. Soc. Rev. 781 (1992); Marcia J. Carlson, Sara S. McLanahan, & Paula England, *Union Formation in Fragile Families,* 41 Demography 237 (2004); Diane K. McLaughlin & Daniel T. Lichter, *Poverty and the Marital Behavior of Young Women,* 59 J. Marriage & Fam. 589 (1997).

18. Kathryn Edin & Maria J. Kefalas, Promises I Can Keep: Why Poor Women Put Motherhood before Marriage (2005).

19. Beyond Same-Sex Marriage: A New Strategic Vision for All Our Families & Relationships (July 26, 2006), *available at* www.beyondmarriage.org (last visited Oct. 28, 2009).

20. Law Commission of Canada, Beyond Conjugality: Recognizing and Supporting Close Adult Personal Relationships 113 (2001).

21. Amato, *supra* note 2, at 167, 173.

22. *See* Cherlin, Marriage-Go-Round, *supra* note 6.

23. Stanley v. Illinois, 405 U.S. 645 (1972).

24. Michael H. v. Gerald D., 491 U.S. 110 (1989).

25. *Id.*

26. *See* R. McG. v. J.W., 615 P.2d 666 (Colo. 1980) (finding that a denial of standing to the putative father violated the equal protection clause of the Colorado constitution); Callender v. Skiles, 591 N.W.2d 182 (Iowa 1999) (determining that a denial of standing to the putative father violated his due process rights under the state constitution); *In re J.W.T.,* 872 S.W.2d 189 (Tex. 1994) (ruling that a statute denying the putative father standing to challenge paternity violated the due process clause of the state constitution; superseded by statute in Tex. Fam. Code Ann. § 160.101(a)(3) (West 1996)); State of West Virginia ex rel. Roy Allen S. v. Stone, 474 S.E.2d 554 (W. Va. 1996) (holding that a biological father who has developed a substantial relationship with the child gains a liberty interest

in the father-child relationship that is protected by the due process clause of the West Virginia constitution).

27. *See* Willmon v. Hunter, 761 S.W.2d 924, 926 (Ark. 1988) (finding that the statute permits a man alleging to be the biological father of the child to assert paternity and that such an action does not violate any public policy of the state); Johnson v. Studley Preston, 812 P.2d 1216, 1219–20 (Idaho 1991) (finding that the statute permits the alleged biological father to bring action); K.S. v. R.S., 669 N.E.2d 399, 401 (Ind. 1996) (determining that the statute permits the alleged biological father to bring a paternity action despite the intact marriage of the mother and presumed father); Rafferty v. Perkins, 757 So. 2d 992, 995–96 (Miss. 2000) (determining that the results of scientific paternity testing are adequate to overcome the marital presumption).

28. *See* Cal. Fam. Code § 7540 (1994); la. civ. code ann. art. 189 (West Supp. 2001) (enforcing the time limitation strictly unless the child is born more than 300 days after the parents are legally separated). Oklahoma limits actions to establish or disestablish paternity to two years, where the child lived for those two years with the mother and her husband as a member of the family. Okla. Stat. Ann. tit. 10 § 3 (West 1998). Judson v. Judson, 1995 WL 476848 (Conn. Super. Ct. July 21, 1995) (refusing to permit husband to deny paternity of 12- and 6-year-old children in divorce proceeding, although it is unclear whether the court was applying estoppel or best interests of the child).

29. *See, e.g.,* Theresa Glennon, *Somebody's Child: Evaluating the Erosion of the Marital Presumption of Paternity,* 102 W. Va. L. Rev. 547 (2000).

30. Cherlin, The Marriage-Go-Round, *supra* note 6, at 134 (describing the tolerance of American religions for divorce, even if they preach that it's sinful). For empirical research on the effect of different rules governing divorce, see Stéphane Mechoulan, *Divorce Laws and the Structure of the American Family,* 35 J. Leg. Studies 143, 144–47, 165–66 (2006).

31. *See, e.g.,* Nancy Polikoff, Beyond (Straight and Gay) Marriage: Valuing All Families under the Law (2008); Laura A. Rosenbury, *Friends with Benefits?* 106 Mich. L. Rev. 189, 191 (2007).

32. American Law Institute, *Principles of the Law of Family Dissolution: Analysis and Recommendations* (LexisNexis 2002), § 6.03(1), at 916.

33. For a summary of this debate, see Carbone, *supra* note 11, at chapter 21.

34. Katherine Shaw Spaht, *Covenant Marriage: An Achievable Legal Response to the Inherent Nature of Marriage and Its Various Goods,* 4 Ave Maria L. Rev. 467, 482 (2006).

35. Rick Lyman, *Trying to Strengthen an "I Do" with a More Binding Legal Tie,* N.Y. Times, Feb. 15, 2005, *available at* http://www.nytimes.com/2005/02/15/national/15marriage.html.

36. Jonathan Mummolo, *Va. Foundation Seeks to Reduce Divorces,* Wash. Post, July 26, 2007, at B1.

37. Steven L. Nock, Laura A. Sanchez, & James D. Wright, Covenant Marriage: The Movement to Reclaim Tradition in America 3, App. A (2008).

38. *Id.* at 117.

39. *Id.*, at 117–19.

40. U.S. Dep't of Health & Human Services, Administration for Children and Families, *Healthy Marriage Initiative, available at* http://www.acf.hhs.gov/healthymarriage/about/mission.html (last visited Mar. 31, 2009).

41. Vivian Hamilton, *Will Marriage Promotion Work?* 11 J. Gender Race & Just. 1 (2007).

42. *Id.* at 15.

43. Martin, *supra* note 5, at 106.

44. Dr. James Dobson, *Eleven Arguments against Same-Sex Marriage,* Citizenlink.org (May 23, 2004), *available at* http://www.citizenlink.org/FOSI/homosexuality/maf/A000004753.cfm (citing a column by Steve Blow in the Dallas Morning News).

45. *Id.*

46. *See* Robert & Post & Reva Siegel, *Roe Rage: Democratic Constitutionalism and Backlash,* 42 Harv. C.R. - C.L.L. Rev. 373, 424 n. 232 (2007) (emphasizing that conservative groups see abortion and same-sex marriage as essentially the same issue).

47. Maggie Gallagher, *Re: Marriage Proposal,* national review online, Mar. 10, 2009, http://corner.nationalreview.com/post/?q=OWY3ODRhNDFjNzQoM zkoNDI2YjM4Y2YyOGVjMGVkNDU=.

48. Bonnie Azab Powell, *Framing the Issues: UC Berkeley Professor George Lakoff Tells How Conservatives Use Language to Dominate Politics,* UC-Berkeley News, Oct. 27, 2003, *available at* http://www.berkeley.edu/news/media/releases/2003/10/27_lakoff.shtml.

49. Martha C. Nussbaum, Hiding from Humanity: Disgust, Shame, and the Law (2004).

50. Religious Coalition for Marriage, Top 10 Social Scientific Arguments against Same-Sex Marriage (2006). On the other hand, several studies refute the idea that gay men are much more promiscuous than heterosexual men. Jonathan Rauch, Gay Marriage: Why It Is Good for Gays, Good for Straights, and Good for America 143 (2004); Dale Carpenter, The Myth of Gay Promiscuity (2003), *available at* http://www.marriagedebate.com/2003/08/myth-of-gay-promiscuity-dale-carpenter.htm.

51. Andrew Sullivan, Virtually Normal: An Argument about Homosexuality (1995).

52. Sondra E. Solomon, Esther D. Rothblum, & Kimberly F. Balsam, *Money, Housework, Sex, and Conflict: Same-Sex Couples in Civil Unions, Those Not in Civil Unions, and Heterosexual Married Siblings,* 52 Sex Roles 561 (May 2005) (observing that 50% of the gay men in contrast with 15% of the heterosexual men had sex outside of their primary relationship).

53. Pew Research Center, As Marriage and Parenthood Drift Apart, Public Is Concerned about Social Impact 2 (2007), *available at* http://pewresearch.org/assets/social/pdf/Marriage.pdf

54. In this argument, marriage reassumes its traditional role in channeling sexual expression and restraining promiscuity. *See* William N. Eskridge Jr., The Case for Same-Sex Marriage: From Sexual Liberty to Civilized

Commitment 8–9 (1996). *See generally* William N. Eskridge & Darren
R. Spedale, Gay Marriage: For Better or for Worse? What We've
Learned from the Evidence (2006).

55. *See* Douglas W. Allen, *An Economic Assessment of Same-Sex Marriage Laws*, 29
Harv. J.L. & Pub. Pol'y 949, 951–54 (2006).

56. Popenoe, *supra* note 3, at 21.

57. Ryan T. Anderson & Sherif Girgis, *A Real Compromise on the Same-Sex
Marriage Debate: An Invitation to Rauch and Blankenhorn*, Public Discourse:
Ethics, Law, & Common Good (Feb. 24, 2009), *available at* http://www.
thepublicdiscourse.com/viewarticle.php?selectedarticle=2009.02.24.001.
pdart.

58. Religious Coalition for Marriage, *A Letter from America's Religious Leaders
in Defense of Marriage* (2006), *available at* http://www.nhclc.org/about/pdf/
defenseofmarriage.doc; *see also* Maggie Gallagher, *(How) Will Gay Marriage
Weaken Marriage as a Social Institution: A Reply to Andrew Koppelman*, 2 U. St.
Thomas L. Rev. 33 (2005).

59. Hernandez v. Robles, 855 N.E.2d 1 (N.Y. 2006).

60. The data in this paragraph are drawn from Pew Research Center, As
Marriage and Parenthood Drift Apart, Public Is Concerned about
Social Impact 27 (2007), *available at* http://pewresearch.org/assets/social/
pdf/Marriage.pdf.

61. *Id.*

62. Richard Thompson Ford, *Analogy Lesson: Racism Is the Wrong Frame for
Understanding the Passage of California's Same-Sex Marriage Ban*, Slate.com,
Nov. 14, 2008, *available at* http://www.slate.com/id/2204661.

63. William Meezan & Jonathan Rauch, *Gay Marriage, Same-Sex Parenting,
and America's Children*, 15 Future of Child. 97–113 (2005); *see also* Fiona
Tasker & Susan Golombok, Growing Up in a Lesbian Family (1997); Lisa
Saffron, "What about the Children?" Sons and Daughters of Lesbian
and Gay Parents Talk about Their Lives (1996).

64. Hernandez v. Robles, 855 N.E.2d 1 (N.Y. 2006).

65. *See, e.g.*, Naomi R. Cahn, *The Moral Complexities of Family Law*, 50 Stan. L.
Rev. 225, 270–71 (1997); Vivian Hamilton, *Principles of U.S. Family Law*, 75
Fordham L. Rev. 31 (2006).

66. Religious Tolerance.org, *Two California Laws Regarding Sexual Minorities*,
*available at* http://www.religioustolerance.org/hom_mar13.htm; *see also*
American Enterprise Institute, AEI Studies in Public Opinion:
Attitudes about Homosexuality and Gay Marriage (2004), *available
at* http://www.aei.org/docLib/20050121_HOMOSEXUALITY.pdf
(summarizing poll results that find between 57% and 74% disapprove of
criminal sanctions against homosexuality, depending on the polls' wording).

67. *But see* Martha Albertson Fineman, The Neutered Mother, the Sexual
Family and Other Twentieth Century Tragedies (1995); Nancy D.
Polikoff, Beyond (Straight and Gay) Marriage: Valuing All Families
under the Law (2008); Katherine Franke, *Emancipation Approximation*
(forthcoming) (manuscript on file with authors).

68. *See* Naomi Cahn, Test Tube Babies (2009).

69. *See, e.g.*, Rauch, *supra* note 50, at 6.

70. Goodrich v. Dep't of Public Health, 798 N.E.2d 941 (Mass. 2003).

71. CBS News Poll, *The Public's Views on Same-Sex Marriage*, CBS News, June 15, 2008, http://www.cbsnews.com/htdocs/pdf/MAYB-GAYMARRIAGE.pdf.

72. Jeffrey Lax & Justin H. Phillips, *Gay Rights in the States: Public Opinion and Policy Responsiveness* (forthcoming, Am. Pol. Sci. Rev., current version on file with authors).

73. *See, e.g.*, Red and Blue Nation? Characteristics and Causes of America's Polarized Politics (Pietro S. Nivola & David W. Brady eds., 2006) (evaluating claims of polarization and distinguishing between polarized parties and public attitudes); Wayne Baker, Purple America (2005), *available at* http://webuser.bus.umich.edu/wayneb/pdfs/culture/Purple%20America%20June%202005.pdf (emphasizing that there is greater polarization among the political parties and political activists than among the public as a whole).

74. Debra Rosenberg & Karen Breslau, *Culture Wars: Winning the "Values" Vote*, Newsweek, *available at* http://www.msnbc.msn.com/id/6401635/site/newsweek. *But see* Gregory B. Lewis, *Same-Sex Marriage and the 2004 Presidential Election*, 38 Pol. Sci. & Politics 195–99 (2005) (suggesting that other issues may have been more critical to the outcome).

75. *See* Goodridge v. Dep't of Pub. Health, 798 N.E.2d 941 (Mass. 2003); Mass. Gen. Laws chap. 207 (2007).

76. Lawmakers Approve Same-Sex Marriage in N.H., Maine, CNN Politics .com, May 6, 2009, http://www.cnn.com/2009/POLITICS/05/06/maine.same.sex.marriage.

77. Vermont (civil unions, 2001); California (domestic partnerships, last amended in 2006); New Hampshire (civil unions, effective Jan. 2008); New Jersey (civil unions, 2007); Oregon (domestic partnerships, effective Jan. 2008). Human Rights Campaign, *Relationship Recognition in the U.S.*, *available at* http://www.hrc.org/Template.cfm?Section=Your_Community&Template=/ContentManagement/ContentDisplay.cfm&ContentID=16305 (updated May 31, 2007).

78. Hawaii (reciprocal beneficiaries, 1997); Maine (domestic partnerships, 2004); Washington (domestic partnerships, July 2007); District of Columbia (domestic partnerships, implemented in 2002). *Id.*

79. *See* National Gay and Lesbian Task Force, http://www.thetaskforce.org/downloads/reports/issue_maps/GayMarriage_04_09; Andrew Koppelman, Same Sex, Different States; When Same-Sex Marriages Cross State Lines xi (2006).

80. The Alaska constitution states: "To be valid or recognized in this state, a marriage may exist only between one man and one woman" (Ala. Const. art. 1, § 25); the Nebraska constitution provides: "Only marriage between a man and a woman shall be valid or recognized in Nebraska. The uniting of two persons of the same-sex in a civil union, domestic partnership, or other similar same-sex relationship shall not be valid or recognized in Nebraska" (Neb. Const. art. 1, § 29); and in Nevada, the constitution states: "Only a marriage between a male and female shall be recognized and given effect in this state" (Nev. Const. art. 1, § 21).

81. Julie L. Davies, *Family Law Chapter: State Regulation of Same-Sex Marriage*, 7 Geo. J. Gender & L. 1079, 1086 (2006).

82. *Id.* at 1087.

83. *Id.*

84. Christine Vestal, Gay Marriage Legal in Six States *Tetons Handily Press Gay Marriage Ban*, Stateline.org, April 8, 2009, *available at* http://www.stateline .org/live/details/story?contentId=347390.

85. E. J. Graff, *Marital Blitz*, Am. Prospect, Feb. 20, 2006, http://www.prospect .org/cs/articles?articleId=11177.

86. Human Rights Campaign, *State Prohibitions on Marriage for Same-Sex Couples* (Nov. 2006), *available at* http://www.hrc.org/Template.cfm?Section =Home&CONTENTID=28225&TEMPLATE=/ContentManagement/ ContentDisplay.cfm. These provisions vary, but they are potentially more immediate in their impact.

87. Human Rights Campaign, *supra* note 77.

88. *See* Religious Tolerance.org, http://www.religioustolerance.org/hom_ marrnm.htm (last visited Oct. 28, 2009); and *Human Rights Campaign, Domestic Partner Bill Stalls in New Mexico State Senate*, HRC.org, Feb. 29, 2009, http://www.hrc.org/issues/marriage/domestic_partners/12182.htm (updating reports on the progress in passing a domestic partnership bill).

89. The Pew Forum on Religion and Public Life, *Religious Beliefs Underpin Opposition to Homosexuality* 5 (2003), *avilable at* http://pewforum.org/ publications/surveys/religion-homosexuality.pdf.

90. Human Rights Campaign, *supra* note 77.

91. Indeed, even opponents of the anti-same-sex-marriage ballot propositions herald their impact on the level of political organization of the forces opposed to them. *See, e.g.*, Graff, *supra* note 85.

## *Chapter 9*

1. *See* Barbara A. Babb, *Reevaluating Where We Stand: A Comprehensive Survey of America's Family Justice Systems*, 46 Fam. Ct. Rev. 230 (2008).

2. *See* June Carbone, From Partners to Parents: The Second Revolution in Family Law, chapter 20 (2000).

3. States vary considerably, however, as to whether they allow fault to be considered for some purposes in the financial allocations at divorce. *See* Ira Mark Ellman, *The Place of Fault in a Modern Divorce Law*, 28 Ariz. St. L.J. 773 (1996) (summarizing and cataloging the different state approaches).

4. *Id.*

5. *See, e.g.*, Jarrett v. Jarrett, 400 N.E.2d 421 (Ill. 1979), *cert. denied*, 449 U.S. 927 (1980); Dockins v. Dockins, 475 So. 2d 571 (Ala. Civ. App. 1985) (mother was denied custody; she entertained her paramour in the home when children were present).

6. *See, e.g.*, Lasseigne v. Lasseigne, 434 So. 2d 1240 (La. Ct. App. 1983) (restricting the father's visitation on the grounds that having children exposed to his relationship with "his concubine" would undermine respect for the family as an institution).

7. Dunn v. Dunn, 609 So. 2d 1277 (Miss. 1992) (it was an error for the chancellor to prohibit the presence of the father's lover during visitation with his children, because there was no evidence of any detriment to the children, and harm could not be presumed from the lover's presence alone); Buschardt v. Jones, 998 S.W.2d 791 (Mo. Ct. App. 1999), *rehearing and/or transfer denied* (June 1, 1999), *and transfer denied* (June 29, 1999) (moral misconduct is insufficient to deprive a parent of the right to continuing contact with the child); Rushing v. Rushing, 724 So. 2d 911 (Miss. 1998) (it was an error to restrict the mother's visitation to the absence of male visitors without a showing of detriment to the child); *In re Marriage of Pleasant*, 628 N.E.2d 633 (Ill. App. Ct. 1993) (the parent's open involvement in a lesbian relationship is not grounds to restrict visitation in the absence of evidence of inappropriate behavior in the child's presence).

8. See, e.g., *Dunn*, 609 So. 2d 1277 6; Robin Cheryl Miller, *Restrictions on Parent's Child Visitation Rights Based on Parent's Sexual Conduct*, 99 A.L.R.5th 475 (2002) (citing only four states—Florida, Louisiana, Vermont, and Virginia—that do so). Virginia has reaffirmed this practice. *See* Carrico v. Blevins, 402 S.E.2d 235, 237 (Va. Ct. App. 1991) (upholding the restriction that the child could not be kept overnight where the mother and her lover lived together); A.O.V. v. J.R.V., No. 0219-06-4 (2007 Va. App.), LEXIS 64, at *18–19 (Feb. 27, 2007) (upholding restrictions on overnight guests and displays of affection in front of the children).

9. See, e.g., T.C.H. v. K.M.H., 784 S.W.2d 281, 284 (Mo. Ct. App. 1989); *In re Marriage of Birdsall*, 243 Cal. Rep. 287, 289 (Cal. Ct. App. 1988); Pryor v. Pryor, 714 N.E.2d 743, 745 (Ind. Ct. App. 1999); Scott v. Scott, 665 So. 2d 760, 766 (La. Ct. App. 1995).

10. See, e.g., *A.O.V.* (2007 Va. App.), LEXIS 64, at *18–19 (upholding restrictions on overnight guests and displays of affection in front of the children).

11. Tallese Johnson & Jane Dye, Indicators of Marriage and Fertility in the United States from the American Community Survey: 2000 to 2003, Table 1 (2005), *available at* http://www.census.gov/population/www/socdemo/fertility/mar-fert-slides.html.

12. *Id.*

13. *See* Goodridge v. Dep't of Pub. Health, 798 N.E.2d 941 (Mass. 2003); Mass. Gen. Laws chap. 207 (2007).

14. *See* Lewis v. Harris, 908 A.2d 196 (N.J. 2006); An Act Concerning Civil Unions, Substitute Senate Bill No. 963 (Apr. 14, 2005), *available at* http://www.cga.ct.gov/2005/fc/2005SB-00963-R000379-FC.htm (Connecticut civil unions).

15. Doe v. Doe, 452 N.E.2d 293, 296 (Mass. 1983).

16. Bezio v. Patenaude, 410 N.E.2d 1207, 1211 (Mass. 1980).

17. *Doe*, 452 N.E.2d at 296.

18. 401 N.Y.S.2d 636 (N.Y. App. Div. 1978). In *Di Stefano*, the appellate court upheld a grant of custody of the couple's three children to the father and conditioned the wife's visitation on the absence of her lesbian partner, finding that the lower court's decision "reasonably may be read to conclude that the wife's conduct in failing to keep her lesbian relationship with . . . [her partner]

separate from her role as a mother has had, and predictably will have, a detrimental effect upon the children." *Id.* at 638.

19. 380 N.Y.S.2d 848 (Sup. Ct. 1976).
20. *See, e.g.,* Kallas v. Kallas, 614 P.2d 641, 645 (Utah 1980).
21. 380 N.Y.S.2d at 859.
22. M.A.B. v. R.B., 510 N.Y.S.2d 960 (Sup. Ct. 1986).
23. *Id.* at 965–66.
24. *See* Gottlieb v. Gottlieb, 488 N.Y.S.2d 180, 182 (App. Div. 1985). In this case, the court excised portions of the judgment that conditioned the father's visitation privileges upon the total exclusion of his lover or any other homosexuals during visitation. The court said, "[T]he daughter must be fully conversant with the fact that her father has a live-in male lover, and…excluding the lover as a condition of visitation serves no real purpose other than as a punitive measure against the father." *Id.* at 182 (Kupferman, J. P., concurring).
25. Parrillo v. Parrillo, 554 A.2d 1043, 1045 (R.I. 1989).
26. Logan v. Logan, 763 A.2d 587, 589 (R.I. 2000).
27. Rubano v. DiCenzo, 759 A.2d 959 (R.I. 2000).
28. Gallo v. Gallo, 440 A.2d 782, 787 (Conn. 1981). It nonetheless limited the restriction to the woman about whom the trial court had made specific findings with respect to the impact on the child rather than including all women.
29. Duffany v. Duffany, No. FA990151366 (Conn. Super. Ct. 2000), LEXIS 2821, at *8–10, 12 (Oct. 17, 2000).
30. Zienka v. Zienka, No. FA000505452 (Conn. Super. Ct. 2004), LEXIS 1638, at *11–12 (June 1, 2004).
31. Laspina-Williams v. Laspina-Williams, 742 A.2d 840, 844 (Conn. Super. Ct. 1999) (holding that the lesbian co-parent had standing to petition for visitation).
32. *In re J. S. & C.,* 324 A.2d 90, 97 (N.J. Super. Ct. Ch. Div. 1974).
33. Lewis v. Harris, 908 A.2d 196, 213 (N.J. 2006).
34. M.P. v. S.P., 404 A.2d 1256 (N.J. Super. Ct. App. Div. 1979) (holding that the children's best interests were to remain with defendant and that they could best learn how to cope with her homosexuality by confronting its existence rather than being sheltered).
35. 614 P.2d 641 (Utah 1980).
36. The trial court had excluded testimony on the subject because both factors had existed at the time of the divorce (although the father did not know about them at the time).
37. *Kallas,* 614 P.2d at 643.
38. *Id.*
39. *Id.* at 645. Two justices dissented, suggesting that the trial court was fully aware of the sensitive nature of the evidence, and no abuse of discretion had occurred.
40. 881 P.2d 948 (Utah Ct. App. 1994), *rev'd,* 910 P.2d 1209 (Utah 1996).
41. *Id.* at 1214. The trial court found:

> [The mother] has chosen to act out her sexual preference by conduct-ing a relationship with a woman companion involving cohabitation

without benefit of marriage in the same home with the minor child. The court finds that this can be analyzed and should be analyzed similarly to a situation involving cohabitation with a member of the opposite sex without benefit of marriage in the presence of a minor child. The court finds that this conduct on the part of [the mother] during the pendency of this action and prior to the custody trial in this matter demonstrates a lack of moral example to the child and a lack of moral fitness. This conduct is unlawful in the State of Utah. (*Id.* at 1213)

42. *Id.* at 1217–18. The case was followed by *Thomas v. Thomas*, 987 P.2d 603 (Utah Ct. App. 1999). A 15-year marriage ended after the wife had an affair with her jiu jitsu instructor, who was also married. The trial court found that, although the mother's role as primary caretaker would have ordinarily justified an award of custody to her, recent gun and domestic violence charges against her lover and her continuing involvement with him justified the award to the father. The court of appeals emphasized that this was not a case based solely on the fact of the nonmarital affair nor on the character of the parties, but the decision was based on a combination of factors related to the children's best interests. *Id.* at 608.

43. 99 P.3d 111 (Idaho 2004).

44. *Id.* at 117.

45. *Id.*

46. The court observed: "She simply alleges that his living openly as a homosexual needed to be appropriately explained to the children through the help of professional counseling and a cooperative effort by both parents—not an unreasonable request." *Id.* at 118. The father, however, who became visibly angry in the mother's presence, maintained that she had difficulty accepting his sexual orientation and had refused to work with him. *Id.*

47. 110 S.W.3d 731 (Ark. 2003).

48. *Id.* at 732.

49. *Id.*

50. *Id.* at 732–33.

51. *Id.* at 734. The court cited the *Taylor* decision.

52. *Id.* at 737.

53. *Id.* at 739.

54. Holmes v. Holmes, 255 S.W.3d 482, 488 (Ark. Ct. App. 2007). The initial order prohibiting cohabitation occurred in response to the father's first motion to modify custody, when the mother was living with a man to whom she was engaged. The trial court, explaining the change of custody, emphasized the mother's purposeful lack of compliance with the court order and the fact that the non-cohabitation order was designed to provide stability in the child's life. The trial court found that the mother's frequent change of partners showed a "lack of residential, employment, financial and moral stability manifest[ing] an overall lack of stability in [the child's] life warranting a change of custody."

55. *See* Alphin v. Alphin, 219 S.W.3d 160, 165–66 (Ark. 2005). The trial court relied explicitly on the mother's "illicit sexual relationship" in changing custody and viewed her marriage to the boyfriend "as a ruse" because the

partners testified that they moved up the date to look better in front of the court. *Id.* at 165. The Arkansas Supreme Court, in affirming the trial court's order, observed: "It is true that this court and the court of appeals have held that extramarital cohabitation in the presence of children 'has never been condoned in Arkansas, is contrary to the public policy of promoting a stable environment for children, and may of itself constitute a material change of circumstances warranting a change of custody.'" *Id.* (citations omitted). The court then noted that other cases in which the courts transferred custody involved violations of non-cohabitation orders. It nonetheless upheld the transfer of custody in this case on the basis of the court's specific findings that the mother's frequent changes of residence (and romantic partners) involved instability not in the best interests of the child. *Id.* at 166. Justice Betty C. Dickey dissented, accusing the trial court of applying a "blatant double standard" as it criticized the mother's "illicit sexual relationship" before her remarriage, but not the father's relationship with his new wife, who was three months pregnant with his child at the time they married. *Id.* at 167 (Dickey, J., dissenting). The dissent also noted that the mother's residential instability was caused in part by the father's failure to contribute to their daughter's care. *Id.* at 167–68.

56. S. v. S., 608 S.W.2d 64, 66 (Ky. Ct. App. 1980).

57. Sosh v. Sosh, No. 88-CA-2401-S (Ky. App. 1989), LEXIS 72, at ˙4–5 (June 16, 1989) (discussing the mother's extramarital affair with an overnight guest).

58. B.F. v. T.D., 194 S.W.3d 310, at ˙311–12 (Ky. 2006).

59. 904 P.2d 66 (Okla. 1995).

60. *Id.* at 70.

61. See especially New Jersey and Massachusetts decisions on marriage, *supra*.

62. See, e.g., *Holmes*, 255 S.W.3d at 488 (construing the trial court's finding as not having anything to do with sexual orientation at all, only with the mother's instability in having many different partners and her defiance of the trial court's order forbidding cohabitation); *cf. In re Marriage of Wicklund*, 932 P.2d 652, 655 (Wash. Ct. App. 1996) (parental conduct may be restricted only if the child's physical, mental, or emotional health would be endangered).

63. See, e.g., the following rulings from other red states only slightly below the five red states with the lowest median ages at marriage: Fulk v. Fulk, 827 So.2d 736 (2002 Miss. App.) (court should not have restricted lesbian mother's parental visitation rights unless the visitation seriously endangered the child); Moses v. King, 637 S.E.2d 97 (Ga. Ct. App. 2006), *cert. denied*, King v. Moses, No. S07C0272 (Ga. 2007), LEXIS 84 (Jan. 8, 2007) (overturning the trial court's ruling that placed too much emphasis on the mother's affair with another woman and inappropriately restricted her visitation rights). Georgia and Mississippi have systems for the nonpartisan election of judges. American Judicature Society, *Judicial Selection in the States: Appellate and General Jurisdiction Courts: Summary of Initial Selection Methods* (2007), *available at* http://www.ajs.org/selection/docs/Judicial%20 Selection%20Charts.pdf.

64. *See Alabama Ousts Justice Moore*, WORLDNETDAILY, Nov. 13, 2003, http://www.worldnetdaily.com/news/article.asp?ARTICLE_ID=35566 (reporting that Chief Justice Roy Moore had been removed from the court halfway through his elected term for "defiance of a federal judge's order to move his Ten Commandments monument from the rotunda of the state courthouse").

65. 830 So. 2d 21 (Ala. 2002).

66. *Id.* at 23.

67. *Id.* at 24–25.

68. *Id.* at 25.

69. *Id.* at 26 (Moore, C.J., concurring).

70. *Id.*

71. *See Ex parte* J.M.F., 730 So. 2d 1190 (Ala. 1998) (holding that where the father had remarried and the mother had changed from involvement in a discreet affair to open cohabitation with her lesbian partner, the trial court could transfer custody to the father on the basis of a best interests finding without a showing of detriment to the child); *see also Ex parte* D.W.W. (R.W. v. D.W.W.), 717 So. 2d 793 (Ala. 1998) (holding that even without evidence of adverse effect, the trial judge would have been justified in restricting the mother's visitation in order to limit her children's exposure to her "lesbian lifestyle." The court noted that exposing children to a "lifestyle...that is illegal under the laws of this state and immoral in the eyes of most of its citizens, could greatly traumatize them"). *Id.* at 796.

72. *Ex parte* H.H., 830 So. 2d 21, 26, 31 (Moore, J., concurring).

73. *Ex parte* Pankey, 848 So. 2d 963 (Ala. 2002).

74. Pankey v. Pankey, 848 So. 2d 958, 961 (Ala. Civ. App. 2002).

75. *Id.* at 962.

76. *Id.; Ex parte* Pankey, 848 So. 2d at 963.

77. *Id.* at 968.

78. We thank political scientist Jane Curry for the observation that whether or not justices are elected might affect decision making in this area. Oklahoma, which has gone the furthest toward a blue state approach of our five red states on nonmarital cohabitation, has an appointed judiciary. Arkansas, which has taken the largest number of cases involving nonmarital cohabitation, has an elected judiciary, as do Alabama, Idaho, and Kentucky. *See* American Judicature Society, *supra* note 63; *see also* Institute for Legal Reform, State Resource Center, http://www.instituteforlegalreform.com/component/ilr_states/18.html (last visited Apr. 10, 2009). Utah justices are appointed. American Judicature Society, *supra* note 63. In the five blue states—Massachusetts, Connecticut, New York, New Jersey, and Rhode Island—all of the justices of each state's highest court are appointed. *Id.*

79. Lower Alabama courts have dealt with issues of nonmarital cohabitation during this time period. In *Pankey v. Pankey*, 848 So. 2d 958, 961 (Ala. Civ. App. 2002), the court referred to the mother's adultery, the existence of the child she bore with her boyfriend, and the boyfriend's financial support but, nonetheless, did not change custody to the father. *Id.* at 961–62. In the one appellate decision to raise the issue of homosexual conduct during this time period, the court

went out of its way to emphasize that the trial court had not based its decision transferring custody to the father solely on the mother's cohabitation with a lesbian partner, but rather on an unweighted variety of factors, including allegations of neglect and interference with the father's visitation, affecting the child's best interests. L.A.M. v. B.M., 906 So. 2d 942, 947 (Ala. Civ. App. 2004). The court underscored the father's testimony that he would have had the same concerns for the child's well-being if the mother's partner "was a man" and that the "visitation disputes, neglect, and a concern for the child's safety, as well as the mother's relationship with P.M., gave him reason to file the modification petition." *Id.*

80. The courts have been more willing to do so in the cases of heterosexual cohabitation. In another case decided in 2002, the intermediate appellate court reversed a trial court decision that had transferred custody to the father solely on the basis of the mother's cohabitation in the presence of the child with men to whom she was not married. The appellate court reversed, holding that for "heterosexual misconduct" to be a basis for a change of custody, there must be a showing of detriment to the child. Riley v. Riley, 882 So. 2d 342, 346 (Ala. Civ. App. 2002). Although the opinion was issued in November 2002, it was not released for publication until mid-2004. *See also* Davis v. Davis, 883 So. 2d 1252 (Ala. Civ. App. 2003) (reversing the trial court's modification of a custody order on the basis of the mother's nonmarital cohabitation, finding that it was insufficient as the sole basis for modification of custody in a case in which the mother married her boyfriend and the father also had an intimate partner stay overnight in the house in the presence of the children).

81. For example, in 1998, the Alabama Supreme Court baldly stated: "[e]ven without this evidence that the children have been adversely affected by their mother's relationship, the trial court would have been justified in restricting R.W.'s visitation, in order to limit the children's exposure to their mother's lesbian lifestyle.... Restrictions such as those at issue here are common tools used to shield a child from the harmful effects of a parent's illicit sexual relationships—heterosexual or homosexual." *Ex parte* D.W.W., 717 So. 2d 793, 796 (Ala. 1998).

82. Ann Estin, *Family Law Federalism: Divorce and the Constitution*, 16 Wm. & Mary Bill Rts. J. 381 (2007).

83. *Id.* at 390–91; *see also* Edward Stein, *Past and Present Proposed Amendments to the United States Constitution Regarding Marriage*, 82 Wash. U. L. Q. 611 (2004) (noting that Theodore Roosevelt called for the federalization of marriage and divorce laws in 1906).

84. *See* Jill Hasday, *Federalism and the Family Reconstructed*, 45 UCLA L. Rev. 1297, 1319 (1998).

## Chapter 10

1. *See* Andrew J. Cherlin, The Marriage-Go-Round: The State of Marriage and the Family in America Today (2009).

2. James Q. Wilson, The Marriage Problem: How Our Culture Has Weakened Families 216 (2002).

3. *Id.* at 217.

4. *See, e.g.*, David Holman, *A New Covenant*, Am. Spectator, Mar. 4, 2005, *available at* http://spectator.org/archives/2005/03/04/a-new-covenant.

5. *See, e.g.*, Paul Peachey, *Family, Society & State in the USA: Some Reflections*, *in* Private and Public Social Inventions in Modern Societies (Leon Dyczewki, John Kromkowski, & Paul Peachey eds., 1994), *available at* http://www.crvp.org/book/Series04/IVA-2/chapter_iv.htm ("Conventionally we view the family as prior to the society, both genetically and historically; genetically, because the family provides the human material from which the state and other social formations are constructed; historically, because as we well know the family precedes the state").

6. *See, e.g.*, Loving v. Virginia, 388 U.S. 1, 12 (1967) (finding marriage to be "fundamental to our very existence and survival").

7. Maynard v. Hill, 125 U.S. 190, 210–11 (1888).

8. Reynolds v. United States, 98 U.S. 145, 165–66 (1878).

9. Laura Kipnis, Against Love: A Polemic (2003).

10. Linda M. Burto & M. Belinda Tucker, *Romantic Unions in an Era of Uncertainty: A Post-Moynihan Perspective on African-American Women and Marriage*, 621 Annals Am. Acad. Pol. & Soc. Sci. 132, 135 (2009).

11. For a more-comprehensive review of these arguments, see Maxine Eichner, *Marriage and the Elephant: The Liberal Democratic State's Regulation of Intimate Relationships between Adults*, 30 Harv. J.L. & Gender 25 (2007).

12. For a thorough examination of such an approach, see, e.g., Nancy D. Polikoff, *Ending Marriage as We Know It*, 32 Hofstra L. Rev. 201 (2003).

13. Goodridge v. Dep't of Pub. Health, 798 N.E.2d 941, 954–55 (Mass. 2003).

14. Chai R. Feldblum, *Gay is Good: The Moral Case for Marriage Equality and More*, 17 Yale J. L. & Feminism 139, 144 (2005); *see also* Marc R. Poirier, *Same-Sex Marriage, Identity Processes, and the Kulturkampf: Why Federalism Is Not the Main Event*, 17 Temp. Pol. & Civ. Rts. L. Rev. 387 (2008).

15. *See* Robert Post & Reva Siegel, *Roe Rage: Democratic Constitutionalism and Backlash*, 42 Harv. C.R.-C.L. L. Rev. 373, 424, n.232 (2007) (emphasizing that conservative groups see abortion and same-sex marriage as essentially the same issue).

16. Jeffrey Lax & Justin H. Phillips, *Gay Rights in the States: Public Opinion and Policy Responsiveness* (forthcoming, Am. Pol. Sci. Rev., current version on file with authors).

17. American Enterprise Institute for Public Policy Research, *Attitudes about Homosexuality and Gay Marriage* 2 (2008), *available at* http://www.aei.org/publications/pubID.14882/pub_detail.asp.

18. *See* Kerrigan v. Comm'r of Pub. Health, 289 Conn. 135 (Conn. 2008); Lax & Phillips, *supra* note 16.

19. *See* Ariz. Rev. Stat. Ann. §§ 25–901 to -906 (2006); Ark. Code Ann. §§ 9–11–801 to -811 (2006); La. Rev. Stat. Ann. §§ 9:272–276 (2006).

20. Nat'l Fatherhood Initiative, *With This Ring…A National Survey on Marriage in America* 29 (2005), *available at* http://www.fatherhood.org/doclibrary/nms.pdf.

21. Jeffry H. Larson & Thomas B. Holman, *Premarital Predictors of Marital Quality and Stability*, 43 Fam. Rel. 228, 229–34 (1994); *see also* Paul R.

AMATO ET AL., ALONE TOGETHER (2007) (finding as risk factors: the individual spouses' own personalities and ability to resolve conflict, the stability of the family in which they grew up, demographics, such as their age at marriage, "economic factors (such as education, employment, and earned income), exposure to stressors (such as unemployment, social integration, and social support (such as the number of close friends), and attitudes about marriage and divorce").

22. THEODORA OOMS, STACEY BOUCHET, & MARY PARKE, BEYOND MARRIAGE LICENSES: EFFORTS IN STATES TO STRENGTHEN MARRIAGE AND TWO-PARENT FAMILIES 12 (2004), *available at* http://www.clasp.org/publications/beyond_marr.pdf; *see, e.g.,* UTAH CODE ANN. §§ 30-1-30 to -39 (2006) (requiring couples to participate in premarital counseling before applying for a marriage license, with certain exceptions).

23. Scott M. Stanley, Paul R. Amato, Christine A. Johnson, & Howard J. Markman, *Premarital Education, Marital Quality, and Marital Stability: Findings from a Large, Random Household Survey,* 20 J. FAM. PSYCHOL. 117 (2006). For a review, see Jason S. Carroll & William J. Doherty, *Evaluating the Effectiveness of Premarital Prevention Programs: A Meta-Analytic Review of Outcome Research,* 52 FAM. REL. 105–18 (2003).

24. *See* Pamela Smock & Stephanie Coontz, *Marriage Preparation Prescriptions for Welfare Reform and Poverty Reduction: Take with a Couple of Grains of Salt* (2002), *available at* http://listserv.uh.edu/cgi-bin/wa?A2=ind0212&L=ccf&T=0&P=2375.

25. *See, e.g.,* Sharon S. v. Superior Court, 73 P.3d 554, 568 (Cal. 2003) (noting that between 10,000 and 20,000 second-parent adoptions had occurred in California before the state supreme court ratified the actions of lower-level judges).

26. Lawrence v. Texas, 539 U.S. 558, 574 (2003) (citing *Casey,* 510 U.S. at 851).

27. *Id.* at 602.

28. Lax & Phillips, *supra* note 16.

29. Sara McLanahan, *Fragile Families and the Marriage Agenda, in* FRAGILE FAMILIES AND THE MARRIAGE AGENDA (Lori Kowaleski-Jones & Nicholas Wolfinger eds., 2005).

30. Eric D. Gould & M. Daniele Paserman, *Waiting for Mr. Right: Rising Inequality and Declining Marriage Rates,* 53 J. URBAN ECON. 257–81 (2003).

31. Frank F. Furstenberg, *If Moynihan Had Only Known: Race, Class, and Family Change in the Late Twentieth Century,* 621 ANNALS AM. ACAD. POL. & SOC. SCI. 94, 102–3, 106 (2009).

32. *Id.* at 106; McLanahan, *supra* note 29.

33. Furstenberg, *supra* note 31, at 124–25, 128.

34. *The Transition from School to Jail: Youth Crime and High School Completion among Black Males,* 2nd version, *available at* http://ideas.repec.org/p/pen/papers/08-033.html (last visited Apr. 21, 2009).

35. For further discussion, see chapter 3. For a comprehensive review of the effectiveness of marriage promotion programs and their inability to address low-income populations, see Marsha Garrison, *Reviving Marriage: Could We? Should We?* 10 J.L. FAM. STUD. 279, 327–28 (2008):

The life circumstances that tend to promote nonmarital birth also
suggest that sex education alone will prove unable to produce significant, long-term results. Nonmarital and teenage birth is highly correlated not just with socioeconomic and educational disadvantage, but
also with instability, trauma, and lack of motivation. In one study of
unmarried teen mothers, thirteen percent of the weighted sample had
been raped, forty-seven percent had been in a controlling or abusive
relationship, and twenty-four percent had no life plans; only sixty-one
percent lived with either parent, and most had recently moved.

36. CHERLIN, *supra* note 1, at 50.

37. See discussion at notes 30–32, *supra*; and Steven L. Nock & W. Bradford
Wilcox, *What's Love Got to Do with It? Equality, Equity, Commitment and
Women's Marital Quality*, 84 Soc. FORCES 1321 (Mar. 2006).

38. Denise Previti & Paul R. Amato, *Why Stay Married: Rewards, Barriers,
and Marital Stability*, 65 J. MARRIAGE & FAM. 561, 570 (2003). Few people
identified stigma or disapproval of divorce as a barrier.

39. *Id.* The researchers contrasted the likelihood of divorce for those who
responded to an open-ended question about marital cohesiveness by identifying
barriers (high) with the likelihood of divorce for those who responded to a
fixed list of reasons to stay married, including various barriers (low). *Id.* at 571.

40. *See, e.g.*, Elizabeth Scott, *Marriage, Cohabitation, and Collective Responsibility for
Dependency*, 2004 U. CHI. LEGAL FORUM 225.

41. *See* Michael Selmi & Naomi Cahn, *The Contradictions of Caretaking*, 55
ME. L. REV. 289 (2003); Theodora Ooms, *Commentary: The Role of the
Federal Government in Strengthening Marriage*, 9 VA. J. Soc. POLY & L.
163, 184.

## Chapter 11

1. Steven Martin, *Recent Changes in Fertility Rates in the United States: What Do
They Tell Us about America's Changing Families?* (Feb. 2008), *available at* http://
www.contemporaryfamilies.org/subtemplate.php?t=briefingPapers&ext=brief
ingPaperMartin.

2. KRISTIN LUKER, WHEN SEX GOES TO SCHOOL: WARRING VIEWS ON SEX—AND
SEX EDUCATION—SINCE THE SIXTIES 99 (2006).

3. John S. Santelli et al., *Explaining Recent Declines in Adolescent Pregnancy in the
United States: The Contribution of Abstinence and Increased Contraceptive Use*, 97
AM. J. PUB. HEALTH 150, 152–54 (2007), *available at* http://opr.princeton.edu/
seminars/papers%5CRecent_declines_in_adol_pregnancy_NSFG.pdf.

4. *Id.*

5. Kerry Franzetta, Elizabeth Terry-Humen, Jennifer Manlove, & Erum
Ikramullah, *Trends and Recent Estimates: Contraceptive Use among U.S. Teens*
(Aug. 2006), *available at* http://www.childtrends.org/files/contraceptivesrb.
pdf.

6. Center for Disease Control, *Teenagers in the United States: Sexual Activity,
Contraceptive Use, and Childbearing, 2002: A Fact Sheet for Series 23,
Number 24*, *available at* http://www.cdc.gov/nchs/data/series/sr_23/
sr23_024FactSheet.pdf.

7. Brady E. Hamilton et al., Centers for Disease Control, *Births: Preliminary Data for 2006*, 56 Nat'l Vital Stat. Rep. No. 7, at 2 (Dec. 5, 2007) (revealing that the pregnancy rate among adolescents fell 34% between 1991 and 2005 before it reversed in 2006, rising by 3% among females aged 15–19).

8. *Id.* at 7, Table 2, *available at* http://www.cdc.gov/nchs/data/nvsr56/nvsr56_07.pdf.

9. *See, e.g.*, National Campaign to Prevent Teen and Unplanned Pregnancy, *Unplanned Pregnancy Rates in the United States, 1981–2002, available at* http://www.thenationalcampaign.org/national-data/pdf/Unplanned-pregnancy-rates-by-age.pdf (showing a decline in teen pregnancy rates, but much higher rates of unplanned pregnancy for women in their early 20s); Press Release, Child Trends, *Contrary to Popular View, Birth Rates Increased among Unmarried Women in their Twenties* (2009), *available at* http://www.childtrends.org/_pressrelease_page.cfm?LID=94587AB7–8C17–4EF2–9C1412618B93A649 (showing an increase over the course of the 1990s in the birthrate to unmarried women in their early 20s).

10. Centers for Disease Control, *supra* note 7.

11. Heather D. Boonstra et al., *Abortion in Women's Lives* 26 (2006), *available at* http://www.guttmacher.org/pubs/2006/05/04/AiWL.pdf; *see also* Lawrence B. Finer & Stanley K. Henshaw, *Disparities in Rates of Unintended Pregnancy in the United States, 1994 and 2001*, 38 Persp. Sexual & Reprod. Health 90 (2006) (noting that unintended pregnancies rose 29% among women living below the poverty level while declining 20% among women with higher economic status, and the unintended pregnancy rates rose for high school dropouts and women between the ages of 19 and 24 while dropping for college graduates).

12. Boonstra, *supra*, note 11, at 25–26.

13. *See* http://www.reproductiverights.org/pdf/CERD_12.19.07.pdf.

14. *See* Rachel Benson Gold, *Rekindling Efforts to Prevent Unplanned Pregnancy: A Matter of "Equity and Common Sense,"* 9 Guttmacher Poly Rev. 2 (2006), *available at* http://www.guttmacher.org/pubs/gpr/09/3/gpr090302.html.

15. Guttmacher Institute, *Facts on Induced Abortion in the United States, available at* http://www.guttmacher.org/pubs/fb_induced_abortion.pdf.

16. Rebekah Smith, *Family Caps in Welfare Reform: Their Coercive Effects and Damaging Consequences*, 29 Harv. J.L. & Gender 151, 177 (2006). The overall abortion rate in 2000 in the United States fell to 21 per 1,000 women, a decline of 11% from 1994. Rachel K. Jones, Jacqueline E. Darroch, & Stanley K. Henshaw,, *Patterns in the Socioeconomic Characteristics of Women Obtaining Abortions in 2000–2001*, 34 Persp. Sexual & Reprod. Health 226, 233 (Sept.–Oct. 2002).

17. Smith, *supra* note 16, at 177; Jones, et al., *supra* note 16, at 231–32.

18. Jones, et al., *supra* note 16, at 231–32.

19. Stanley K. Henshaw & Kathryn Kost, *Trends in the Characteristics of Women Obtaining Abortions, 1974 to 2004* (Aug. 2008), *available at* http://www.guttmacher.org/pubs/2008/09/18/Report_Trends_Women_Obtaining_Abortions.pdf.

20. Editorial, *Behind the Abortion Decline*, N.Y. Times, Jan. 26, 2007, *available at* http://www.nytimes.com/2008/01/26/opinion/26sat2.html?_r=1&scp=2&sq=abortion+contraception&st=nyt&oref=slogin.

21. *See, e.g.,* Cicely Marston & John Cleland, *Relationships between Contraception and Abortion: A Review of the Evidence*, 29 Int'l Fam. Plan. Persp. 6–13 (2003). Compare Janet Smith, *The Connection between Contraception and Abortion* (1993), *available at* http://www.goodmorals.org/smith4.htm ("The connection between contraception and abortion is primarily this: *contraception facilitates the kind of relationships and even the kind of attitudes and moral characters that are likely to lead to abortion; emphasis in original*").

22. *See* Judith E. Koons, *Motherhood, Marriage, and Morality: The Pro-Marriage Moral Discourse of American Welfare Policy*, 19 Wis. Women's L.J. 1, 22–23 (2004).

23. Catholics for a Free Choice, *The Facts Tell the Story: Catholics and Contraception* (2006), *available at* http://www.catholicsinpubliclife.org/pdfs/factscatholicsandcontraception.pdf.

24. *See* Press Release, NARAL Pro-Choice America, http://www.prochoiceamerica.org/news/press-releases/2006/pro6232006_poll.html; *Large Majorities Support More Access to Birth Control Information, and Agree That It Is a Good Way to Prevent Abortion*, 5 Harris Interactive (June 2006), *available at* http://www.harrisinteractive.com/news/newsletters/wsjhealthnews/WSJOnline_HI_Health-CarePoll2006vol5_iss10.pdf.

25. *See* Koons, *supra* note 22, at 22–23.

26. Gary Langer et al., *ABC News Poll: American Sex Survey*, ABC News, Oct. 21, 2004, http://abcnews.go.com/primetime/pollvault/Story?id=156921&page=2.

27. *See, e.g.,* Center for American Values, Marriage and the Law: A Statement of Principles, http://center.americanvalues.org.

28. Regnerus reports, for example, that white evangelicals begin sexual activity at younger ages than do mainstream Protestants, Catholics, Mormons, or Jews, that the difference in timing between more religious and less religious is just under a year, and that the more religious are less likely to use contraception. Mark D. Regnerus, Forbidden Fruit: Sex & Religion in the Lives of American Teenagers 127, 128, 145 (2007).

29. Maher v. Roe, 432 U.S. 464 (1977); Harris v. McRae, 448 U.S. 297 (1980).

30. *See* David J. Garrow, *Abortion before and after Roe v. Wade: An Historical Perspective*, 62 Alb. L. Rev. 833, 834 (1999) (emphasizing that middle-class women with resources and contacts had ready access to abortion before *Roe*, while poorer women did not); David J. Garrow, Liberty and Sexuality: The Right to Privacy and the Making of Roe v. Wade 418–21 (1994; reprint, 1998).

31. Regnerus, *supra* note 28, at 99 ("the pledge works by embedding adolescents into a minority, 'self-conscious' community that gains strength from identifying itself as "embattled'").

32. William Saletan, *This Is the Way the Culture Wars End*, N.Y. Times (Feb. 22, 2009).

33. *The 5% Solution: Reversing the Rise in Teen Births*, National Campaign to Prevent Teen Pregnancy (May 2009), *available at* http://www

.thenationalcampaign.org/media/events/5percent_solution/Rate_Increasing.
pdf (indicating that approximately 30% of teens fear STDs more than
pregnancy).

34. For a comprehensive analysis of state-by-state efforts, see Guttmacher
    Institute, *Contraception Counts: Ranking State Efforts* (2006), *available at* http://
    www.guttmacher.org/pubs/2006/02/28/IB2006n1.pdf.

35. The Kaiser Family Foundation, for example, documents declining
    enrollment in Medicaid family-planning services. Kaiser Family Foundation,
    *Medicaid's Role in Family Planning* 8 (Oct. 2007), *available at* http://www
    .guttmacher.org/pubs/IB_medicaidFP.pdf (last viewed Feb. 2, 2008).

36. On the issue of private insurance coverage, see Guttmacher Institute, *State
    Policies in Brief: Insurance Coverage of Contraceptives* (2006), *available at* http://
    www.guttmacher.org/statecenter/spibs/spibICC.pdf.

37. The Deficit Reduction Act of 2005 had the unintended effect of creating
    disincentives that have led pharmaceutical companies to discontinue the
    provision of steeply discounted drugs to colleges and family-planning
    clinics. The result has been to dramatically raise prices at 400 centers around
    the country serving 3 million college students and 500,000 low-income
    women. National Campaign to Prevent Teen and Unplanned Pregnancy,
    *Policy Brief: Restoring Affordable Birth Control* (2008), *available at* http://www
    .thenationalcampaign.org/policymakers/PDF/Briefly_Policy%20Brief_
    AffordableBC.pdf.

38. Adam Sonfield & Rachel Benson Gold, *New Study Documents Major Strides
    in Drive for Contraceptive Coverage*, 7 Guttmacher Rep. Pub. Pol'y 4 (2004),
    *available at* http://www.guttmacher.org/pubs/tgr/07/2/gr070204.html.

39. *See* Boonstra et al., *supra* note 11 (discussing the greater availability of
    abortion earlier in pregnancy as the number of abortion providers has
    declined).

40. *See* Rachel Benson Gold, *Stronger Together: Medicaid, Title X Bring Different
    Strengths to Family Planning Effort*, 10 Guttmacher Pol'y Rev. 13 (2007);
    Rachel Benson Gold, *Lessons for Family Planning Providers from Transitions in
    Maternal and Child Health Funding*, 10 Guttmacher Pol'y Rev. 2 (2007).

41. E.g., Carey v. Pop. Servs. Int'l, 431 U.S. 678, 694–95 (1977).

42. Guttmacher Institute, *State Policies in Brief: Minors' Access to Contraceptive
    Services* (2009), *available at* http://www.guttmacher.org/statecenter/spibs/
    spib_MACS.pdf.

43. *Id.*

44. Cynthia Dailard & Chinue Turner Richardson, *Teenagers' Access to Confidential
    Reproductive Health Services*, 8 Guttmacher Rep. on Pub. Pol. 6, 7 (2005)
    *available at* http://www.guttmacher.org/pubs/tgr/08/4/gr080406.pdf.

45. Alabama, Illinois, Louisiana, Michigan, Missouri, North Carolina,
    Oklahoma, and Wyoming limit the program to women over 19. New
    Mexico, Texas, and Pennsylvania offer services to those over 18. The other
    states (Arizona, Arkansas, California, Delaware, Florida, Iowa, Maryland,
    Minnesota, Mississippi, New York, Oregon, Rhode Island, South Carolina,
    Virginia, Washington, and Wisconsin) do not have age limits. Guttmacher
    Institute, *State Policies in Brief: State Medicaid Family Planning Eligibility*

*Expansion* (2009), *available at* http://www.guttmacher.org/statecenter/spibs/
spib_SMFPE.pdf.

46. *Poll: School Birth Control OK*, NEWSDAY, Nov. 2, 2007, at A8.

47. U.S. Government Accountability Office, *Food and Drug Administration
Decision Process to Deny Initial Application for Over-the-Counter Marketing
of Emergency Contraception Drug Note: The Imposition of an Age Restriction
on Over-the-Counter Access to Plan B Emergency Contraception: Violating
Constitutional Rights to Privacy and Exceeding Statutory Authority Plan B Was
Unusual* (Nov. 2005), *available at* http://www.gao.gov/new.items/d06109.pdf.
Information about Plan B is drawn from the Plan B Web site: http://www
.go2planb.com/plan-b-pharmacists/faqs.aspx.

48. Sydney Kokjohn, 9 MINN. J.L. SCI. & TECH. 369, 389–90 (2008).

49. Gardiner Harris, *"Morning After" Pill Is Cleared for Wider Distribution*, N.Y.
TIMES (Aug. 24, 2006).

50. L. L. Wynn & James Trussell, *Images of American Sexuality in Debates over
Nonprescription Access to Emergency Contraceptive Pills*, 108 OBSTETRICS
& GYNECOLOGY 1272 (2006) (quoting from the deposition of Curtis J.
Rosebraugh).

51. Ricardo Alonso-Zaldivar, *FDA Has a Deal for Plan B*, L.A. TIMES (Aug. 1,
2006), at A1.

52. Government Accountability Office, *supra* note 47, at 5.

53. Tummino v. Von Eschenbach, 427 F. Supp. 2d 212, 231–32 (E.D.N.Y. 2006).

54. *Nightline*, Sept. 27, 2005.

55. *Tummino*, 427 F. Supp. 2d at 228 (quoting Davidoff).

56. Harris, *supra* note 49.

57. Population Council, *Emergency Contraception Block[s] Fertilization, Not
Implantation, Studies Show* (May 2, 2005), *available at* http://www.popcouncil
.org/mediacenter/newsreleases/ecdisruptsovulation.html.

58. FDA, *Joint Meeting of the Reproductive Health Drugs and Nonprescription Drugs
Advisory Committee* (Dec. 16, 2003), at 181, *available at* http://www.fda.gov/
OHRMS/DOCKETS/ac/03/transcripts/4015T1.DOC (statement of James
Carroll); *see* p. 193 (statement of Dr. Daniel Hussar: "I think the availability of
Plan B without restrictions would increase or would reduce safe sex precautions
which could lead to the increase in consequences, such as STDs").

59. Wendy Wright, Senior Policy Director, Concerned Women for America,
Letter to FDA Advisory Committee on Reproductive Drugs (Dec. 16, 2003),
*available at* http://www.cwfa.org/images/content/ww-maptest.pdf.

60. U.S. Conference of Catholic Bishops, Fact Sheet, http://www.usccb.org/
prolife/issues/contraception/contrafactsheet0207.shtml (last visited Oct. 28,
2009).

61. *See* U.S. Conference of Catholic Bishops, Fact Sheet, Contraceptive
Mandates, http://www.usccb.org/prolife/issues/abortion/contfac2.shtml.

62. *E.g.*, Press Release, American Congress of Obstetricians and Gynecologists,
(Aug. 24, 2006), *available at* http://www.acog.org/from_home/publications/
press_releases/nr08–24–06.cfm.

63. National Partnership for Women and Families, *Testimony* (Dec. 2003),
*available at* http://www.nationalpartnership.org/site/DocServer/portals_p3_
library_ReproHealthMedicalTech_PlanBTestimony.pdf?docID=583.

64. Tina R. Raine et al., *Direct Access to Emergency Contraception through Pharmacies and Effect on Unintended Pregnancy and STIs*, 293 J. Am. Med. Assoc. 54 (2005).

65. Drew Westen, The Political Brain 405 (2007).

66. Guttmacher Institute, *State Policies in Brief: Insurance Coverage of Contraceptives* (2009), *available at* http://www.guttmacher.org/statecenter/spibs/spib_ICC.pdf.

67. Guttmacher Institute, *State Policies in Brief: Emergency Contraception* (2009), *available at* http://www.guttmacher.org/statecenter/spibs/spib_EC.pdf.

68. Westen, *supra* note 65, at 405.

69. Pew Center for the People & the Press, *Pragmatic Americans: Liberal and Conservative on Social Issues* (Aug. 3, 2006), *available at* http://people-press.org/report/283/pragmatic-americans-liberal-and-conservative-on-social-issues.

70. Bill Bishop, The Big Sort 26 (2008).

71. Lydia Saad, *More Americans "Pro-Life" than "Pro-Choice" for First Time*, Gallup (May 15, 2009), *available at* http://www.gallup.com/poll/118399/More-Americans-Pro-Life-Than-Pro-Choice-First-Time.aspx?CSTS=tagrss.

72. Rachel K. Jones, Mia R. S. Zolna, Stanley K. Henshaw, & Lawrence B. Finer, *Abortion in the United States: Incidence and Access to Services, 2005*, 40 Persp. Sexual & Reprod. Health 1, 13 (2008).

73. *See* Heather D. Boonstra, *The Heart of the Matter: Public Funding of Abortion for Poor Women in the United States*, 10 Guttmacher Pol'y Rev. 12 (2007), *available at* http://www.guttmacher.org/pubs/gpr/10/1/gpr100112.html.

74. *See* Physicians for Reproductive Choice & Health, The Guttmacher Institute, An Overview of Abortion in the United States (Jan. 2008), *available at* http://www.guttmacher.org/presentations/abort_slides.pdf.

75. *See* Boonstra, *supra* note 73.

76. Dep't Health & Human Services, *2006 Assisted Reproductive Technology Success Rates* (2008), *available at* http://www.cdc.gov/ART/ART2006/508PDF/2006ART.pdf.

77. *See* Naomi Cahn, Test Tube Families: Why the Fertility Market Needs Legal Regulation (2009).

78. *See id.*

79. *Id.*

80. On Catholic Church opposition, see, e.g., Ramesh Ponnuru, *Out of the Freezer—At Last, Some Questions on In Vitro Fertilization*, Nat'l Rev., Apr. 6, 2009. California requires insurance coverage of most treatments for infertility but excludes IVF procedures. *See* Cal. Health & Safety Code Ann. 1374.55 (West 2000); Cal. Ins. Code Ann. 10119.6 (West 1993).

81. *See* Russell Korobkin, *Stem Cell Research and the Cloning Wars*, 18 Stan. L. & Pol'y Rev. 161, 176 (2007) (suggesting that the United Nations' broadly worded provisions allow each nation to interpret the language as it chooses); Alexander Morgan Capron, *Placing a Moratorium on Research Cloning to Ensure Effective Control over Reproductive Cloning*, 53 Hastings L.J. 1057, 1064 (2002) (describing the "stalemate" in Congress over cloning legislation).

82. *See generally* Karey Harwood, The Infertility Treedmill: Feminist Ethics, Personal Choice, and the Use of Reproductive Technologies (2007).

## Chapter 12

1. *See* CLAUDIA GOLDIN & LAWRENCE F. KATZ, THE RACE BETWEEN EDUCATION AND TECHNOLOGY (2008); MCKINSEY & COMPANY, THE ECONOMIC IMPACT OF THE ACHIEVEMENT GAP IN AMERICA'S SCHOOLS (Apr. 2009).

2. But see this article by Michael Selmi, who argued that empirical analysis does not show men losing out more than women when they attend to family responsibilities. *The Work-Family Conflict: An Essay on Employers, Men and Responsibility*, 4 U. ST. THOMAS L.J. 573, 586–87 (2007).

3. Indeed, for an ironic examination of how "family values" fuel support for the economic policies that exacerbate economic inequality, *see* THOMAS FRANK, WHAT'S THE MATTER WITH KANSAS? (2004).

4. Russell Shorto, *No Babies*, N.Y. TIMES MAG, June 29, 2008.

5. U.S. CENSUS BUREAU, AVERAGE MONTHLY INCOME BY EDUCATION, SEX, AGE, AND RACE AND HISPANIC ORIGIN, 2004: SURVEY OF INCOME AND PROGRAM PARTICIPATION, Table 2B (released Jan. 29, 2008), *available at* http://www.census.gov/population/www/socdemo/education/sipp2004w2.html.

6. National Campaign to Prevent Teen and Unplanned Pregnancy, *Why It Matters: Teen Pregnancy and Education, available at* http://www.thenationalcampaign.org/why-it-matters/pdf/education.pdf.

7. Heather Boushey, *Are Women Opting Out? Debunking the Myth* 11–12, Tables 5–6 (2005), *available at* http://www.cepr.net/documents/publications/opt_out_2005_11_2.pdf.

8. *See* Saul Hoffman, National Campaign to Prevent Teen and Unplanned Pregnancy, *By the Numbers: The Public Costs of Teen Childbearing* 14–16 (Oct. 2006), *available at* http://www.thenationalcampaign.org/resources/pdf/pubs/BTN_Full.pdf; National Campaign to Prevent Teen and Unplanned Pregnancy, *Jamie Lynn Spears and Teen Pregnancy* (2009), *available at* http://www.thenationalcampaign.org/media/jls.aspx.

9. For an example of such an approach to higher education, see ENRICHING THE MIX: RESPONDING TO THE NEEDS OF STUDENT PARENTS AT THE UNIVERSITY OF MICHIGAN, FINAL REPORT TO THE PROVOST FROM THE STUDENT TASK FORCE APPOINTED BY THE CENTER FOR THE EDUCATION OF WOMEN AND THE RACKHAM SCHOOL OF GRADUATE STUDIES (2001), *available at* http://www.umich.edu/~cew/PDFs/pubs/stuparrept.pdf.

10. *See, e.g.*, eLearners.com, Project Working Mom ... and Dads, Too, *available at* http://www.elearners.com/projectworkingmom (last visited May 2, 2009).

11. *See* Joan C. Williams & Stephanie Bornstein, *The Evolution of "FReD": Family Responsibilities Discrimination and Developments in the Law of Stereotyping and Implicit Bias*, 59 HASTINGS L.J. 1311 (2008) (documenting the persistence of employment discrimination against those with significant family responsibilities and the effectiveness of the legal response in combating it).

12. National Campaign to Prevent Teen and Unplanned Pregnancy, *Unplanned Pregnancy and Community College* (2009), *available at* http://www

.thenationalcampaign.org/resources/pdf/briefly-unplanned-pregnancy-and-community-colleges.pdf.

13. Alicia C. Dowd, *From Access to Outcome Equity: Revitalizing the Democratic Mission of the Community College*, 586 Annals Am. Acad. Pol. & Soc. Sci. 92 (2003).

14. Center for Community College Student Engagement, *Imagine Success: Engaging Entering Students* 10 (2009), *available at* http://www.ccsse.org/sense/survey/SENSE_2008_National_Report_March_18.pdf.

15. *See* Bridges to Opportunity Initiative, Bridges to Opportunity for Underprepared Adults: A State Policy Guide for Community College Leaders 16 (2008), *available at* http://communitycollegecentral.org/BridgesStatePolicyGuide.pdf.

16. Joan C. Williams, *Class Acts and Gender Works: Rethinking the Electoral and Everyday Politics of Work and Family* (forthcoming) (manuscript at part II, p. 12).

17. Williams & Bornstein, *supra* note 11.

18. U.S. Equal Employment Opportunity Comm., *Enforcement Guidance: Unlawful Disparate Treatment of Workers with Caregiving Responsibilities*, *available at* http://www.eeoc.gov/policy/docs/caregiving.html (last visited May 3, 2009).

19. Joan Williams, Unbending Gender: Why Family and Work Conflict and What to Do about It 71–72 (2000); Williams, *supra* note 16.

20. Suzanne M. Bianchi, *Maternal Employment and Time with Children: Dramatic Change or Surprising Continuity?* 37 Demography 401–14 (2000); *see also* Mark Aguiar & Erik Hurst, *Measuring Trends in Leisure: The Allocation of Time over Five Decades* 3 (Fed. Reserve Bank of Boston, Working Paper No. 06–2, Jan. 2006), *available at* http://www.bos.frb.org/economic/wp/wp2006/wp0602.pdf (showing an average decline in women's time spent on household tasks of 11 hours a week and an increase in family time spent with children).

21. Jerry A. Jacobs & Kathleen Gerson, *Who Are the Overworked Americans?* 56 Rev. Soc. Econ. 442, 457 (1998) (since 1970, the percentage of men and women working either long or short work weeks has increased. Approximately one in four men (25.2%) and one in ten women (10.8%) work at least 50 hours per week. Additionally, one in ten men and one in five women work 30 hours per week or less); *see also* Jody Heymann, The Widening Gap: Why America's Working Families Are in Jeopardy and What Can Be Done about It 164 (2000).

22. *See* Cynthia Fuchs Epstein et al., The Part-Time Paradox: Time Norms, Professional Life, Family and Gender (1998).

23. *See* Joan C. Williams & Holly Cohen Cooper, *The Public Policy of Motherhood*, 60 J. Soc. Issues 849–65 (2004).

24. Jacobs & Gerson, *supra* note 21.

25. Aguiar & Hurst, *supra* note 20, at 3; see also Paul R. Amato et al., Alone Together 168, 173 (2007), on the higher rates of dissatisfaction of women with traditional expectations and the corresponding increase in divorce risk; Elizabeth Warren & Amelia Warren Tyagi, The Two-Income Trap: Why Middle-Class Mothers and Fathers Are Going Broke 8–9 (2003)

(arguing that two incomes are increasingly needed to support a family so the loss of one income now puts families at greater financial risk than in the past, when middle-class fathers could earn a "family wage" and at-home mothers could get jobs to tide the family over economic rough patches).

26. Jerry A. Jacobs & Kathleen Gerson, The Time Divide: Work, Family, and Gender Inequality (2004).

27. *See, e.g.*, National Partnership for Women and Families, *Where Families Matter: State Progress toward Valuing American Families* 10–11 (2007), *available at* http://www.nationalpartnership.org/site/DocServer/Final_2006_Round_Up.pdf?docID=2161.

28. *See* http://www.johnmccain.com/Issues/JobsforAmerica/workplaceflex.htm; http://www.gop.com/2008Platform/Economy.htm#4.

29. Economy: Work/Family Balance, http://www.barackobama.com/issues/economy/#family-balance (last visited May 2, 2009).

30. Many economists argue that increasing the minimum wage improves family life without necessarily reducing the overall number of jobs. *See* Stephen E. Landsburg, *The Sin of Wages: The* Real *Reason to Oppose the Minimum Wage*, Slate.com, July 9, 2004, http://www.slate.com/id/2103486 (summarizing the literature and concluding that the earned income tax credit is more effective because increases in the minimum wage impose disproportionate burdens on small employers).

31. *E.g.*, Vicki Schultz, *Life's Work*, 100 Colum. L. Rev. 1881, 1957 (2000); Vicki Schultz & Allison Hoffman, *The Need for a Reduced Workweek in the United States* 8 (Yale Law Sch. Pub. Law & Legal Theory Research Paper Series, Working Paper No. 91, 2004), *available at* http://www.ssrn.com/abstract=618801; *see also* Gillian Lester, *A Defense of Paid Family Leave*, 28 Harv. J.L. & Gender 1, 4–5 (2005) (proposing a shortened work week).

32. *See State Policymakers: Supporting Low-Income Working Families* (Policy Leadership Series, Sloan Work and Family Research Network, 2007), at 3, *available at* http://wfnetwork.bc.edu/pdfs/policy_makers12.pdf.

33. Tracee Sioux, *Change America in an Hour and a Half* (2008), *available at* http://www.blisstree.com/tag/momsrisingorg.

34. *See* Naomi Cahn & Michael Selmi, *The Class Ceiling*, 65 Md. L. Rev. 435, 461–63 (2006).

35. Wealthier children often attend summer camps, which cost hundreds of dollars per week per child. *See* Jolayne Houtz, *Get Packing; It's Time to Enroll in Summer Camp: One Answer to Child-Care Needs*, Seattle Times (Apr. 11, 2004), at E1.

36. *See* Annette Lareau, Unequal Childhoods: Class, Race, and Family Life 250–51 (2003) (describing how children adjust differently to schedules). It is worth noting that, for many children in day care, a day that begins before and ends after the typical work day is already the norm.

37. *See* Mary Becker, *Caring for Children and Caretakers*, 76 Chi.-Kent L. Rev. 1495, 1527 (2001) (noting "mounting evidence that children in quality daycare do as well or better than children raised by stay-at-home mothers on every imaginable indicator of well-being").

38. For a catalog of 19 of these proposed changes, see Williams & Cooper, *supra* note 23, at 857.

39. U.S. Dep't of Labor, Bureau of Labor Statistics, Women in the Labor Force: A Databook (2007 ed.), *available at* http://www.bls.gov/cps/wlf-intro-2007.pdf.

40. Pew Research Center, *Fewer Mothers Prefer Full-Time Work, 1997–2007* (2007), *available at* http://pewresearch.org/pubs/536/working-women.

41. Debbie N. Kaminer, *The Work-Family Conflict: Developing a Model of Parental Accommodation in the Workplace*, 54 Am. U. L. Rev. 305, 352 (2004).

42. Williams, *supra* note 16, at chapter 6.

43. 29 U.S.C. §§ 2601–54 (2000).

44. *Id.* at § 2612(a)(1).

45. Jodi Grant, Taylor Hatcher, & Nirali Patel, Expecting Better: A State by State Analysis of Parental Leave Programs 7 (2005), *available at* http://www.nationalpartnership.org/site/DocServer/ParentalLeaveReportMay05.pdf?docID=1052.

46. *Family and Medical Leave Act Regulations: A Report on the Department of Labor's Request for Information*, 72 Fed. Reg. 35550, 35622 (June 28, 2007), *available at* http://www.dol.gov/esa/whd/FMLA2007Report/2007FinalReport.pdf.

47. Grant et al., *supra* note 46, at 7.

48. *Id.* at 8.

49. *Id.*

50. Ann O'Leary, *How Family Leave Law Left Out Low-Income Workers*, 28 Berkeley J. Emp. & Lab. L. 1, 8 (2007) (internal citations omitted):
    In March 2005, 54% of workers who made more than $15 per hour had access to a short-term disability policy, while only 28% of workers earning less than $15 per hour had access to a short-term disability policy. Similarly, 46% of workers who made over $15 per hour had access to long-term disability leave, while only 16% of workers making less than $15 per hour had access to long-term disability leave. There are similar disparities in access to paid sick leave and paid holidays. Eighty-eight percent of workers making more than $15 per hour had access to paid holidays, and 75% of these workers had access to paid sick leave. Meanwhile, 68% of workers earning less than $15 per hour had access to paid holidays, and only 47% had access to paid sick leave.

51. Joan C. Williams, One Sick Child Away from Being Fired: When "Opting Out" Is Not an Option 8 (2006), *available at* http://www.uchastings.edu/site_files/WLL/onesickchild.pdf.

52. Grant et al., *supra* note 46, at 7–8.

53. Julia O. Johnson & Barbara Downs, *Maternity Leave and Employment Patterns of First-Time Mothers: 1961–2000*, Current Population Rep. 11, Table 7 (Oct. 2005), *available at* http://www.census.gov/prod/2005pubs/p70-103.pdf.

54. *See* National Partnership for Women and Families, *Working Families Need Paid Family and Medical Leave* (n.d.), *available at* http://www.nationalpartnership.org/site/DocServer/WF_PL_FactSheet_PaidFamilyLeave_2009.pdf?docID=4682&autologin=true.

55. *See* Mary C. Still, *Family Responsibilities Discrimination and the New Institutionalism: The Interactive Process through Which Legal and Social Factors Produce Institutional Change*, 59 HASTINGS L.J. 1491 (2008).

## Conclusion

1. Maggie Gallagher, *Re: Marriage Proposal*, NATIONAL REVIEW ONLINE, Mar. 10, 2009, *available at* http://corner.nationalreview.com/post/?q=OWY3ODRhN DFjNzQoMzkoNDI2YjM4Y2YyOGVjMGVkNDU=.

# Index

abortion
  in blue paradigm, 92
  conflation with murder, 4, 93, 95
  contraception conflated with, 8, 182
  declines in 1990s, 8, 173–74
  and delayed marriage rates, 38, 84
  Democrats on, 4, 93, 94, 95, 185
  effect of contraception access on, 174,
    175, 176, 183, 184–85, 186
  facilities for, 185
  as fallback in family planning, 92,
    176, 184
  federal funding for, 104, 178
  late-term, 8, 185–86
  lower birthrates from, 8, 27
  by low-income women, 103–5, 173,
    184–85
  by minority women, 23, 104, 172,
    173, 184, 185
  nonsurgical (RU-486), 8, 180, 185
  parental notification laws for, 96–103
  as polarizing political issue, 4, 5, 7–8,
    91, 92–95, 160–61, 184, 185, 208
  rates of, 23–24, 27–28, 104, 161, 172,
    173–74
  in red paradigm, 92, 93, 105, 115
  Republicans on, 4, 93, 94, 95, 185
  restricting access to, 104, 105, 184–85
  in sexual revolution, 37
  Supreme Court decisions on, 83,
    95–96, 98–100, 104, 176
  by teens, 23–24, 172

Abortion Access Project, 104
abstinence
  and drop in teen births, 172
  by minorities, 175
  by religious teens, 4, 43, 115, 174
  as unrealistic, 2, 110
  virginity pledges, 177
abstinence-only education
  cultural conflicts in, 7, 106–8,
    112–15, 116
  government programs for, 107,
    109–10, 112–15
  impact on poor women, 3, 8,
    111–12
  ineffectiveness of, 7, 110–12, 115, 116
  opponents of, 112–15
  in religious communities, 43, 116
"abstinence-plus," 107
  *See also* sex education
Adolescent Family Life Act (AFLA), 109
adolescents
  and birth control law, 87, 89–91
  cognitive development in, 47, 48, 49,
    52–54
  from lower-income families,
    166–67
  pathways into adulthood, 20, 49–52,
    57–58
  peer relationships of, 90
  *See also* births, teen; pregnancy, teen;
    teen sexuality
adoption, 81, 218n.31

adultery. *See* infidelity
adulthood, pathways into, 20, 49–52, 57–58
African-Americans
  abortion rates for, 23, 173
  and abstinence-only education, 111–12
  and birth control law, 87
  community changes during 60s and 70s, 166
  divorce rates for, 118
  educational attainment, 221n.16
  employment prospects for, 51
  family formation by, 11
  impoverished, 11, 86–87
  incarceration rates, 221n.17
  infertility in, 45
  in middle class, 11
  non-homogeneity among, 11
  nonmarital birthrates in, 29, 86–87, 118, 166, 179
  social conservatism in, 4
  teen births in, 8, 22, 23, 172
  tolerance of homosexuality, 137
  at turn of twentieth century, 119
  unplanned pregnancies in, 173
  views on unwed motherhood, 11
*Against Love: A Polemic* (Kipnis), 157
Aid to Dependent Children, 86
Akerlof, George, 50
Alabama
  cohabitation in, 119
  custody decisions in, 140, 149–50
  household composition in, 28
  marriage rates in, 118
  on same-sex unions, 136, 137
Alaska, 28, 118, 136, 236n.57
Amato, Paul R., 57
American Civil Liberties Union, 113, 114
*American Conservative*, 31
American Law Institute, 124
American National Election Survey, 70
American Psychological Association, 110
anti-obscenity campaign, 78–79
Arizona
  ban on same-sex unions, 136
  covenant marriage in, 125, 162
  household composition in, 28
  state funding for abortion, 104
  teen birthrates in, 21, 22

Arkansas
  age at marriage in, 25, 30, 141, 144
  age of mother at first birth, 25, 30
  birth control law, 83
  cohabitation in, 28, 119
  contraception restrictions, 183
  covenant marriage in, 125, 162
  custody disputes in, 146–47, 148
  divorce rates in, 28
  and marital presumption of paternity, 123
  marriage rates in, 118
  on same-sex unions, 136, 137
  teen abortion in, 24
  teen birthrates in, 21, 22
atheism, 72
*Ayotte v. Planned Parenthood of New England*, 100, 180, 235n.51, 236n.57

Baird, Abigail, 47, 49–50, 53–54
Baird, Bill, 82–83
Barnhizer, David, 228n.50
Becker, Gary, 34–35
*Bellotti v. Baird*, 98–99
Berg, Harold, 82
*Beyond Conjugality*, 121
*The Big Sort* (Bishop), 30, 67–68
birth
  age of mother at first, 19–20, 25–27
  in earlier eras, 19–20, 119
  *See also* birthrates; births, nonmarital; births, teen
birth control. *See* contraception; family planning
birthrates
  between 1950s and present, 81
  baby boom, 37, 38, 79
  baby bust, 38
  nonmarital, 29, 74, 86–87, 118, 166, 170, 179
  relationship of abortion to, 8, 27
  teen, 21–22, 23–24, 25, 30, 170, 172, 219n.42
  for women over age 30, 170
births, nonmarital
  to cohabiting couples, 118
  current increases in, 3, 8, 33, 118, 172–73, 206–7, 218n.26

genetic basis for, 65, 227n.22
as issue in custody disputes, 141–50
liberal vs. conservative beliefs, 65
shifting attitudes toward, 161, 164, 165
tolerance of by racial group, 137
*See also* same-sex unions
Huckabee, Mike, 125
Hyde Amendment, 104
Hyde Park, Ill., 68

Idaho
abortion rates in, 27
age at marriage in, 25, 141, 144
ban on same-sex unions, 136, 137
custody disputes in, 145–46, 148
divorce rates in, 28
and marital presumption of paternity, 123
marriage rates in, 118
nonmarital birthrate in, 29
parental notification laws, 236n.57
teen birthrates in, 23
Illinois, 28, 83, 104, 236n.57, 236n.59
income inequality
family structure as factor in, 19
and marriage rates, 165–66
in new economy, 3, 39
Indiana, 29, 123
individualism, 34, 63–64
industrial economy, 34–36, 197
infertility
in African-Americans, 45
assisted reproduction for, 13, 186–89, 209
from deferred childbearing, 45, 167, 186
in lower-income Americans, 45, 187–88
infidelity, 157, 166, 223n.42
information economy
American shift to, 34, 35, 190
economic inequality in, 46, 57–58, 193
educational attainment required for, 36, 190
family transformations in, 1, 3, 190–91
impact on family formation, 190–92

moral values in, 35
wealth generation in, 35
women in, 35, 36–37
*In re Jane B.*, 142
Institute for American Values, 43, 48
insurance plans. *See* health care
Iowa, 11, 123, 135

Jenkins, John, 181
Jews, 115, 219n.48, 228n.48, 260n.28
Johnson, Lyndon B., 86
Johnston, Levi, 9–10, 52, 110

*Kallas v. Kallas*, 144, 145
Kansas
age at marriage in, 25
ban on same-sex unions, 136
cohabitation in, 119
diverse communities in, 11
household composition in, 28
parental notification laws, 235n.55
Katz, Lawrence, 80, 83–85
Katz, Michael, 50
Kennedy, Anthony, 122, 163
Kent, James, 117, 119
Kentucky
abortion rates in, 24, 27, 28
age at marriage in, 141, 144
ban on same-sex unions, 136, 137
custody disputes in, 147, 148
divorce rates in, 28
household composition in, 28
lesbian parents in, 147
teen birthrates in, 22, 23
Kipnis, Laura, 157, 159

Lakoff, George, 61–62, 64, 93, 94, 129
*Larry King Live*, 110
Larson, Jane, 35–36
Latinos/Latinas
abortion rates in, 173
and abstinence-only education, 111–12
contraception use by, 173, 177–78
family formation by, 11
nonmarital birthrates in, 29, 179
social conservatism in, 4
teen births among, 22
tolerance of homosexuality, 137

Texas (*continued*)
  criminalization of homosexuality in, 129, 163–64
  and marital presumption of paternity, 123
  and parental notification laws, 101
  teen birthrates in, 21, 22, 23
*Texas, Lawrence v.*, 129
Title V of Social Security Act, 109, 110–11, 112
Title X of Public Health Service Act, 87, 89, 90, 178, 179
traditionalists
  in red states, 74
  response to change in family form, 41–42, 72
  security important to, 71
  v. modernist world views, 61–67, 70–71, 72–73, 106–7
  *See also* red family paradigm
traditional values. *See* moral values
*Tucker v. Tucker*, 145
Tuttle, Robert, 114–15
Twenty-sixth Amendment, 83

United States
  changes from technological revolution, 19
  chronology of demographic transformations, 34–37
  hours worked in, 198–99
  increasing divisiveness in, 66–67
  safety net in, 13
  *See also* United States Congress; United States Supreme Court
United States Congress
  Aid to Dependent Children, 86
  Deficit Reduction Act, 261n.37
  family law legislation in, 151
  funding for abstinence-only education, 107, 109–10
  Title V programs, 109, 110–11, 112
  Title X, 87, 89, 90, 178, 179
United States Supreme Court
  abortion rulings, 83, 95–96, 100, 104, 176
  on abstinence-only education, 112–13
  on contraception, 82–83, 87, 88–89, 96, 176, 179

  on criminalization of gay sex, 129
  on marital presumption of paternity, 122–23
  parental notification rulings, 98–100, 102, 149, 180
  on polygamy, 156–57
  under Obama administration, 105
  views of marriage, 156–57
  welfare rulings, 86
  *See also individual justices*
University of Chicago, 68
Utah
  abortion rates in, 24, 27
  and adolescent access to birth control, 90, 179
  age at marriage in, 25, 30, 141, 144
  ban on same-sex unions, 136, 137
  custody disputes in, 144–45, 148
  household composition in, 28
  marriage promotion programs in, 162
  marriage rates in, 118
  Mormons in, 11, 157
  nonmarital birthrates in, 29
  and parental notification laws, 101
  support for same-sex marriage in, 134
  teen birthrates in, 23, 25, 30

values. *See* moral values
Vermont
  abortion rates in, 28
  cohabitation in, 29, 119
  domestic partnership legislation in, 137
  household composition in, 28
  nonmarital birthrate in, 29
  and parental notification laws, 100, 236n.58
  and same-sex marriage, 135, 137, 161
  teen birthrates in, 21
Vietnam War, 66, 67
Virginia
  age of mother at first birth, 25
  ban on same-sex unions, 136, 137
  shift from Republican to Democrat, 25–27
*Virtually Normal* (Sullivan), 129
voting patterns
  correlation with family structure, 31
  and religious affiliation, 69–70

War on Poverty, 86, 87
Washington
    abortion rates in, 27, 28
    cohabitation in, 119
    domestic partnership legislation in,
        137
    family leave legislation, 204
    and parental notification laws, 100,
        236n.58
Wax, Amy, 58
Waxman, Henry, 110
The Way We Never Were (Coontz), 79
wealth
    in blue regions, 45–46
    in information economy, 35
    mobility from, 66–67
    role in family formation, 29
    See also earning potential
welfare
    denial to poor women, 86
    increase in recipients of, 86–87
    reform efforts for, 44, 109, 124–25,
        126–27
    for unmarried teen mothers, 194
Welfare Reform Act, 109
the West, 112, 133, 134
West Coast, 74
Westen, Drew, 4, 93
West Virginia
    and marital presumption of paternity,
        123
    marriage rates in, 118
    nonmarital birthrate in, 29
    and parental notification laws, 101,
        103, 237n.66
    poverty in, 29
White, Byron, 123
Whitehead, Barbara Dafoe, 6, 218n.27
whites
    abortion rates for, 104, 172, 173
    nonmarital birthrates in, 29, 179
    and sex education, 111
    teen birthrates for, 21–22, 172
    teen pregnancy rates in, 173
    tolerance of homosexuality, 137
    views on unwed motherhood, 11
    on welfare rolls, 86
Williams, Joan, 196, 197
Wilson, James Q., 156

Wisconsin, 11, 112, 136, 137, 235n.56,
    236n.60
women
    achieving work/family balance,
        190–96
    "child penalty" for, 194
    educational attainment from 1950s to
        present, 79–81
    employment prospects for, 51
    feminism, 37, 93
    and first demographic transformation,
        35–36
    growing financial independence
        in, 58
    historical dependence on men, 50–51,
        58
    incentives to work, 38–39
    income based on educational
        attainment, 193–94
    in information economy, 35
    investment in education by, 38, 39,
        41, 193–96
    likelihood of marriage for, 118
    in old England, 33, 220n.4
    peak fertility in, 50
    in pre-industrial societies, 50
    premarital sexual activity from 1940s
        to present, 80–81
    and second demographic
        transformation, 36–40, 216n.6
    traditional pathways into adulthood,
        49–51, 57–58
    at turn of twentieth century, 119
    working class, 57–58, 193
Woodcock, Janet, 181
Wood, Susan, 182
work/family balance
    for blue families, 191, 192
    critical need for, 190–92
    family and medical leave, 203–5
    family-friendly workplaces, 9, 195–96,
        197–98, 199
    government role in achieving,
        198–200
    maintaining educational flexibility for
        women, 193–96
    part-time work, 202–3
    for red families, 191–92
    restructuring schools for, 200–201

work/family balance (*continued*)
  support for men entering workforce,
    196–97
  workplace accommodations for, 9,
    200–205, 209
  *See also* workplace
working class
  dependence on dual incomes, 52, 193,
    203
  dependency of women in, 57–58
  employment opportunities in, 9, 51,
    57–58, 196–97

workplace
  changes since World War II, 193
  occupational status of men v. women
    in, 51
  proposals for work/family balance,
    200–205, 209
  responsiveness of families to, 9, 14
  *See also* work/family balance
Wyoming, 11, 23, 28, 101, 118

Yale, 63, 82
Yellen, Jane, 50